BIRDS
AND
BIRDWATCHERS

100 Brief Essays

BIRDS
AND
BIRDWATCHERS

100 Brief Essays

by

Gerry Rising

W. R. PARKS
Hershey, PA

ISBN-13: 978-1537160016

ISBN-10: 153716001X

Library of Congress Control Number: 2016913715

Published by William R. Parks

Hershey, Pennsylvania

WRParksPublishing@gmail.com

www.WRParks.com

Twitter: www.twitter.com/WParksPublisher

Facebook: www.facebook.com/wparkspublishing

Cover

A black-capped chickadee taking a sunflower seed from the author's left hand while he holds the camera in his right. The photograph was taken in Algonquin Park, Ontario Canada where nearby boreal chickadees and gray jays were more wary.

BIRDS AND BIRDWATCHERS

On a May morning in 1937 I joined my older brother, a boy scout working on his bird study merit badge, on one of his bird hikes. That outing captured my interest and initiated my 80-year love affair with birds.

I remind readers that birdwatching is an avocation and not a vocation for me. My professional life was spent as a mathematics teacher. I have, however, edited a state ornithological journal, *The Kingbird*, contributed species essays to *Bull's Birds of New York*, participated in a wide range of data-gathering activities including for *The Second Breeding Bird Atlas of New York State* and interacted with many outstanding professional ornithologists including Roger Tory Peterson and Charles Sibley. (Essays about each will appear here.)

While those activities have contributed to these essays, most of which appeared as my weekly "Nature Watch" columns in the *Buffalo News* over a 25-year period, my writing remains that of a birdwatcher, an amateur who ventures out most weekends with others who share his interests to observe the local avian community and to add to his year and regional lists.

And that is, I believe, exactly the value of these informal essays. They represent what I would like to have had available to read over the years as I participated in this popular activity. In them I speak to others like me who seek to extend their knowledge about this wonderful avocation and who wish to share with me my many interesting personal experiences.

The essays that follow are not ordered. I invite you to read the essays in sequence, choose topics of interest to you from the index or simply dip in at any point in this book.

Gerry Rising
September 2016

DEDICATION

This book is dedicated to those young men and women, especially those who are teenagers and even younger, who separate themselves from the crowd, as I did, to become birdwatchers, and for whom the cry, "Look! Look!" is not a trick to divert attention, because there really is a tanager in that tree or a kettle of hawks circling those clouds.

CONTENTS

1. Our Smallest Heron

Most of us are familiar with the great blue heron, the largest and most commonly seen of our local herons. We often observe this large bird either standing absolutely still at the edge of a marsh or slowly flying overhead, its neck folded back into an S-shape and its long legs trailing behind.

Far fewer know the heron at the opposite end of the size scale: the least bittern. And fewer still have ever seen this tiny swamp dweller.

Tiny indeed. The least bittern is scarcely larger than a robin. Even that scrawny great blue heron weighs over forty times as much and the heron nearest its size, the green heron, is still three times as heavy.

For that reason, even though I am familiar with the least bittern, seeing one always comes as a surprise to me, even a shock. It is so remarkably downsized it seems like an escape from a circus sideshow; it is the Tom Thumb of the herons, a tiny model of what we have come to expect.

Look for least bitterns in cattail marshes. Like the rails that frequent the same areas, they occasionally venture out to the pond edge. Scan those edges regularly and you will occasionally see one either stepping daintily on the muck, wading in shallow water or straddling between two reeds.

You'll know it by its heron-like appearance and its size. It has a dark back and crown, light buff-colored breast and a matching buffy wing patch. That wing patch will distinguish it from the similar-sized all-dark rails. It appears as a light forewing and is especially apparent when the bird is in flight. And one sometimes pops up out of the cattails to fly a few dozen yards before dropping down out of sight again.

There is also a rare chestnut-breasted color phase that was formerly called the Cory's least bittern, but that race has not been recorded for many decades.

The least bittern is a bird more often identified by its call. Although it has other notes, its three syllable dove-like *coo-coo-coo* is distinctive. In spring it responds readily to a taped or even human imitation. This call is an extreme departure from the bog-pumping *ung-ka-chunk* call of its relative, the American bittern.

The least bittern is listed by the U.S. Fish & Wildlife Service as a "species of management concern" and in New York it is considered threatened. I am pleased therefore to read in an article about this species by Heidi Bogner and Guy Baldassarre published in a recent *Wilson Bulletin* that they were able to find and study dozens of these birds in the Iroquois-Oak Orchard-Tonawanda marshlands. I find this another response to those who believe that these state and federal lands serve only the hunting, fishing and trapping communities. As former Iroquois manager Bob LaMoy regularly insisted: refuges serve wildlife first, people second.

In both 1999 and 2000, Bogner and Baldassare recorded two dozen successful and one dozen unsuccessful nests, which suggests that these birds are doing reasonably well in these marshes. But life is threatening to the tiny chicks: they must avoid a litany of enemies including hawks, raccoons, snapping turtles, coots and geese. Of the average five eggs per nest less than half matured to be able finally to fly on their own.

A more serious concern: none of the birds trapped one year were recaptured the next indicating a very low over-winter survival rate.

2. Audubon and Wilson

Recently William Souder came to the University at Buffalo to read from his new book *Under a Wild Sky: John James Audubon and the Making of the Birds of America*. On my bookshelves are three other very good and quite recent Audubon commentaries: Alice Ford's 1988 *John James Audubon: A Biography*, Shirley Streshinsky's 1993 *Audubon: Life and Art in the American Wilderness* and the Library of America 1999 *John James Audubon: Writings & Drawings*.

Why then do we need another Audubon biography?

I for one am quite happy to have this new volume about our remarkable ornithologist and artist. Aside from the fact that millions of bird watchers — and in particular Audubon Society members — will always enjoy another book about their patron saint, Souder approaches Audubon quite differently.

Of most interest to me is his focus on Audubon's relationships with another important early American ornithologist, his contemporary, Alexander Wilson.

Here is what Elsa Allen has to say about Wilson in her authoritative *History of American Ornithology before Audubon*: "With Alexander Wilson (1766-1813) a new era in American ornithology opens. He has given us 320 figures of American birds, representing 262 species. Of these, 39 were new to science, and 23 others were sufficiently described to differentiate them from European species with which they had been confused.

"How is it, then, that the name of Alexander Wilson is so unfamiliar? There are two principal reasons for this: his untimely death at forty-seven, before he finished his proposed ten-volume work; and his close juxtaposition in time to the great bird artist, John James Audubon (1785-1851). The brilliance of the Audubon fame, with the inordinate commercialization which it has undergone, has blinded us to the hard-working Scot who came to America in 1794 without a friend or a farthing to aid him. A man of meager ability we are told, of unattractive personality his biographer says, with a quixotic scheme of writing and illustrating a great work on American birds; surely such a man, though a fund of genius lay hidden in his work, was no match for the talented Audubon.

"It would he vain to attempt to remold the judgment of a century, but it should be pointed out that Wilson never took the position to which he was entitled both by priority and by certain scientific powers. Instead, Audubon, riding on the wave of bird interest that swept the late nineteenth century, has been lavished with praise, to the almost complete exclusion of a very able ornithologist."

Of course, Souder sees the inevitable comparison of the two from Audubon's side but he is, I believe, quite fair in his consideration of their very different talents.

Of special interest is the first meeting of Wilson and Audubon because it seems to me such a shocking event for Wilson.

Think of yourself in Wilson's role. The year is 1810 and you are developing a reputation as an ornithologist with publication of the second volume of your *American Ornithology*. As an artist, however, you are self-trained and the drawings you have produced appear today flat and lifeless.

You are now on an extended tour of this young country to sell subscriptions to your work and to collect more information about birds — mainly by shooting them as was the standard practice then. You've ridden horseback and boated from Philadelphia all the way through the wilderness to Cincinnati and now you stop at a local store to try to talk one of the managers into purchasing your series.

The manager declines but he shows you his own bird

paintings. They put your meager art to shame for the man you have approached is Audubon himself.

That experience must have been like a hard blow to the stomach.

And their reaction? Audubon later bragged about this confrontation. Wilson, on the other hand, seemed to hide it. Here are his journal entries: "March 19 Rambling round the town with my gun; examined Mr. —'s drawings in crayons - very good." March 20: "Went out shooting this afternoon with Mr. A." And finally on March 22: "Science or literature has not one friend in this place."

The two were very different, both touchy, each to make major contributions to North American ornithology. Today Audubon is best remembered for his paintings, Wilson for his natural history, but there is significant overlap. Both deserve our recognition and esteem.

3. Snowy Owl Incursion

I didn't keep count, but I estimate that I received over a hundred reports of snowy owls in our region during the winter of 2013-2014. That was quite remarkable, but not entirely unprecedented. Mike Galas reminded me that, back in the 1980s during another incursion, we watched five snowy owls at once on the Bird Island Pier.

But ours in 2013-2014 were only a small measure of the thousands of snowies — the affectionate term by which they are known by birders — that retreated that winter from the far north into the northeastern states. In fact they were being reported as far south as the Carolinas and even Bermuda.

This was, in any case, a major incursion. And the natural question arises. Why did this take place?

But first, let's back up a bit. Consider some general information about these owls.

The snowy owl is our largest owl. Although the great gray owl, an even rarer visitor here, is a bit longer, the snowy owl outweighs it by 70%. We generally think of these birds as feeding on rodents, but this owl is twice the size of our common ducks and waterfowl more often serve as prey for the ones frequenting our waterfront. These owls have even been known to take Canada geese, which are among the few birds in our region that weigh more than they do.

This white owl is not an albino like the white squirrels and deer we occasionally see here. Unlike albinos, the snowy owl has bright yellow eyes.

Its range is circumpolar. The species was named *Bubo scandiacus* by Carolus Linnaeus, the Swedish naturalist known for developing that binomial nomenclature for he found it on his own trips to northern Scandanavia. It is normally considered a permanent resident of the open tundra north of 60° latitude, thus over a thousand miles north of us here. That is about as far north of us as Key West is to our south. If you have been to Alaska or to Churchill, Manitoba, you have been to snowy owl country.

It was formerly thought that these irruptions from their normal range were caused by low points in the cycle of lemming populations.

Lemmings are small rodents hard to distinguish from our meadow and red-backed voles. The range of two lemming species is restricted to the far north, but Wayne Gall once pointed out another lemming species to me in a Southern Tier bog. A folk tale falsely enhanced by an early Disney film has them committing suicide in large numbers when they become overpopulated. Although the story has been dismissed, lemmings do migrate and some drown when they cross large bodies of water.

The theory that appears to fit these snowy owl irruptions more closely, however, is that they are caused by high points in the lemming population cycle. When this food source is easy to tap, the owls respond by having large families. Single females been known to lay as many as eleven eggs. Snowy owls are territorial and guard their ranges from other owls and this overproduction forces many, especially young owls, out of their normal territory. Most of our visiting owls are these young birds.

These young owls have quite a bit of black barring among their white feathers. Only older males are all white. The few pure white owls being seen here may be elderly owls that have lost their territories to younger, more robust birds.

Some of these birds from the far north become diseased here. Two afflictions rehabilitators are finding among them are aspergillosis, a respiratory mold infection that inhibits their breathing and can cause death, and bumblefoot, a nasty swelling of the feet that can debilitate a bird. The normal species of our region have developed immunities to these diseases but the owls lack those defenses. They don't get shots before they come south the way we do when we visit tropical countries.

Chris Hollister, Scott Meier and I travelled to the Town of Yates to see one of these owls that had been reported at a farm there. It had snowed then very little and the landscape looked like it did for so much of that winter: it was green and brown instead of white.

We scoped the fields and barns for several minutes before Chris finally found our target bird. Once he did, there was no trouble seeing the owl as it stood out like white paper against a colored background. It was an adult snowy owl, its feathers completely white. Only this bird's staring yellow eyes broke the solid ivory. As I watched, it turned its head away in a smooth move that left only white where those eyes had been. The owl had identified us as a bit large for prey and thus of no interest.

I saw several more snowy owls that winter but my experience could in no way match that of a local high school art teacher.

Melissa Mance Coniglio teaches in the Byron-Bergen Central Schools and her heart was captured by the first snowy owls she saw that winter near the Genesee County airport in Batavia. She soon learned that these were just two of an unusual number of these birds and she decided that she would try to see and photograph as many of them as she could. So began a winter of driving back roads looking for owls before and after school, travel that added over 30,000 miles to her car odometer.

Early on, Melissa met bird bander David Genesky, who sought to band these owls, and they formed an alliance. They not only traded information about where they found the owls but she also assisted him in banding some of them.

Even more important to her was the influence her search had on Melissa's teaching. The word spread through her school about how she was looking for the white owls and she was soon better known among her students and colleagues school-wide as the Owl Teacher.

When I asked her about this late that winter, she told me, "Even today I had a fifth grade student come to me with a report of an owl on a barn near his house. Many have seen them this year at the Genesee Airport and come in to school very excited to tell me. It is thrilling to see them so engaged in the natural world. Even the bus drivers give me reports of owls. I had a sign on my door recording the number I had seen and the kids were watching the count closely. They were rooting for me to reach 100 but I only made it to 89. One of the rules of the count was that these birds were only in New York State and most of them came from western New York."

She continued: "One second grade student saw his first owl with his family near his house. He came in so excited and told me that he named the owl 'Snowy Buddy'. Another large family of kids went out sledding. When they reached their backyard an owl that had been roosting on their house flew right over them. They were thrilled at the experience. And kids were seeing owls sitting up on poles as they rode the bus to school. I could imagine them sitting sleepily riding the bus looking out over the snow-covered landscape and being surprised as they suddenly stared into a pair of gold owl eyes. I encouraged them by creating owl artwork and staging an owl art 'invasion' in the school."

A few of the banded owls that winter were also mounted with backpack electronics so that their future location could be monitored. Maps of their movements and current updates are to be found at Scott Weidensaul's ProjectSNOWstorm website. A number of owls returned in what has been termed an echo incursion the following winter.

Some of Melissa's owl paintings are at Melissa's website: mmance.wix.com/mancegallery#!home%/mainPage.

These handsome owls are worth seeking out during any winter. They tend to find a location from which they can hunt and then remain in that area. Local birders look for them on lakeshore breakwalls and at regional airports. If you visit an airport carrying binoculars or telescope, however, expect to be checked by local police.

4. West Virginia Birding

At the beginning of May I drove south against the tide of migrating birds. My destination: the New River Birding and Nature Festival in Oak Hill, West Virginia.

This trip gave me a wonderful opportunity to see birds that occur here in western New York only on rare overflights. Before I explain what is meant by overflights, I'll first describe a few of my experiences in West Virginia, one of the most attractive states I have ever visited.

Experience 1. I'm looking at a beautiful male scarlet tanager in a maple tree and am impressed once again with its gorgeous colors: its jet black wings and tail contrasting with its luminous red body. But then my host for the day, Joey Herron, tells me, "Look about ten feet higher." And there sits an equally gorgeous, all red summer tanager, only the second I have ever seen.

Experience 2. "Now look over in that other maple," Joey tells me and I easily find a third spectacular bird, the familiar orange and black Baltimore oriole at which he is pointing. Then at his direction I notice in the same binocular field a second oriole, this one with chestnut replacing the orange of the Baltimore. It is an orchard oriole, another species uncommon in western New York.

Experience 3. On another day guide Paul Shaw hears a distinctive whistled call and leads me down a steep hillside toward the sound. A notorious skulker is calling from behind a dense rhododendron thicket. Despite that, I focus my binoculars on the hemlocks just beyond the shrubs and, much to my surprise, I locate the bird singing lustily. It is a Swainson's warbler, a species I have never before heard or seen.

Now about overflights: In springtime birds move north from the tropics where they have spent the winter. Their testosterone levels boiling over, these migrants — among them woodpeckers, flycatchers, swallows, thrushes, warblers and finches — are driven to get north as quickly as possible. They seek to establish territories and advertise for mates before competitors of the same species take over the best spots.

The result is like the 1889 Oklahoma Land Rush.

Mixed in with these migrant flocks are many birds whose normal range is well south of us. A few of these birds are so eager that they fail to stop and we record them here on these overflights. Those three species — summer tanager, orchard oriole and Swainson's warbler — are among these overfliers. They rarely stay for more than a few days. I presume that, chagrined, they then retreat to their normal range to compete for those mates but now as latecomers.

There is another way to see these local rarities. Simply go south into their normal range and that is what I did on this trip.

I found several other species there that occur in western New York on similar overflights: white-eyed vireo, yellow-throated and worm-eating warblers, and black vulture.

Of course, those weren't the only interesting birds I saw on this trip. Among the 106 species I listed was the Carolina chickadee, the replacement for our black-capped chickadee at lower elevations in the south and a species that has never been recorded in New York.

On the third day of this expedition I joined Sue Olcutt, a West Virginia Division of Natural Resources naturalist, and

Kevin Dodge, a professor at Garrett Community College, on a visit to Cranesville Swamp, a site listed by the National Wildlife Federation as one of the hundred best birdwatching spots in North America.

Situated on the West Virginia-Maryland border, the geological history of this bog is different from those in western New York because it lies south of the glacial penetration of the Ice Ages. Despite that, I felt very much at home there. Its plants, mammals and birds duplicate those of our northern bogs.

So not everything is different in West Virginia. Their hospitality too is a match for the best we have to offer.

5. Christmas Counts

Through the 19th century anyone who studied birds seriously went afield with gun in hand. For example, the early bird artists, Audubon in particular, thought nothing of shooting dozens of birds of a single species in order make a field sketch for a painting.

Then in 1900, 26 bird watchers joined Frank Chapman, then an assistant curator of mammals and birds at the American Museum of Natural History in New York City, on the first Christmas Bird Count. That field trip initiated what one ornithologist has called a "new epoch in bird study." It represented a first step in the replacement of the gun by binoculars and, more recently, by the camera.

That single count in 1900 has also evolved into an annual international birding adventure. In the 2014-2015 season there were 2462 separate counts tabulated with 72,653 participants. A total of more than 650 species were recorded in North America and a remarkable 2106 species worldwide.

It was not until 1929 that a Christmas Count was organized locally. In that year seven Buffalo Ornithological Society members in three parties counted 5300 birds of 31 species. For comparison, last year on the 61st repetition of the Buffalo count 42 observers in 16 parties tabulated 64,000 birds of 95 species. The record number of species was recorded in 1969 when 86 were seen, and over the years a grand total of 146 have been observed here.

The rules for the Christmas Counts are strict. Each count is organized within a 15-mile diameter circle and within a date period set by the supervising National Audubon Society that always falls between mid-December until early January. Data is carefully recorded for each area, including not only species names and totals but also such details as party hours in the field walking and riding. This latter information provides a measure of the extent of coverage. Clearly, for example, a single party afield for three or four hours could not census an area as completely as several dozen parties birding for longer periods.

My own first Christmas Bird Count was in 1939. Although that was long ago, I recall that December morning as if it were yesterday. One of Rochester's finest field ornithologists, Howard Miller, allowed me, a pre-teen beginning birder, to join him on a visit to Tryon Park at the south end of Irondequoit Bay.

It was a dreary day, the sky overcast and the temperature in the 40s. There was significant snow cover, but it was melting and every breath of wind brought a shower of cold drops, some of which inevitably found their way inside my coat collar.

Our species list that morning was not long, probably less than twenty, but one episode made up for that brevity. A loud whistle greeted us from the woods and Howard imitated it. "Watch carefully now," he warned me and, no sooner had he said that when a bright male cardinal flew up to pose for us. At that time the cardinal was still a rare species this far north and ours may have been the only one on that count.

Times have changed. This year I participated in five Christmas Bird Counts and we saw cardinals on all of them, a total of 80.

But much has also stayed the same. These carefully organized midwinter counts give birders a chance to contribute small-scale information to an annual national survey of the status of birds. Tens of thousands of birders participate across North America. They also provide an opportunity for friends to get out to see how this year's list will compare with what they saw in earlier years.

Here are some random notes taken from the dozen Niagara Frontier count reports over the years.

* Bob Sundell thought that he had chosen the best possible

date for the Jamestown Christmas Count. It was December 15, the earliest Sunday in the count period defined by the National Audubon Society, but when Bob rose at four that morning to join friends for pre-dawn owling, he looked out at a blizzard. A foot of snow blanketed his yard and another foot was to come before the morning was over. It took him almost two hours to shovel his car out of his driveway and he missed the owling entirely.

Despite his miserable start, Bob described that year's Jamestown count as tied for best ever with 74 species, a half dozen more than in any recent year. The morning blizzard with its whiteouts broke up by noon to provide a pleasant afternoon of birding. Among the unusual birds on the count were the first turkey vulture in the 55-year count history and the first bald eagle since the 1950s. And without him Bob's owling friends called up screech and great horned owls as well. The weather even helped. Among the more common birds at Carol Wagner's feeder in Lakewood were Carolina wren, pine siskin, golden-crowned kinglet and brown creeper, as well as a marauding sharp-shinned hawk.

* A loon was found on Green Pond in Orchard Park. Sadly it may not have been able to take off before this narrow stretch of water froze over completely. Two rare white pelicans in Ontario's Jordan Harbor face a similar fate as I write this.

* Beaver Meadow's 51 species included a remarkable 9 barred owls. Among the 148 turkeys also found on this count was a possible albino. Hans Kunze, who recorded this bird, has taken a great deal of ribbing from those who believe that the white turkey was an escaped barnyard fowl.

* Even the police participated this year, appearing at Bill Watson's Tonawanda home late on the Buffalo count day. Bill and I had focused our binoculars on a red-winged blackbird near an apartment building, which led one of the

residents to report to 911 Bill's license number as "the car of two Peeping Toms." Fortunately the accommodating police were amused by his wife's explanation that we were "just bird watchers."

* Each count had its unique contributions. Wilson-Lake Plains: Cooper's hawk, Northern flicker, Eastern bluebird, and two rare hoary redpolls. Remarkably our only wild turkeys were on the Buffalo count as was Eastern mockingbird. Oak Orchard: ring-necked pheasant, American kestrel and red-winged blackbird. East Aurora: our only screech owl, belted kingfisher, yellow-bellied sapsucker and pileated woodpecker. And Beaver Meadow: mute swan, Northern harrier, rough-legged hawk, common raven, Lapland longspur and purple finch. Easily our "best" birds were those hoary redpolls that Mike Galas and Ron Hacker found feeding at roadside. "They were so close," Ron told me, "I could almost have reached out the car window and touched them."

* On the Oak Orchard count I sank into a deep drift and Charles Mitchell had to pull me out.

* Snow buntings and horned larks flew up from a field near where we picked up our third counter, Lewis Crowell. A dozen white-winged crossbills flew into the top of a spruce tree and were almost immediately lost to sight among the thick branches. And later we came upon a big pileated woodpecker quietly tearing apart a dead maple stump. Our totals: 763 birds of 29 species.

* Checking the Niagara River was punishment but we recorded there a few ring-billed and Bonaparte's gulls and a single great black-backed gull, a great blue heron, a dozen mallards, a bufflehead and 15 common mergansers. The male mergansers are handsome black and white ducks with thin, bright orange bills. Before we left the river to head east, we saw our best bird. Flying toward us from the south

Grand Island Bridge came a falcon. I first called it a kestrel but it immediately became obvious that it was far too big. It was one of the fierce peregrine falcons that have adopted those spans, taking their mortal bridge tolls from rock pigeons and other passing birds.

* Our count in East Aurora was the most challenging in which I have ever participated. A good sign of what was to come were the gulls on the high school lawn south of town. They had retreated from the lakeshore. Smart move, because at nine o'clock a front moved in bringing driving rain and winds that shook our car. Trees were down everywhere, at one point nearly trapping us in a cemetery. We went hours without seeing a bird but we did find 20 siskins hugging the ground under a feeder. Our totals: 176 birds of 17 species, less than half our usual count. We'll do better next year.

* Not a pleasant day, but also not the worst CBC I have experienced. I recall one many years ago with Doug Happ that was like birding from a submarine it was raining so hard. To me CBCs represent an interaction between wildlife, recorders and weather and clearly this time weather won out. (We later learned that this Buffalo count was not compiled for only the second time in over a hundred years.)

* We check Lake Ontario from Fort Niagara. At first it appears empty, but our list soon mounts: scoters, scaup, mergansers, goldeneyes, buffleheads and long-tailed ducks — hundreds of birds. Last year we found no birds in the woodlot behind Stella Niagara. This year we find dozens of robins, cedar waxwings, juncos, tree sparrows and woodpeckers there.

* Another dark and drizzly day. We're checked out by the East Aurora police responding to a caller worrying about "possible intruders," but they are friendly, supportive — and amused. Our worst count here in fifteen years, but we

finish on a high note with a Carolina wren in the village cemetery.

* Farther north I come upon a small flock of birds: nuthatches, chickadees, waxwings and woodpeckers including a lone red-bellied woodpecker. A warbler joins them but I get only fleeting views of it before it flits off again. I record it as a yellow-rumped warbler, the species we most often find here in winter, but then I begin to question my observation. This bird's markings were more like those of an American redstart. I search for it for a half hour unsuccessfully. No luck when I return the next day either. Why does this kind of experience only happen when I am alone and have no one with whom to compare notes?

These regional counts provide me with great excuses to spend wonderful days out-of-doors no matter what the weather.

6. Once in a Lifetime

Early one morning too many years ago Howard Miller took a twelve-year-old neophyte bird watcher to Highland Park in Rochester, a park internationally known for its May Lilac Festival. Each spring before the lilac bushes bloom to attract thousands of visitors, you can usually find small numbers of interesting birds there.

But this morning was to prove quite different. The slanting rays of the early morning sun sparkled not on lilac blossoms but instead on hundreds of warblers. Every one of the lilac bushes was ornamented like the plates in a field guide by a half dozen to a dozen of these beautiful birds. Howard pointed out to the excited youngster twenty-one warbler species, about half of which the boy had never seen before. He could hardly record their names fast enough: palm warbler, black-throated blue warbler, Wilson's warbler, cerulean warbler, common yellowthroat, myrtle warbler, chestnut-sided warbler, redstart, the list went on and on. The colors were stunning: yellows, reds, and blues against intricate black and white patterns. And there were twenty to thirty of each kind.

There were other birds as well: rose-breasted grosbeaks, vireos, a brown thrasher, kinglets, thrushes, towhees, purple finches; but the warblers were center stage.

It was a wonderful experience, one I — for I was that youngster — have never matched and will never forget. But the very next day the show was over. I returned hopefully that day to find only a few dozen birds remaining.

What caused this spectacular brief fall-out of migrants? Serious scientists as well as bird watchers have sought the answer to this question for many years. In the April 1991 issue of *Birding*, biologist Kenneth Able of the State University at Albany summarizes much of what is known about this curious phenomenon. Here is a quick summary:

Most birds migrate at night, flying in the first three hours of darkness, some moving shorter distances at low levels just before dawn. "Weather," says Able, "is the single most important factor in determining if the bird will migrate on a given night." Best conditions for spring migration are a flow of warm south or southwest wind following a high-pressure system and just ahead of a cold front. The clockwise winds around the high and the counterclockwise winds around the low combine to enhance these conditions. Such systems occur quite regularly in the northeastern United States in March, April, and May. The night before that May morning when we found those Highland Park birds exactly those conditions occurred.

But this is only part of the story. With these conditions large numbers of birds will simply pass through the region. What is also necessary to produce an event like the one in Highland Park is a local barrier that stops a strong migration flow. Such a local barrier could be rain, opposing northerly winds, low cloud cover, or fog. These conditions occur much less often and usually involve what weathermen call an occluded front, where a warm and cold front meet.

To a lesser extent the Great Lakes provide a migration barrier and so woodlots along the south shore of the Great Lakes are good spring birding spots. But the really spectacular shows require the unusual weather conditions Able describes.

Of course there is one additional requirement: you have to be there at the time all of these weather features coincide in order to take advantage of such a unique turn of events. That is the reason bird watchers pay special attention to national and local weather maps. They're looking for a combination of circumstances that occurs once or — I hope — twice in a lifetime. I'm still waiting.

7. Kinglets

Most of us are familiar with chickadees, those delightful little black-capped sprites that visit our feeders through the winter, one of which enhances the cover of this book. Far fewer know two species that often consort with chickadees: golden-crowned kinglet and its cousin, ruby-crowned kinglet.

Kinglets are even smaller than chickadees. The only still smaller species that occurs here is the ruby-throated hummingbird. A single kinglet weighs less than a quarter ounce, as much as a few pats of butter.

Kinglets are mostly gray birds with white wing-bars. The two species are easily distinguished. Golden-crowns have brightly-colored caps: the male's orange and the female's yellow. In both cases the caps are outlined with black. They also have a black line through their eye.

Ruby-crowns lack these head markings but instead have distinctive white rings around their eyes. Where then does the qualification ruby-crowned come from? If you watch these active little birds closely you will occasionally see the male ruby-crown's bright crest. It is normally hidden by other feathers and when you do see it, it will usually appear only as a thin red stripe. It is, however, raised occasionally to make a quite spectacular display, most often during courtship.

I enjoy the ruby-crown's bubbling warble, but the golden-crowned's song is too high pitched for my ears.

On a winter walk in woodlands that include conifers — especially pines, spruce and hemlocks — you will often come across a troop of birds. Look among the downy and hairy woodpeckers, chickadees and creepers in such flocks to find golden-crowned kinglets. For another week or two you may also find ruby-crowns before they head south.

Near the end of the fall migration kinglets of both species are rather common. During both spring and fall migration kinglets often mix with warblers, creating further identification difficulties for novice birders. In spring the build-up of golden-crowns occurs in early April but in mid-April ruby-crowns arrive and soon outnumber them.

Most kinglets pass through, heading for the forests of Canada. A few golden-crowns stay to nest, however, usually in thick conifer plantations. They have, for example, been recorded nesting in Amherst's Nature View Park and in the Iroquois National Wildlife Refuge. They raise large families, laying as many as ten eggs, each smaller than a child's marble. Their young, when born, are the size of bumblebees.

We would know kinglets better if they came to our feeders. The reason they do not is simple: they are almost exclusively carnivores, meat eaters. That description is a bit strong when that meat is mostly tiny insects and spiders and their eggs. A study of the food of ruby-crowned kinglets found that only six percent of their food is vegetative.

Their insect food makes them useful birds. Early 20th century ornithologist Edward Howe Forbush wrote, "I watched the gold-crest [a name then for the golden-crowned kinglet] hunting its insect food amid the pines. Each one would hover for a moment before a tuft of pine needles, and then either alight upon it and feed, or pass on to another. I examined the needles after the kinglets had left them, and could find nothing on them; but when a bird was disturbed before it had finished feeding, the spray from which it had been driven was invariably found to be infested with numerous black specks, the eggs of plant lice. Evidently the birds were cleaning each spray thoroughly, as far as they went." Another observer told how they saved the pines in her yard from spruce budworms.

Kinglets' few enemies include small hawks and owls. But James Needham found a number of golden-crowned kinglets that had become entangled in the hooks of burdocks. Examining the individual birds, he described how their attitudes suggested their final struggles. He also found the burdocks infested with moth larvae that had evidently attracted them to these deathtraps.

It is remarkable that these tiny birds are able to make it through our cold winters. They are said to huddle together deep in evergreens to share body warmth. Their worst weather enemy is an ice storm covering their insect food.

8. Shearwater Migration

A few years ago I joined a group of birders on a pelagic trip. (Pelagic relates to the open ocean.) We saw many interesting birds on that trip but I was especially impressed with two species. Several flocks of mostly white Northern phalaropes, delicate little shorebirds hardly bigger than sparrows, flew around us like snow squalls. They seemed completely out of their element here not even within sight of land.

The other species, the sooty shearwater, was just the opposite. These birds were clearly at home here.

The sooty shearwater is a big bird. It weighs more than a wood duck and when it sits on the water it looks a little like a duck. But that is where the similarity ends. You don't often see these birds sitting on the ocean surface.

Instead I watched them sailing on their long narrow wings close to the ocean surface. In doing so this otherwise dingy brown bird (brown is the source of the sooty in its given name) becomes quite beautiful. It earns its surname, shearwater, by the way it tips a wing end down to trail within inches of the sea surface. It takes full advantage of wind gusts and wave crests, scarcely moving those wings. I know of no bird more graceful.

It turns out that the sooty shearwater is a bird in the news today. Here's why.

One ornithological fact long known by the general public as well as ornithologists is that the Arctic tern's 22,000 mile migration holds the distance record for birds. One website calls this species the World Champion of Migration. That route takes the tern from its breeding grounds in eastern Canada and Maine across to Europe, down along the coast of Africa to its wintering region in the Antarctic and back up to North America, this time often following the coast of South America.

Ah, but sometimes long-held "facts" turn out not to be true. An eleven-member team of ornithologists, five from the United States, five from New Zealand and one from France, headed by Scott Shaffer of the University of California at Santa Cruz, studied the migration of the sooty shearwater.

They did so by attaching tiny devices called archival tags to 33 shearwaters on their breeding grounds in New Zealand. These tags transmit information not only about the location of the individual birds but also about how far under the ocean surface they dive to feed.

What they found was quite amazing. These shearwaters all migrated more than 33,700 miles, with an average distance of just under 40,000 miles and a maximum of almost 46,000 miles. Thus these sooty shearwaters not only outdid the old Arctic tern record of 22,000 miles, but in some cases they more than doubled that record.

We have then a new World Champion of Migration: the sooty shearwater.

Be sure you understand: this migration distance does not include the wanderings of these seabirds on their breeding or wintering grounds. It includes only their 200 days actually migrating.

The route the birds followed varied but generally formed a figure eight in the Pacific Ocean. In early April they left their New Zealand breeding grounds, headed due east toward

South America, then turned northwest to their offshore wintering area between North America and Asia at the latitude of the United States and Canada. Finally, they headed south again to complete their trip.

These researchers also found that the tagged shearwaters also dove to amazing depths: some down more than 200 feet.

9. Evening Grosbeaks

A reader contacted me recently to ask about an unusual goldfinch visiting his bird feeder. "Do any goldfinches get extra large?" he asked.

What he thought was a bigger-than-usual goldfinch I am certain was in reality an evening grosbeak. This species does have the yellow and black appearance of a goldfinch, but it is much larger, almost twice the goldfinch's length and four times its weight. And the evening grosbeak is not just bigger, it is a robust bird with an especially thick bill for seed cracking. Another adjective appropriately applied is plump.

As I write this, reports are coming in from across the region of these birds appearing at feeders and birders are excited to have them visit. The reason: for almost thirty years they have been rare winter visitors here.

For several earlier decades evening grosbeaks were rather common birds at bird feeders in winter. And after a few days of their visits, birders often were ready to shoo them away. They consume amazing amounts of sunflower seeds at feeders and they clean them out in a matter of minutes. When they are available in nearby woodlots, the seeds of the ash-leafed maple or boxelder serve as an alternate food source.

The longer-term history of this species in the east is interesting. Originally a bird of the western United States and

Canada, the species slowly spread eastward, the first in the eastern Great Lakes region appearing in Toronto in 1854. Until the winter of 1889-90, however, it was reported as "almost unknown in the East." That winter there was a significant eastward movement and the species was even recorded on the Atlantic coast.

Although evening grosbeaks breed south into the forests of western states and even into Mexico, in the east they mostly nest in Canada and in the High Peaks area of the Adirondacks. Exceptions: on the 2000-2005 state breeding bird survey individual nests were found in New York's Wyoming and Chautauqua Counties.

Almost exclusively, however, evening grosbeaks appear here in winter and then not regularly. During the years from the 1950s through the early 1980s, they were common winter birds and during migration flocks of up to two thousand were occasionally recorded. But then their numbers dropped off and they became rare. For example, on May Counts that cover all of the Niagara Frontier the average number of evening grosbeaks recorded each year in the 1970s was 127; the same number for the early 2000s was 5.

I have also recently found them less common on their breeding grounds. After the mid-'80s I rarely saw them when climbing in the Adirondacks or while on canoe trips in the Minnesota Boundary Waters.

These birds are well worth watching as, despite their heavy bills, they are very adept at feeding. Here are some remarks about the care they take in handling seeds that I found in Bent's life history: "In feeding on the maple seed keys, the bird snips off the pod at the basal end, manipulates the winged portion between the mandibles to [separate] the seeds from their compartments, swallows [the seed] and allows the winged pod to flutter to the ground." "It was apparent that the birds had bitten directly over the kernel itself at a point rather nearer the wing than the kernel. But, although by this incision the kernel was expressed, it was never severed and allowed to fall with the wing, as would have been the case had the beak been closed and bite completed. All this, although the process involved the nicest precision, was accomplished with great rapidity, within a second or two." "They [also] eat snow, scooping it up and swallowing it in large quantities after feeding on seeds." If you do have these birds visit your feeder, you should watch this process as it applies to your sunflower seeds.

10. First Outing

Although it happened over fifty years ago, I recall the experience as though it was just yesterday. Three of us, Ambrose Secker, my mother and I, stood on a high bluff overlooking the vast cattail marshes at the foot of Irondequoit Bay east of Rochester. This was my first meeting with Amb Secker who had been assigned by the Genesee Ornithological Society to check me out, to see if I would be the first elementary school student to join their organization.

It was evening and light was quickly fading. From below us came the calls of swamp birds, familiar friends now but then another story entirely. I did know the *konkaree* of the red-winged blackbird and I could associate the *cronk* of the great blue heron with the large bird flapping slowly along Irondequoit Creek, but the rattle of the marsh wren and the *quowk* of the black-crowned night heron were alien to me as were the *kow kow kow* of pied-billed grebes and the chicken-like cackling of moorhens (then called gallinules.)

Even stranger were odd horse whinnies and *kidick kidick* and whinnying sounds that increased in number as twilight descended. Those I learned that evening were the calls of birds I still rarely see, the sora and Virginia rail. Rails are solitary and secretive birds that William Burt, in his evocative book, has aptly named *Shadowbirds*.

I have since seen Virginia rails hardly a dozen times, most often in the reeds at Tifft Nature Preserve where they nest and where one once even stayed through the winter. I have seen soras there too, still less often, and Mandy Galas and I were lucky enough to see a king rail briefly in the Iroquois National Wildlife Refuge. That's it locally for everyone I know, although many of us have seen clapper rails in their Atlantic coastal tideland habitat. Although the tiny black and yellow rails have also been reported here, I know of no recent records, and they are nearly impossible to find anywhere.

Shadowbirds is the perfect term for rails as their costumer certainly knows the art of camouflage. At nine inches the sora and Virginia rail are about the same size and are usually described as chicken-like not only for their shape but for their leg length and the deliberate placement of their outsized feet as they tiptoe among the reeds. Both are drab brown and gray birds with streaks that perfectly blend into the background of brown cattails — shadowlike.

Unless they are out away from the reeds in mud flats — a too rare event — they are not only difficult to see but almost impossible to point out to a friend even when you have them in your telescope field.

That long ago summer evening was one of the most exciting I have ever spent birding. And the life-defining outcome was my admission to the society.

I did not forget that marsh. For years Joe Taylor, Allan Klonick and I started "Big Day" May counts there. At midnight I would light the fuse of a firecracker salute at its edge. The loud bang would bring a cacophony of those barnyard responses, starting our list with at least a half dozen species.

11. Cardinal

My wife's favorite bird is the cardinal and that lovely redbird is one of my personal favorites as well.

Doris missed our neighborhood pair through the entire winter but I heard and occasionally saw the male. Now, however, our backyard resounds almost continuously with his cheery whistles and the female busily searches out nest building material.

The cardinal is one of the few birds I can imitate and that only because its songs are so simple: a series of clear, elided *tee-you* calls, each one sliding downward, often followed by an equally clear series of rising *wheet* notes. If you know no other bird song, learn this one. It is indeed a day-maker.

We had every reason to worry about our cardinals after a winter that seems to have been especially tough on feeder birds. Both Christmas Census and Breeding Bird Survey data show cardinal numbers down. Also friends have been telling me that where there had been five or ten cardinals they were seeing only one or two and sometimes none.

Although we have never had those higher numbers near our home, I had a similar experience on last December's Buffalo Christmas Count. Each year on this count we stop at a house on Tonawanda Creek Road which has a large spruce tree and a bird feeder on its front lawn. In past years a half dozen or more cardinals decorated that tree like beautiful red Christmas ornaments. This winter only a few house sparrows ate lazily at the well-stocked feeder; not a cardinal was to be seen.

Newer birders may not realize that the cardinal is a newcomer to this region. It is a southern species that has moved north, probably encouraged and then sustained by the smorgasbord provided them by bird feeders.

When I was a beginning birder in Rochester I was active for

several years before I saw my first cardinal. I have told this story in an earlier essay but it is worth retelling here. The event was so important to me that I recall it vividly still. I was in Tryon Park at the head of Irondequoit Bay with Howard Miller, a superb birder who was exceptionally kind to me as a novice. It was my first Christmas Count. Winter had come early and harsh and birds were scarce. We had found only a few chickadees and nuthatches when suddenly a clear whistle came from the distance.

It was a song I didn't know and Howard, an excellent teacher as well as birder, said, "Gerry, I'm not going to tell you what that is. Instead let's hike over to where it is singing. I'm sure that you will then identify it for yourself."

We slogged through the deep snow perhaps a hundred yards until we came to a sumac grove. And there he was, sitting tall on top of an ice-encrusted sumac tassel serenading us with his lovely song. I have added many rare and exotic birds to my life list over the years but none have given me more pure pleasure than that perfect cardinal on that winter morning.

I expect that many people like the male cardinal because of its bright red coloration. That is not what makes it so attractive to me. Its red is no match for the deep rich color of the scarlet tanager's breast nor the helmet of the red-headed woodpecker. Instead I think of it as a Cary Grant among birds, its posture erect, its body light, its movements sure and swift and understated, its manners towards its consort impeccable.

We are delighted to have "our" cardinals again beginning a nest in our junipers. Doris is already concerned about protecting the little family from our neighborhood cat.

12. Jordan's Desert

From a mile up it just looked brown, but now, as our plane glides down to the El Paso runway, I notice that the sand is uniformly dotted with the drab green of creosote bush.

This is the Chihuahuan Desert, a largely Mexican desert extending over an area three times that of New York State. Only its northernmost arms reach into Texas, New Mexico and Arizona. It is not our only United States desert: the Sonoran and Mojave claim more of this Basin and Range Province between the Rocky Mountains and the Sierras.

When I was here before I found the land sterile. A walk beyond artificially maintained yards took me into a vast sandbox with little sign of life other than straggly bushes.

But this time I hope for better. I have been promised that I will be shown "his desert" by my eight-year-old grandson, Jordan.

I'm already wilting in the 104° heat when he greets me at the airport with a large poster on which he has mapped his neighborhood and the two morning walks he will lead. Houses appear in profile with lines that trace our half-mile routes looping around them. He has appropriately drawn on sand colored paper.

At six the next morning it is only 83°. It takes me five minutes to rouse my guide, but once Jordan is awake his enthusiasm returns. He unrolls his map and off we go.

This is not the desert I remember. It is now full of life.

As we cross the driveway and step onto the hard caliche, three black-tailed jack rabbits dart off to disappear among the bushes. They seem all ears and hind legs. Later we'll see a desert cottontail, much like our own backyard rabbits.

Through the dry air comes the lovely *Chi-ca'-ga* call of a Gambel's quail, a sound we've all heard in western movies but that represents a real life first for me. There it is! The bobwhite sized bird poses for us, its strange plume rising from its head like one of those women's nineteenth century ostrich feathers. Another joins it trailing a half dozen young, hardly bigger than grapes.

Jordan shows me a prickly pear cactus, its vertical green pancakes now surrounded by pretty pink blossoms. Nearby we find an ocotillo or coachwhip. I shudder as I imagine being beaten by these fierce branches. The brown wands are covered with huge thorns.

Here is the ever-present tumbleweed, in some places a small green shrub, more often a brown tangle captured by a windbreak. Another shrub, western peppergrass, sports tiny white blossoms. And stunted trees that I first assume are locusts turn out to be mesquite, source of that wonderful western aroma and flavor when mixed with charcoal to grill steaks.

My grandson mixes adventure with natural history. I identify his interest in the Hardy Boys when he leads me to what he calls Snake Mountain. It is only a slight rise, but from it we can see the jagged crests of the Chihuahuan Mountains far south of the thin blue ribbon that is the Rio Grande.

On my previous visit I found only grackles. Now we see ash-throated flycatchers, white-winged doves, a pyrrhuloxia (a mostly gray southwestern cardinal), curve-billed thrashers, a Swainson's hawk. Jordan discovers a cactus wren's nest just before we see the bird itself.

We don't find the tarantulas or scorpions or roadrunners or sidewinders my guide had hoped to show me, but I come away with a better appreciation for the remarkably varied life of what I will always recall as Jordan's desert.

13. The Real James Bond

Some time ago two revised editions of the famous Roger Tory Peterson field guide series reached my desk. They are *Birds of Britain and Europe* by Peterson himself together with Guy Mountfort and P. A. D. Hollom and James Bond's *Birds of the West Indies*. Bond had been the sole author of the earlier edition of that second book. Each is in the best tradition of this quite remarkable series that now includes 44 titles: books on everything from minerals to medicinal plants, from seashells to stars, from mammals to moths. All of them represent an extension of the identification scheme developed by Peterson and before him Ernest Thompson Seton.

The second of these new books brought back pleasant memories of an incident many years ago.

I was attending a meeting in Philadelphia. With a morning free, I made my way to the Academy of Natural Sciences, the fine Philadelphia museum. I paid my entrance fee at the door and crossed to the information desk to ask if it would be possible to visit James Bond, the author of this book who was also Curator of Birds at the museum.

I knew Dr. Bond only by reputation, but at the time I was considering a career change and wanted the advice of a senior ornithologist. I hoped that he would be able to spare a few minutes for me.

My request received an immediate and quite unexpected response. The young woman I had approached first, ushered me over to the cashier, retrieved my entrance fee and returned it to me. She then called Dr. Bond and, at his instructions, escorted me up to his office. As we walked along the marble floored corridors, my guide made it increasingly clear that the museum staff held their bird curator in both high regard and personal affection.

Before we reached his office we were met by a slim erect

man, then I expect in his early sixties. He wore a jacket and tie, but the rumpled condition of his clothes gave him an air of informality. Most noticeable were his penetrating eyes: they could have been stern but for the friendly wrinkles that surrounded them and the wide smile of greeting that now creased his face.

When I explained my mission, he responded openly and enthusiastically. He had some time he explained as he walked me to his office and he would be delighted to talk to anyone with an interest in birds. My few minutes turned into one of the most stimulating four-hour periods I have ever spent.

I recall many things from those hours including the excellent advice he gave me, but two other things stand out. I asked something about Darwin's finches, the Galapagos Island birds that contributed so importantly to the 19th Century English naturalist's thinking about evolution. This struck a chord, because, unknown to me, Bond had discovered the only member of this group away from the Galapagos. He had found it, not on mainland South America, but across that continent in the West Indies, something no one had been able to explain. We examined tray after tray of the museum's collection of these unusual birds.

I finally asked Bond if people teased him about the association of his name with Ian Fleming's notorious superspy. "As it happens," he responded smiling, "I am that James Bond." He went on to explain that he was a neighbor and friend of Fleming in Jamaica. When Fleming was writing his first story, he asked his ornithologist neighbor for permission to use his name.

For others James Bond, I suspect, brings to mind the actors Sean Connery or Roger Moore or now Timothy Dalton. Not for me. Even the number 007 will forever be associated in my memory with that kind and gentle man who so generously shared his day with me in Philadelphia.

14. A Migration Interrupted

Like so many other birds, the tiny Wilson's warbler nested unsuccessfully this year. Even though her moss-covered ground home was well hidden in an alder swamp northeast of Sudbury, a chipmunk found it. The little mammal promptly made a meal of her five finely-speckled white eggs.

Now she is on the second night of her flight south toward her winter range in Mexico and her luck is not improving.

Last night the strong winds accompanying a cold front blew her east of her regular flight path along Georgian Bay and across the narrow end of Lake Erie at Point Pelee. She was finally forced down by a pre-dawn shower in a Lake Ontario shoreline woods near Port Weller.

At midnight instinctual drives again propel her into the air with scores of other birds. They rise high into the black sky, join hundreds more and head south. At first the air is clear and the little warbler can even see stars, but ahead the weather is unsettled. She can make out the north shore of Lake Erie, but dense clouds obscure its southern boundary. Because of this, the entire flock drifts still further east to follow the Niagara River and skirt the end of the lake.

But as the Wilson's warbler and her companions fly high over the stacks of Squaw Island, the wedge of clear air ends and they enter the low cloud layer. The birds become disoriented and the flock loses its cohesiveness. Each bird is on its own.

The warbler flutters on, losing altitude and searching for clues in the dense cloud: a ground pattern, wind direction, a star — anything.

Suddenly she does see something: a light ahead. She makes for it.

Her end comes quickly. She never hears the thump as her tiny body hits the lighted City Hall window and she falls lifeless to a distant balcony. At dawn a ring-billed gull finds her limp body, tears it to shreds and gulps it down.

That poor bird? No: those poor birds. A documented estimate of the number of birds killed annually by flying into man-made structures is 80 million. Over 150 species have met this fate. Single location, one-night kills of 30,000 and 50,000 have been recorded.

The volunteer group FLAP (for Fatal Light Awareness Program) patrols the skyscraper canyons of midtown Toronto during spring and fall migrations, from mid-April to early June and from mid-August to early November. FLAP volunteers each pick up over 3,000 birds a year. A few of the birds they find are only stunned; those they carry to the edge of the city for release.

Meanwhile, efforts are being mounted to reduce this carnage. Birds are most attracted on stormy or foggy nights to steady, bright lights and white floodlit objects; less to colored or filtered lights. They tend to ignore flashing strobe lights. Such prime killers as lighthouse beacons and airport ceilometers have been modified accordingly.

Birds often fly into windows during the day as well. One glass-paneled downtown Buffalo building has proved a killing magnet to songbirds. In its panes the birds see the reflection of trees across the street.

Mounting cardboard falcon silhouettes solves some of these daytime problems of picture windows and glassed-in porches.

Buffalo's skyscrapers don't present as severe a nighttime problem as those of Toronto; however, if you must light a room in a high building during migration, you should draw the shades or close the blinds.

Such small gestures could help to slow the steep population decline of these beautiful songbirds.

15. Tanager

Is there such a thing as being too beautiful? If there is, my candidate is the scarlet tanager.

We all admire the cardinal's bright flash of red as it dashes across a yard or pops up to snatch seeds from a feeder. But cardinal red is almost harsh beside the soft deep red of the male tanager's head and body. And the tanager's black wings set off that red to additional advantage. Whenever I focus binoculars on one of these shy treetop dwellers, I have great difficulty moving my eyes away.

I have known this species since childhood when my father pointed one out to me in the Adirondacks. And I have seen — and more often heard — them hundreds of times since then. The scarlet tanager is in fact rather common on the Niagara Frontier.

That statement will no doubt surprise many readers who may never have seen even a single tanager. This is a case of finding something only when you know how to look. I offer help here.

If you know the robin's oft-repeated *cheery-up cheery-ee*, you can easily learn the tanager's song. It sounds like a hoarse robin. Its song has the same cadence, but the notes have a burry quality. The yellow-throated vireo has a similar song, but its phrases are widely separated.

Now where do you listen? Tanagers are most often found in deciduous woodlots where tree crowns are over 50 feet high. They forage in those treetops, but at this time of year will sometimes descend and even approach you if you imitate that sushing sound librarians use to keep you quiet. Since that *shh shh* is also the noise that nestlings make, birders use it to attract many species. (At the time this column was written the way we could attract birds by sound was limited. Today, of course, we can use technology to play a recording of a tanager's song to entice a male to approach to defend his territory.)

Of course not every woodlot produces tanagers. On a survey for the Cornell Laboratory of Ornithology I found only two in eight woodlots; thus you'll need luck if you have only one place to look.

For those who seek a sure thing, here are directions to two male tanagers that are easy to find. Drive north on Cedar Street from Alden until you pass Swift Mills and Martin Roads. Cedar Street will then pass between two woodlots. Near the north end of the lot to your left are the tanagers.

Do not enter either woodlot as they are posted. Instead listen from the road. You should locate at least one of the two males by zeroing in on that song. One often sings from a branch that overhangs the road itself.

Finding the two male tanagers together is quite unusual. Normally you would expect territorial behavior at this time of year. As one is only a year old, it may be last year's offspring of the older pair and not yet independent of them.

You can look for these birds at any time of day. Warning: get ready for mosquitoes if they bother you! Prepare also for a shock if you have never seen a scarlet tanager before. The sub-adult retains a small area of orange wash, but that hardly detracts from its glorious red.

You will probably not see a female. She is much less conspicuous with the male's red replaced by olive green and she is probably brooding by now anyway.

(Although those directions were written over twenty years ago and the age of the birds will certainly differ today, they remain accurate because new tanager generations continue to inhabit this small woodlot.)

Three other tanager species are found in the United States: the summer tanager of the South and the hepatic tanager of the Southwest, both all red, and the red, yellow and black western tanager. All but the hepatic tanager have been recorded in New York, yet very rarely. Those too are handsome birds, but they are no match for our own scarlet tanager.

16. Pelagic Trip

This is my idea of excitement!

It is 10:30 a.m. on December 3 and I am wedged between the rail and the cabin bulkhead of a 90-foot motor launch. I have to maintain that position because the boat rolls and pitches in ocean swells. One minute I'm deep in a trough, the seas towering above me, the next I'm ten feet higher on a wave crest, the broad expanse of the ocean open to my view. The sensation is that of a carnival ride.

But I'm not here for the ride. We're in the Atlantic 100 miles southeast of New York City looking for pelagic birds and mammals.

We set out from Captree on Fire Island just before 5:00 and I slept hunched uncomfortably over a cabin table until dawn. I was never seasick in the navy but when I awoke this morning my stomach lurched, bringing to mind an old bos'n's warning: "Battleship sailors have trouble on destroyers. Each ship has its own brand of discomfort." But when I stumbled out on deck the queasiness passed.

On the way out we saw dozens of kittiwakes among more common gulls. A kittiwake is a sea-going version of our Bonaparte's gull, another delicate tern-like flier. Each winter one or two kittiwakes visit the Niagara Gorge, but the sight of so many is exhilarating.

Now we're wallowing in quartering seas at the edge of the Continental Shelf where the ocean floor beneath us drops off from hundreds of feet to the thousands of the Hudson

Canyon. A few trawlers are nearby, each with its flurry of attendant gulls.

A crew member begins chumming: that is, he tosses fish parts high in the air from our stern. In response hundreds of gulls join us, some flying in from the other boats. Among them are a few intriguing brown-backed birds whose small bodies make them appear almost all wings. They are shearwaters. That Shakespearean name suits them because they sail close to the water surface, one wing tip constantly appearing to shear the waves. I watch one glide for ten minutes expecting to see the water cleft or the feathers ruffled. I never do. The tips of their primaries always stay a centimeter or two clear.

Shearwaters are made for this element. They use the air with consummate skill. Nearby one sits lightly on the water surface where it has caught and devoured a fish. It paddles its feet rapidly for a second or two and simply raises its wings: up and off it sails. How unlike the furious struggle of a loon to rise from a lake.

Suddenly something hurtles down through a crowd of gulls to slice into the surf. Others follow: each dive a perfect Olympic ten. These are gannets, bigger and heavier-bodied than the gulls, but like them generally white with black wing ends. They are so close I can see their blue-gray bills without binoculars.

And now a spine-tingling thrill. The water surface is broken by a bulbous black head and a 20-foot dark body, single-finned, follows it along a wave crest. It is a pilot whale. Sailors have called this dolphin relative a pothead since well before the 1960s when that name was appropriated for another use. For ten minutes a dozen of them play about us so close that we can hear them breathe. A single calf closely accompanies one of the cows.

By the end of the long day I'll see other birds new to me — among them my first auks: a razorbill and a dovekie — but those pilot whales alone make the trip one I'll never forget.

17. Saw-whet

In a hallway of our home hangs a painting of a saw-whet owl by Guy Coheleach. It is a valued possession since its subject is one of my favorite birds. Out of the painting stares a seven-inch long, fluffed out, tawny butterball with its yellow irises almost covered by big black pupils.

But this painting in no way represents the saw-whet owl that my wife and I found hidden in a pine grove of the Tifft Nature Preserve in mid-March. This bird seemed much thinner, perhaps a distant, less affluent cousin of the little fatty of the painting. To gain some sense of the size of this diminutive owl, hold up together three fingers of one hand: the bird could easily hide behind those fingers.

This is always a difficult bird to find. Although we had been given specific directions to a half dozen small pine trees, it took us several minutes to locate the owl. It suddenly materialized like Alice's Cheshire cat where I was certain I had looked before.

I had a similar experience several years ago cross country skiing through a thicket along Ellicott Creek on the University at Buffalo campus. Straightening up from bending under a low snag, I found myself blinked at sleepily by one of these little owls from a distance of less than three feet. It never even flushed as I awkwardly pushed on through the brush.

As this suggests, the saw-whet owl is an extremely tame little bird. We were able to approach the Tifft owl closely before its increasing concern caused us to back away to a less threatening distance. If you ever find one of these birds — and dozens of them quietly pass through this region in March and April — I also encourage you not to disturb it.

Unthreatened, it will often remain in the same area for days and even weeks. You will be well rewarded. Even my wife, who is only marginally tolerant of birds, was charmed by this Lilliputian representative of the notoriously vicious strigiform order.

Larger raptors like barred and great horned owls occasionally prey on saw-whet owls, but the smaller owls are hunters too. Their food is most often rodents and frogs; however, at this season this saw-whet almost certainly thinned the numbers of the juncos and white-throated sparrows that foraged the ground nearby. The only prey I ever observed in the talons of a saw-whet was a junco, but bigger (still only eight inch) females have been known to kill and devour red squirrels.

Saw-whet owl is a strange name. It sounds like something someone dreams up toward the end of the cocktail hour, like left tern or O'Hara cardinal or coffee chat, but there is a reason for this one. Only once have I heard the repeated metallic, whistled snee'-awww notes of the courtship song of this species. They wafted down from the midnight forest of Calamity Mountain to our Adirondack campsite at Flowed Land, and they did indeed sound like the working of a file back and forth, back and forth across the serrations of a saw. The saw-whet has another song as well, a one-note whistle repeated every second for minutes on end. Its quality is very different, yet it too could be taken for saw filing.

Although many of the saw-whet owls seen here at this time of year are migrants, some do nest in the region, most often in the deep, often boggy and pine-covered recesses of such sanctuaries as Bergen Swamp and Allegany State Park. Evening visitors to these and other heavily wooded areas, especially in March and April, should listen for their eerie notes.

18. A Bird with Two Heads

Late last spring I spent about fifteen hours over a three-day period sitting in a Monroe County backyard watching a bird feeding station. Coming and going to and from the feeders were cardinals and house finches, downy woodpeckers and chickadees, chipping sparrows and even an indigo bunting. A chipmunk joined grackles, red-winged blackbirds, mourning doves and house sparrows below the feeding trays. In the recently mown field beyond the lawn yellow and chestnut-sided warblers searched the grass for seeds and insects.

But I never saw what I was looking for. I was watching for a chipping sparrow with two heads.

I had learned of this remarkable possibility from an Internet bird chat line. The message called attention to the report, gave the address and added, "I question this but it might be worth checking out."

Despite that disclaimer, I phoned the Hilton couple, Bob and Grace Carson, to ask about their sighting. Yes, they had seen the bird several times and had photographed it through their kitchen window. They were afraid, however, that even taken with a telephoto lens the pictures would not be definitive. Would I come to confirm their observation? I went — I watched — but I failed to see the bird.

A two-headed bird would be the wildlife equivalent of conjoined human twins and would be at least as rare. Bird abnormalities have been reported, of course. A 1934 study of 100,000 starlings, for example, turned up over five percent with various deformities but they were things like malformed bills, unusual size or missing eyes, legs, feet or toenails. Other observers have noted wild birds with extra pairs of legs or wings — a phenomenon called duplicity that is also found occasionally in domestic fowl. But I turned up no record of a two-headed bird.

However, I did come across an interesting and detailed description of a two-headed black rat snake. The ethologists who studied the snake called it IM, the letters representing instinct and mind. Gordon Burghart writes, "The snake's frequent conflicts over prey, usually mice, vividly reminded me of the perennial conflict between those two concepts.... Regardless of whether one or both heads struck, both heads often simultaneously attempted to swallow the prey."

The Carsons described their sparrow as having the second head facing backwards, the bills thus pointing in opposite directions. Grace told me how it twisted so that each head could feed in turn. But Bob's later reports indicated that the second head became inactive and drooped lifeless down the bird's back.

I never saw any of this although I missed one reported appearance by only ten minutes. I did see a few feathers on one bird's nape raised by the breeze and I tried to convince myself that was what the Carsons were seeing.

But now finally the photographs have been printed and Bob has forwarded copies. Although none are ideal, I believe that they confirm the Carsons' observations of this bizarre anomaly. The best shows the bird perched opposite a house finch at a tube feeder, its body facing away from us, one head turned to the left, the other to the right. The left head is fully plumaged with the red cap of an adult chippy, the right retaining the characteristics of an immature bird. In two photos taken later that immature plumaged head has lost its vitality and lies lifeless against its back.

After a week of those late May visits the bird failed to return. By now it has almost certainly died, but its brief appearance at the Carson feeder might have represented an extraordinary ornithological first.

Postscript

Several weeks after this column appeared, the two best photographs of the sparrow were enhanced by Don Trainor, a

University at Buffalo graphic arts specialist. Although the improved pictures were still far from perfect — recall that they were taken by telephoto lens through a kitchen window — they appear to me to be definitive.

Unfortunately — or perhaps fortunately for the little chipping sparrow — the photos do not confirm my earlier belief that it had two heads. The second appears to be a ball of some kind of woolly material that gives only the appearance of another head.

What confirms this reanalysis for me are two facts: (1) No bill appears on the "second head" in either picture. And (2) In the second picture which was taken several days later (when the second "head" appeared to have "died") that "head" not only lies down the sparrow's back but it has rolled around from the right shoulder to the left and gray feathers show to the right where the strange material had earlier been stuck.

Now that the false second head has been identified, I am able to look back on how the Carsons and I had allowed ourselves to be misled. We should have been immediately put off by two things. First, this is an adult chipping sparrow which meant that it is in at least its second year. To manage that full year — including two migrations — with that additional burden would have been virtually impossible. And second, the additional head should also have been that of an adult bird. Now I can see how my enthusiasm and the seeming photographic evidence, no matter how foggy, overwhelmed those very serious concerns.

It is interesting to note, however, what looks very much like an eye in the lower black stripe of the first picture. This osceli is, according to the photographic specialist, almost certainly a visual aberration.

So the Carsons and I lost our chance of announcing a real first for ornithology. That loss was at least balanced by the fact that my dismal prognosis for the bird's future was very possibly wrong. I expect that after a time the material would have freed itself from the bird's feathers — during molt if at no other time — and the little sparrow would then have been free of its irritating "extra head." The evidence of the second photograph suggests that that process had already started.

In any case, once again I have managed a near miss. Most of us know the feeling that the great ones always seem to get away, but that is one of the challenges of bird watching.

Second Postscript

On June 23, 1998 bird bander Bob McKinney of Rochester, New York sent me the following e-mail message:

Hi Gerry, I may have the answer to your Chipping Sparrow with two heads. This morning I caught a Chipping Sparrow with an enormous, ugly growth on the side of the head. I have never seen anything like it. The bird certainly would not have a normal liklihood of survival so I released it immediately. The growth was almost as large as the head itself. Anyone seeing this bird may very well suspect it had two heads. I didn't enjoy handling the bird and thoroughly washed my hands after doing so. Thought you would be interested.

While this is almost certainly not the same bird I saw a year earlier — surely that bird could not have survived even our mild winter of 1997-1998 — it does suggest another possibility for the appearance of the bird observed at the Carson's feeder.

19. Oriole

Early May is a time of anticipation for birders. The addicted among us are already reciting our mantra, "The warblers are coming, the warblers are coming," but it will be several days before those tiny jewels will appear in good numbers. Meanwhile we are delighted by other songbirds as they return to decorate our shade trees.

One species that gives me much pleasure each year when it returns is the Baltimore oriole. (I am happy to be able to call it that again after a number of years when it was referred to as the northern oriole. Reversing an earlier combining of these species, ornithological systematists just last year split northern orioles back into our familiar Baltimore oriole and the western Bullock's oriole.) My enjoyment in that first sighting is shared with ornithologist Winsor Tylor who claims that the "greatest day of the whole year is in early May when the apple blossoms are opening. On this day the Baltimore oriole makes his dramatic entrance."

The vagaries of weather affect the migration timing of these beautiful birds in their long trip from Central America. My records, accumulated over eight years canvassing Williamsville Glen, show our oriole arriving as early as April 30 (in 1990 and 1994) and as late as May 11 (in 1995), with an average arrival date of May 6. Although the Glen is not a place where birders go for earliest records — Tifft Nature Preserve and Times Beach are probably best for them — mine compare closely with those of Beardslee and Mitchell's *Birds of the Niagara Frontier*, which is the local standard. May 1 is their expected first arrival and May 8 the date when they become numerous.

Each spring the oriole's clear rounded whistle first attracts my attention. His cheery notes greet me as I enter Glen Park. From the top of a tall cottonwood he's proclaiming to us common folk his majestic arrival on the Niagara Frontier. And because he is so much a creature of habit, I know exactly where to look for him. Indeed there he is, singing from his usual perch.

Now he leaves that high branch and flies across to the top of a maple. Like the cardinal he combines beauty of appearance with his melodious voice. As he flies overhead in the early morning sunlight I get a spectacular view of the rich orange of his breast in contrast with his black head. Unlike his darker and rarer congener, the orchard oriole, the male Baltimore oriole also shows a white chevron in each wing. He's about the same length as another relative, the red-winged blackbird, but he appears to this prejudiced observer slimmer and more graceful.

In a few days his olive-colored consort will arrive and they will mate. Then their remarkable nest will be constructed high in an elm, maple, or other hardwood tree. An opportunity to watch the intricate nest-building process is a great experience. After gathering and dangling a mass of material from the end of a branch, in just two or three days the female will feverishly weave the strands into a soft hanging basket — a unique nest. (You can sometimes attract orioles by stringing pieces of yarn and twine in your shrubbery.) In late May or early June four or five grayish white eggs will be laid and the family raising process begun.

Orioles' preferred food is caterpillars, which with other insects makes up five sixths of their diet. Later they will also feed on wild berries. As those who feed birds have found, they are especially attracted to grape jelly.

Welcome back to this colorful aristocrat. You'll do fine whether or not those warblers stop by.

20. Sumac Storehouse

Among the easiest to identify of our native trees in winter is the staghorn sumac. Often found in disturbed areas along highways or railroads, the species appears at this time of year as a thicket of 10-15 feet high leafless vertical branches topped with red candles. Up close those candles turn out to be clusters of hairy reddish berries gathered into ten-inch upright cones.

The name staghorn is well chosen. Individual branches do look like deer antlers and this species differs from smooth sumac by the velvety surface of its upper branches. This quality is similar to that of newly grown deer horns before their fuzz is worn off.

A sumac grouping is comprised of clones growing from a common root. Just as deer are aged by counting their antler divisions, you can tell the age in years of an individual stem by the number of its branchings. You can use this technique to determine the mother stem.

For many years I have checked sumac clusters for birds because of an experience I had when I lived near Binghamton, New York. A group of a dozen pine grosbeaks, one of our rarest visitors from the far north, spent several weeks that winter feeding in a single sumac grove south of the city. The birds were so tame that we could approach to within a few feet to take pictures. Unfortunately that encounter was not repeated.

Almost a hundred bird species have been recorded feeding on sumac, among them grouse and turkeys, bluebirds, hermit thrushes and robins, cardinals, crows and starlings. But sumac fruit serves these species only as a last resort — like spinach to a starving child — and it is a rare winter that drives birds to these trees. This winter on the Niagara Frontier, for example, the wild fruit crop is excellent so you won't find many birds resorting to these berries.

Something else about sumac was discovered by Syracuse teacher Kathy Schwab's fourth-graders several years ago. Her students wrote to naturalist Ben Burtt: "Our class has been studying plants found in a field near our school. One of the plants that we studied was the staghorn sumac. When we dissected the red seed clusters, we found something we didn't expect."

They went on to tell Burtt that they found kernels of corn, sunflower seeds and some unusual three-sided seeds in the candles and they wondered if he knew where they came from. "Could some kind of bird be responsible?" they asked.

Unfamiliar with this kind of sumac warehousing, Burtt checked with specialists at the Syracuse College of Forestry and he posted the students' inquiry on the Internet. No one had had the students' experience. But Burtt investigated sumac himself and found similar seeds. (The students' "unusual" seeds turned out to be beechnuts.)

Burtt quickly ruled out mice, chipmunks and squirrels. Although they do cache food, he decided that "it would hardly be worth the climb" for them to store and retrieve it. A literature search indicated that, of regional birds, jays, nuthatches, titmice and chickadees commonly hoard food. His report on this episode continues: "From the large size of the beechnuts, I tend to rule out chickadees, titmice and nuthatches. The blue jay seems the most likely candidate." But he adds, "So far, I have found no one who has seen the jays actually doing this."

I join Burtt in saluting these students. Their investigation contributed both to their own understanding and to that of the scientific community.

But the story remains incomplete. Watch for birding activity in sumac groves and you too may add to our understanding of this phenomenon.

21. Lark Bunting

When I was seventeen and a World War II Navy seaman, I hitchhiked most of the way across the country alone, making my way in eight days from Great Falls, Montana to Rochester. It was a wonderful adventure. I was given rides by many families with sons my age serving in battle zones around the world and by a few who had already lost children: for a few miles I served as a stand-in for them. I was also picked up by truckers man-handling huge rigs, rough-looking men but every one of those I met on that 2500 mile trek intelligent and good humored. One, I recall, enjoyed very much a small restaurant with blackboard chalked menus on which he pointed out two variant spellings of the same word: "sandwitches" and "sandwhiches". I hadn't expected to meet an orthographer in the cab of an eighteen-wheeler.

But I also spent many hours mostly in Montana and Wyoming walking across vast open rangeland where hours sometimes passed between cars — to say nothing of rides. It was like hiking across a vast moonscape bisected by the highway.

To a boy raised in the suburbs some of the experiences were intimidating. For example, topping a rise I came upon a herd of perhaps a hundred long-horned cattle. Every one of them turned its white forehead toward me. All the time they were in sight I wondered if they might stampede over me, but looking back from the next hill I could see them still standing there staring in my direction.

Over the miles I walked, however, more cheerful companions regularly accompanied me. They were lark buntings — sparrow-sized birds, all black except for large white wing patches. I could sometimes see as many as six or eight at the same time, not in flocks but rather evenly distributed over the barren land. They were delightful songsters, their outpourings reminding me a little of song sparrows — several clear notes at first, followed by a jumble of phrases.

While they often sang from the bare ground or the tops of the few small bushes, they also occasionally flew up fifteen to twenty feet to pour out their notes as they coasted back down to earth. It seemed clear that this kind of territory defining display represented the best they could do without taller bushes and trees for perches.

These pretty little songsters seemed to be outdoing each other for my benefit. The female birds for whom they were really displaying must have been sitting on nests as I never saw any of them.

The memory of this experience was brought back to me vividly when I joined a number of birders just south of Iroquois National Wildlife Refuge last week. We were there looking for a reported lark bunting. It would be the first of this western species to visit this area since 1967.

Sure enough, after about fifteen minutes of waiting in the early morning drizzle, we were rewarded. Out of the bushes popped the little black finch to perch atop a trash pile from which he proceeded to entertain us with his singing. A half dozen telescopes were immediately focused on the bird, some with cameras attached.

Why this bird of the western prairies is here we can only guess. Most likely it was blown off course on its flight north from its wintering grounds in Texas and Mexico. Whatever the reason, however, its visit has made a Genesee County farm a mecca for birders from all over the northeastern states.

22. Loon Story

Each of us who has spent time in the North Woods has a favorite loon experience. Most of these stories relate to the wildly varying calls of this big waterfowl. We all know its Woody Woodpecker-like shrieking laugh that reverberates across the wilderness lakes to awaken us in the morning or to alert us later in the day of an approaching storm. Guides tell us, "When a flying loon calls, tighten your tent lines and prepare for a blow." We know too its nighttime wails that carry even from distant lakes — calls that are often misidentified by neophyte campers as wolf howls. There is a solemn, even mournful quality to them that can sends shivers up your spine.

Now I have come across a true story about the calling of loons that will, I am certain, remain my favorite forever. It appears in an excellent biography, *Joseph Banks: A Life*, by Patrick O'Brian. O'Brian is also the author of the superb Aubrey Maturin sea novels. I commend both book and author to you.

Banks was a wealthy 18th century English naturalist, perhaps best known for his service for over 40 years as president of the Royal Society and his circumnavigation of the world with Captain Cook. In 1766 an earlier voyage took him to Newfoundland where the following event occurred.

As he did throughout his life, Banks recorded his many experiences in his unpunctuated and idiosyncratically capitalized and spelled style. Deciphering this writing is half the fun and I quote Banks' narrative, as does O'Brian, directly:

"Some birds there are that I must mention Particularly one Known here by the name of Whobby he is of the Loon Kind & an Excellent Diver but Very Often amuses himself especially in the night by flying high in the air and making a very Loud & alarming noise at least to those who do not know the Cause of it as the following circumstance will shew

"In August 1765 as Commodore Paliser in the Guernsey a 50 gun ship Lay in this Harbour Expecting the Indians one Dark night in a thick fog the Ships company were alarmed by a noise they had not heard before Every one awoke Conjecturd what it could Possibly be it came nearer & nearer grew louder & louder the first Lieuftenant was calld up he was the only man in the Ship Who had Ever seen the Esquimaux immediately as he heard the noise he declard he rememberd it well it was the war whoop of the Esquimaux who were certainly Coming in their Canoes to board the Ship & Cut all their throats the Commodore was acquainted up he Bundled upon the Deck orderd ship to be cleard for Engaging all hands to Great Guns arms in the Tops Every thing in as good order as if a french man of war of Equal Force was within half a mile Bearing down upon them

"The Niger which Lay at some Distance from them was haild & told the indians were Coming when the Enemy appeared in the shape of a Troop of these Whobbys swimming & flying about the Harbour which From the Darkness of the night they had not seen before all hands were then sent down to Sleep & no more thought of the indians till the Nigers People came on board next morning who will Probably never Forget that their Companion Cleared Ship & turned up all hands to a flock of Whobbies"

I would not wish to have been Commodore Paliser or his first lieutenant or in fact any member of the crew of the unlucky HMS Guernsey as that story made the rounds of the fleet.

No wonder the loons are laughing.

23. Charles Sibley

This essay is about a friendship that was much too short.

Charles Sibley died last year and I have only now come to terms with that personal loss. Although we met only briefly forty years ago and we corresponded by e-mail only for the last four years before his death, I considered Sibley a close friend. Moreover, I was deeply honored by our friendship.

Our 1950s meeting was at Cornell where Sibley presented a talk about the relationships among ducks. Most observers notice that female puddle ducks — black, mallard, gadwall and pintail, for example — all look alike, only the males differing in colorful plumage. Sibley pointed out that a Caribbean drake that did not compete with other species for females did not exhibit colorful plumage and, in fact, differed from the female not at all. Thus, he claimed, it was interspecific competition that led to the development of those striking plumage differences among our familiar ducks.

I was deeply impressed by that controversial talk and I was impressed too with Sibley's convincing responses to his critics at that meeting.

Professor Sibley soon moved from Cornell to Yale where he pioneered studies of bird interrelationships through use of DNA evidence. This completely new approach to avian systematics brought him into further controversy with conservative ornithologists and he was often the subject of personal as well as academic attacks.

That is where I came in. On the Internet I defended Sibley against one of those personal attacks and a student of Sibley copied and forwarded my message to him. He promptly wrote a long and quite moving response thanking me for my intercession on his behalf. It was clear that Sibley was hurt by the personal attacks but he felt that it was inappropriate to respond to them himself.

That began our regular correspondence. For those four years I served as a kind of foil for this outstanding ornithologist, a man I rank among the very finest of his profession.

It was during those very years that Sibley's paradigm began to gain favor, especially as independent research confirmed his findings. The most noticeable result of his work has been a major revision of the relationship hierarchy of bird species, a reordering driven by his genetic evidence.

An example of the striking changes that have already been accepted was his move of vultures away from hawks to be relocated between storks and swans. Perhaps today Hans Christian Andersen's ugly duckling would grow up to become a vulture instead of a swan.

Two other examples will show Sibley's penchant for raising the hackles of his opponents. He wrote: "It's difficult to find 'pure' species, which is evidence for...evolution by natural selection. If all species were neat, sharp, and with no fuzzy edges — they would be evidence for creation!" And he pointed out that DNA evidence relates man more closely to chimpanzees than it does the red-eyed vireo to the white-eyed vireo.

My role in our correspondence was mostly one of asking questions which Sibley answered generously. It was clear that he enjoyed doing so and that my inquiries stimulated him. But he also enjoyed sharing with me the confirmations that supported his theories. I am delighted that acceptance of his evidence came to him before he died. Too many fine scientists — Mendel is a good example — went to their graves, their enormous contributions not yet recognized.

Shortly before he died, Sibley sent me a copy of his *Birds of North America*, which he developed as a computer CD so that it could be easily revised. It is a gift that means a great deal to me but I would far rather have my good friend back.

24. Blue Birds

Our recent trip to Alabama had a bittersweet quality. This would be our last visit to my mother-in-law's home. For thirty years my wife and I have spent a few days each year there but now her mother has moved into a retirement home. In two weeks Doris cleaned out the house and distributed its contents among her family.

I will remember this country home with its broad lawn, its hay fields, its grove of long-needled pines, its sweetgums and oaks for many things but among the best of those memories will be its remarkable number of blue birds.

Of course, first among those blue-plumaged birds is the one carrying that name, the eastern bluebird. A half-dozen of these most beautiful of birds live in or near this yard and their mournful churring *tru-ly* calls provide a softer background to the strident songs of mockingbirds, thrashers and Carolina wrens.

There is, I believe, no blue to compare with that of the male bluebird. It is a rich color that seems to glow especially in the South's bright sunlight. When one flies across the lawn and rises to perch on the phone line near the porch where I sit, I cannot take my eyes off it. Hesitantly it looks around at me, exposing its chestnut throat and breast. No photograph could capture this color.

What is so remarkable about the presence of these birds is the fact that they are not nesting in bluebirdhouses. There are many old trees here and the birds make their homes in abandoned woodpecker holes. There is one nesting now in the pine grove.

But bluebirds are only one of the blue species. Indigo buntings sing their doubled phrases – *chi chi fee fee ti ti* – from the poplars across the hay field. Their blue is metallic and in indirect light they often appear dark gray or even black.

Common in the South, these birds are common on the Niagara Frontier as well but few people notice them. Once you know their song, however, you can locate them feeding in treetops often accompanying goldfinches.

And those omnipresent blue jays are regularly heard, often seen flying but only occasionally to be noticed quietly skulking in the undergrowth. I think of them together with crows as the delinquents of the forest — always on the lookout for nests to rob or food to steal.

Three swallows that dash through the air lanes over the yard show various shades of blue, the tree swallow a greenish blue, the barn swallow a grayer shade and the purple martin a deep violet.

All those birds we in New York share with Alabama, but one other species seldom occurs this far north. Even in the South I do not see them very often, but this year I again find a pair of blue grosbeaks in Mattie Copeland's yard. They sit quietly in a small bush near a brush pile that awaits burning. One year I heard the male sing a rather attractive purple finch-like, warbling song, but this time he poses silently with his mate.

The male at first appears all blue but on closer examination I pick out his chestnut wing bars and the black area around that thick bill that identifies it as a grosbeak. The female is a drab brown bird and, seen without its consort, I would probably misidentify it as a female cowbird.

25. Spring Arrival Dates

To everything there is a season, and a time to every purpose.

That lovely verse from Ecclesiastes has a special meaning at this time of year. When I pause in writing this column, I can look out my window on a winter landscape, snow piled on the bare limbs of leafless trees, more falling to add to the depth, the only birds in evidence a few finches and chickadees scratching for feeder seeds and the ubiquitous neighborhood crows. It is a bleak time, yes, but some of those snow-covered trees are budding and remarkably the bird migration season is already underway. Spring, thank goodness, is just around the corner.

Flocks of migrating blackbirds are being seen and many of the male ducks along our river and lake shorelines are displaying before prospective mates. Testosterone is flowing and migration pressure is heating up.

The driving forces behind migration are not well understood but we do know, from records gathered over many years, that birds arrive on fixed schedules. Those swallows of Capistrano are not the only finely-tuned migrants. I share with you here some of those schedules, the approximate dates drawn from Beardslee and Mitchell's *Birds of the Niagara Frontier* and from the *Seasonal Checklist of the Birds* prepared by a Buffalo Ornithological Society committee.

I mention first, because many observers still go to see them there, the timing of peak Canada goose numbers — often over 100,000 — at the Iroquois National Wildlife Refuge. According to refuge biologist Paul Hess the best dates are usually the last week of March or the first week of April. At that time there are 5,000 to 10,000 ducks as well. It is difficult to realize that 50 years ago Canada geese were uncommon.

Here then are the dates when many other species will return:

March 11-20: tundra swan, Northern pintail, redhead, Eastern bluebird, American robin, song sparrow, red-winged blackbird

March 21-30: great blue heron, snow goose, gadwall, American wigeon, Northern shoveler, ring-necked duck, hooded merganser, red-breasted merganser, ruddy duck, Northern harrier, killdeer, American woodcock, fox sparrow, Eastern meadowlark, common grackle, brown-headed cowbird, purple finch

April 1-10: pied-billed grebe, horned grebe, turkey vulture, green-winged teal, blue-winged teal, lesser scaup, Cooper's hawk, American coot, greater yellowlegs, common snipe, belted kingfisher, yellow-bellied sapsucker, northern flicker, eastern phoebe, tree swallow, brown creeper, hermit thrush

April 11-20: American bittern, wood duck, osprey, sharp-shinned hawk, pine warbler, field sparrow, savannah sparrow, swamp sparrow

April 21-30: double-crested cormorant, lesser yellowlegs, blue-headed vireo, purple martin, Northern rough-winged swallow, barn swallow, blue-gray gnatcatcher, brown thrasher, yellow-rumped warbler, palm warbler, Eastern towhee, chipping sparrow, white-throated sparrow

May 1-10 green heron, Virginia rail, sora, common moorhen, spotted sandpiper, black tern, chimney swift, ruby-throated hummingbird, least flycatcher, yellow-throated vireo, warbling vireo, bank swallow, house wren, wood thrush, gray catbird, golden-winged warbler, Tennessee warbler, Nashville warbler, yellow warbler, Cape May warbler, black-throated blue warbler, black-throated green warbler, blackburnian warbler, cerulean warbler, black-and-white warbler, prothonotary warbler, ovenbird, northern waterthrush, common yellowthroat, hooded warbler, white-crowned sparrow, bobolink, Baltimore oriole, American goldfinch

May 11-20: least bittern, semipalmated plover, black-billed cuckoo, great crested flycatcher, Eastern kingbird, red-eyed vireo, marsh wren, blue-winged warbler, chestnut-sided warbler, magnolia warbler, bay-breasted warbler, American redstart, mourning warbler, Wilson's warbler, Canada warbler, scarlet tanager, rose-breasted grosbeak, indigo bunting

May 21-30 yellow-billed cuckoo, willow flycatcher, blackpoll warbler

By then, of course, it will be a different world entirely.

26. Craigheads

Recently someone called my attention to an essay by Vicki Constantine Croke about the Craighead brothers in the *Washington Post Magazine*. Coke's evocative story, "The Brothers Wild," follows the careers of Frank and John as they gained international reputations through their World War II survival training programs, their field studies of grizzly bears in Yellowstone Park including the development and use of radio transmitters and immobilization with tranquilizers, and their writing the National Wild and Scenic River Act.

But I knew the Craighead twins for a different reason. Croke's essay led me to recall reading their stories and photographs in *National Geographic Magazine* and in their book, *Hawks in the Hand*, which was published when I was in junior high school.

Fortunately that book was reissued in 1997 and is available through the Buffalo and Erie County Library system. It tells how they and their friends learned and practiced falconry and photography while they were high school and college students. I ordered the library's copy, opened to the first page and rewound my personal history 75 years, immediately finding myself just as engrossed in the adventures of those amazing youngsters as I was when I first came upon this book.

Those were very different pre-World War II times. Hawks and owls were shot and trapped, because they were seen as killers of both farm animals and wildlife, the latter reducing the numbers available to hunters. Buteos and accipiters were known as chicken hawks and hen hawks. Protection for raptors would not be achieved until the Migratory Bird Treaty Act was amended to include them in 1972.

Even ornithologists' names for raptors were different. I still often use the older ones: sparrow hawk for today's kestrel, pigeon hawk for merlin, duck hawk for peregrine falcon, marsh hawk for harrier. Jamestown native Roger Tory Peterson made an important contribution to that change using the new names in a revision of his famous *Field Guide to the Birds*.

And those too were years before the post-war use of DDT and other pesticides so severely reduced the populations of animals and birds.

So I rejoined the pre-teen Craighead brothers to remind myself how their interest in raptors was stimulated. John tells us that they were hiking with their dad along the Potomac River near Chevy Chase (still wild lands then) when they flushed a big bird. Their father identified it as a barred owl and suggested that it might be nesting nearby in the hole he pointed out in a sycamore tree. "No longer were we tired," John says. "The fishing rods, the stringer of catfish were all dropped in a heap as we raced to see who would be the first to climb the tree."

John managed with some difficulty to climb the sycamore and with even more difficulty extract the owl from its nest five feet below the entrance hole. The boys raised that owl as a pet before releasing it a year later as they often did other raptors.

But by then they were committed falconers.

They describe in subsequent chapters their adventures with

bald and golden eagles; duck, pigeon, sparrow, red-tailed, red-shouldered, broad-winged, Cooper's and sharp-shinned hawks; great horned, barn, screech, long-eared, short-eared and burrowing owls; ospreys and ravens as their activities turned increasingly from capturing and raising the raptors to photographing them at their nests.

But those adventures were not like those of modern rehabbers: they had to climb trees and rappel down cliffs to reach the nests of these birds. Fortunately, they brought physical strength to these activities as they did to their school and college wrestling. They needed that strength as many of their climbs were very challenging.

They also spent many hours photographing these birds, not the way we do today with digital cameras enhanced by powerful lenses and automatic focusing or even with smartphones. Frank and John had to take photos one at a time, changing plates after each exposure, and then developing and printing them in the darkroom they constructed.

Although Tom Killip and I tried to follow their lead in photographing birds, in no way could we match their efforts.

Interestingly, their younger sister Jean Craighead George was also an author. Her award-winning children's book, *My Side of the Mountain*, is another must read.

27. Yellow-rumped Warbler

When I approached Mirror Lake in Forest Lawn Cemetery, I found more than a dozen people standing with binoculars and cameras pointed at a willow tree that had not yet leafed out.

I could see six or eight small birds hopping about among the willow branches. One of them was a ruby-crowned kinglet; the rest appeared to be yellow-rumped warblers. These were the warblers to be expected at that time in early May and I could hear other individuals singing in the trees behind me.

When these first yellow-rumped warblers flood into the region, they soon become what birders call "trash birds." The reason: when you look for the other twenty-nine warbler species that occur here at this time of year, you find every bird you see is this one species instead. Further denigrating it, this bird's unattractive name is often shortened by jaundiced observers to yellow-rump.

While I recognize the problem of overabundance, I still find myself attracted to these handsome little birds. After a winter spent watching drab finches and sparrows, they are a welcome sight.

I followed one as it hopped about, appearing to pick food from the willow twigs, and occasionally dashed out to snap up a flying insect. It was a bright male in what is now called alternate plumage. Its back was mostly a bluish-gray striped with black, its eyes were covered with a black mask and its white throat and belly were separated by another band of black. But the field marks that distinguish this species in all but juvenile plumages are its four bright yellow markings: the top of its head, its sides and, as the name implies, its rump.

That word rump certainly conveys the location of that fourth spot because we think of it in comparison with our own rear end, but this bird's rump is more accurately described as its upper tail-coverts. Of course, no one would like this bird to be designated the yellow-upper-tail-coverts warbler, but I wish we were still calling this delightful little bird the myrtle warbler, the name I knew it by when I first began birding.

In fact myrtle warbler is the name now assigned to the eastern sub-species of the yellow-rumped warbler, so I can certainly justify using it. (The reason most birders avoid that subspecies name is because only species count on their lists.) It derives from this species' feeding on wax-myrtle berries (also called bayberries or sweet gale) especially along beaches in its southeastern United States winter range. As it migrates through this region, however, it feeds almost exclusively on insects.

The western subspecies is called Audubon's warbler. It is easily distinguished from the myrtle warbler by its fifth yellow area: its throat is yellow whereas the myrtle's is white.

Where do these names come from? The American Ornithologists Union has a Committee on Classification and Nomenclature that has since 1886 published editions of the Check-List of North American Birds. The most recent edition, the seventh, was published in 1998. Between editions the committee each year publishes a supplement to which birders refer. This series does much more than provide Latin and common names for bird species and subspecies that occur here. It also determines the order in which they are listed which is supposed to reflect their evolutionary history. This changes as new information is discovered. When I began birding the first listed bird was the common loon and the last was the bluebird. Today those listed species occurring regularly here are Canada goose and house sparrow.

That 1886 edition included 768 species; the 1998 edition, 2099. That remarkable accumulation is due to a number of factors: new species identified, the area covered extended (to Hawaii, for example), species splits (cackling goose from Canada goose is one), and new arrivals.

Back at that willow tree I asked the man standing next to me why all the attention was being paid to these birds. "There's a Cape May warbler among the yellow-rumps," he responded and he added, "There it is," pointing it out to me.

28. Cats and Birds

My wife woke me. "You must have been having a terrible nightmare," she said. And indeed I had. In my dream someone had released all the lions and tigers and leopards from the Buffalo Zoo and I was running from them.

I know why I had that dream. I had been upset by recent local activities supporting feral housecats that is referred to as TNR for trap, neuter and return. That process and the associated supported cat colonies are wreaking havoc on the populations of birds and small mammals. My dream served as a perfect metaphor for what was happening to these defenseless animals.

David Suzuki's television program, "Songbird SOS", addressed serious problems faced by songbirds today. He offered four examples of the steep decline in numbers of songbirds over the past 20 years: wood thrush down 62%; Baltimore oriole 46%; bobolink 64%; and purple martin 67%. The program identified problems related to migrating birds such as building strikes, forest loss, neonicotinoid pesticide effects and problems related to climate change.

I can add to that data. For New York State, based on June Breeding Bird counts, some declines for field birds from the 1960s to the 2010s are: brown thrasher down 79%, Eastern towhee 83%, meadowlark 91%, field sparrow 80%, grasshopper sparrow 97%, Henslow's sparrows gone, the last one recorded in 2006. (Those field birds are the ones often predated by cats.)

Professor Bridgit Stutchbury of York University in Toronto, who has been using radiotelemetry to determine songbird survival, worries that we may be reaching a tipping point after which these already severe declines will steepen and we will begin to face extinctions.

Most important to the concern I have raised, one section of Suzuki's program spoke to the problems cats create. In the program Peter Marra, director of the Smithsonian Migratory Bird Center, tells us: "Cats have been around and part of human civilization for a long time. That said, it doesn't mean that they have been moved to places where they are natural components of this fragile ecosystem. They are as invasive as kudzu vines or zebra mussels."

And Marra goes on to detail the extent of the problem this alien species creates:

* An estimated between 30 and 80 million feral cats (those are housecats living in the wild)
* An estimated 80 million pet housecats, a substantial portion of which are allowed to run wild
* Based on the most conservative estimates, a resulting 1.4 billion birds killed annually by these cats

That 1.4 billion per year is a very large number so consider it translated into a number you can better understand. It is equivalent to over 2500 songbirds killed every minute day and night all year long.

What does that have to do with TNR? Increasingly today, responsible housecat owners are keeping their cats indoors or allowing them outside only in enclosures often referred to as catios. But meanwhile well-meaning but misled cat lovers are creating situations that support numbers of feral cats. These free-roaming cats are often fed by their sponsors, but this does not in any way reduce their hunting instinct.

Carefully designed studies that use tiny cameras called

KittyCams hanging around cats' necks show that even well-fed pet cats that are allowed to roam kill more than two animals per week. (They also show that only about one in four of these birds or other animals are brought home.)

The American Veterinary Medical Association policy states, "All free-roaming abandoned and feral cats that are not in managed colonies should be removed from their environment and treated in the same manner as other abandoned and stray animals in accord with local and state ordinances."

The association also encourages state and local agencies to adopt ordinances that prevent the establishment of managed cat colonies in wildlife-sensitive ecosystems.

For this state the applicable ordinance is New York Conservation Law Section 11-0529: "1. Any person over the age of twenty-one years possessing a hunting license may, and environmental conservation officers and peace officers, acting pursuant to their special duties, or police officers shall humanely destroy cats at large found hunting or killing any protected wild bird or with a dead bird of any protected species in its possession." And "5. No action for damages shall lie against any authorized person for the killing of a cat, dog or coyote as provided in this section."

Okay, so what is happening locally? TNR supporters are browbeating local politicians into supporting their programs. So far they have won over the Erie County Legislature, the City of Tonawanda, the Town of Amherst and the Village of Williamsville, the University at Buffalo Law School, the Erie County SPCA and the Niagara County Board of Health. (That Health Board has wisely since withdrawn its support.) According to TNR proponents the City of Buffalo has gone so far as to budget $50,000 to the support of such programs. Only Lackawanna has held out and as a result council president Hank Pirowski has been the subject of *ad hominem* attacks and a petition has been circulated to fire the city's animal control officer, Frederick Grasso.

Why is this happening? Because our representatives have been led to focus only on protecting these stray cats. They are not told about the other species affected.

The TNR supporters claim that by neutering cats they stop them from adding to the cat population, but this claim fails for two reasons: (1) Studies have shown that it is necessary to neuter over 70% of the cats in a locale just to maintain the cat population and that level is rarely reached. (2) Despite thousands of these TNR programs even the cat supporters admit that less than 4% of all feral cats are neutered. Thus these well-meant programs lead inevitably to an exponential increase in the overall cat population and delay in responding to the problem.

And the population problem is indeed real. You need only consider a regional headline, "Cats Outnumber People in Niagara Falls" and a story about a single neighborhood of Rochester that harbors a thousand cats.

All support for stray cats should be withdrawn except where they are maintained in well-designed enclosures.

Answering a Reader

In a long delayed response to that 1998 column (which has been updated in what preceded here) I received the following message in 2004 from a reader who asked not to be identified: "A while back one of your articles listed cats as the worst predators of birds. I found the enclosed bit of information in a book by Walter Chandoha in 1963 [evidently *Walter Chandoha's Book of Kittens and Cats*]:

"Cats: They are everywhere efficient rodent exterminators as required. They catch mice and rats for man — man feeds them. It's a good relationship. Admittedly, they catch some birds too. But actually cats are not nearly as proficient at catching birds as is generally believed. The Audubon Society once printed a list of enemies of birds in this order: disease, automobiles, weasels, humans, parasites, hawks, starvation, cats.

"So, if cats are to help man by hunting for rodents, we must expect also to lose some birds. When I hear people complain of the way birds are bothered by cats, I feel compelled to remind them that man is not without fault in this respect either. I am reminded of a piece of dialogue I once read somewhere: 'That horrible cat caught another sparrow today,' said the duchess to the duke as she sat down to her quail and he to his pheasant.'"

I have recently read Ellen Perry Berkeley's well-written *Maverick Cats: Encounters with Feral Cats* which makes an even better case for my correspondent than does Chandoha, but I remain unconvinced.

First, my correspondent quotes old data. Here are the best current estimates I find of birds killed annually through non-natural causes:

* glass windows in homes and commercial buildings: 97 to 976 million
* electric power lines: 130 to 174 million
* hunting: over 100 million
* cars and trucks: 60 to 80 million
* agriculture (harvesting and pesticides): 67 million
* lighted communication towers: 4 to 10 million
* cats: 2.4 billion

Here is a way similar results are illustrated in a scientific publication that draws together evidence from many studies: Scott R. Loss, Tom Will and Peter P. Marra, Direct Mortality of Birds from Anthropogenic Causes. *Annual Review of Ecology, Evolution, and Systematics* 2015. 46: 99–120. (Anthropogenic means human related.) The following bar graph taken from that publication compares various causes of bird mortality:

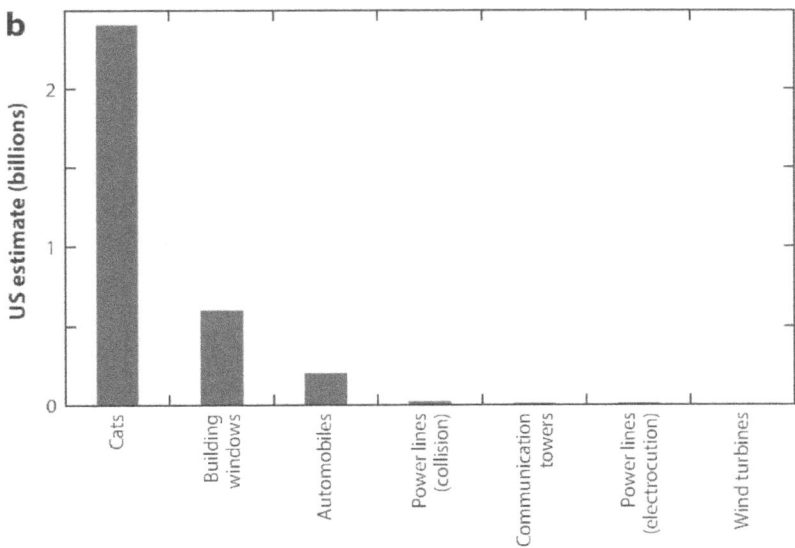

Note how most of those causes of bird mortality are so small in comparison with cats that they don't even show on the graph. (Among them is deaths from the often damned by birdwatchers, wind turbines.)

In this response I have not even discussed a more serious problem *for us* related to cats: disease. When considering animal-borne disease most people think only of rabies and cats are the number one domestic animal source of this disease. They passed dogs years ago. But another disease, toxoplasmosis, is also very serious. The disease is rated "the second leading cause of deaths attributable to foodborne illness." Originating in cats and spread through their feces, over a quarter of us are now infected. And yet the response to this disease so far is only defensive: Cover your sandboxes, for example.

Now let me restate my position. I consider myself a reasonably serious birder, but I also like cats. I admire both their grace and their independence; however, I believe that they should be kept indoors. My position is in agreement with that of the National Audubon Society and American Bird Conservancy.

Pet cats kept indoors are healthier, they avoid the traffic accidents that claim 1.5 million cats each year and they live longer because they are not subject to predation and disease.

Meanwhile, feral cats need to be removed from our environment. Those that cannot be adopted should be contained in catios or euthanized.

Whenever a cat steps outside it reverts to its inborn compulsion to hunt. It is far better to have it make passes at birds through your windowpane than from your bushes.

29. Snipe and Woodcock

When I was a youngster, to me March and April were distressful months. I couldn't wait until "real" birding would begin with the return of the land bird migrants. Of course, a few species had already shown up: robins, grackles, killdeer, bluebirds, red-winged blackbirds, song and white-throated sparrows, but they weren't especially exciting.

I soon learned, however, that these months too can be entertaining. And in particular two birds can be found at this time but rarely at any other. Those birds are the common snipe and the American woodcock.

My Rochester backyard then was bounded by extensive open fields, hundreds of acres of grassland that are filled with houses today. Standing at the edge of that vast meadow in late March I heard a strange, rapid *who-who-who-who-who-who-who...* sound. It seemed to go on forever and it sounded as though it came from high above those fields.

Finally with binoculars I found the source. It was a bird flying at least a hundred yards high. All I could make out was its fluttering pointed wings.

I called my friend Howard Miller to ask for identification help. "That's a Wilson's snipe," Howard told me, "and that winnowing is the sound made by the motion of its outer tail feathers during its courtship flight." (The name has since been changed to common snipe.)

A boy scout at the time, all I knew about snipes was a camp prank sending some foolish tenderfoot out in the night after them armed with a spear and a banana. Now I could tell my friends that there really is such a bird and that I had seen it. I never could convince them, however, that I wasn't simply extending the joke.

It was much later when I had my first close look at a snipe, a squat, robin-sized fatso, mostly brown with a long bill. It was so well camouflaged that it was almost impossible to observe. I rarely see more than one or two a year and those only during their fall migration.

Even more exciting in springtime is a woodland inhabitant, the American woodcock or, as it is colloquially known, the timberdoodle.

One April evening Chris Hollister and I visited the Tillman Preserve in Clarence to seek one of these birds. We must have walked a mile without success. But when we had given up and were returning to our car, we heard the high-pitched twittering made by the woodcock's wings as it rose in its strange courtship display. Then we heard it drop rapidly emitting even louder chirps. And finally, we listened to its very different Bronx cheer-like *pzznt* call from its so-called singing ground where it landed to display for its mate.

Birdwatchers armed with flashlights often listen for these flight take-offs and rush up to within a few yards of their origin. Then when the timberdoodle returns, they turn on the light and watch the bird's display antics. An intervening fence prevented us from doing so. A good time to do this is when the moon is out and nearly full. On those nights the woodcock sometimes continues his flights through the night.

Although the woodcock's coloration differs significantly from that of the snipe, they appear quite similar hidden on the ground. The woodcock too is squat and brown-backed and its bill is equally long. Both birds have flexible bill-tips that help them probe the earth for worms and other insects.

Both snipe and woodcock are game birds with fall hunting seasons but their erratic flight makes them a challenge. I once went along with two Alabama relatives hunting quail and woodcock. Mistake. When their dog put up a bird and they swung those guns around to follow its flight I hit the dirt. I can understand Harry Whittington's experience hunting with Dick Cheney. I stuck it out that day but have not accepted more recent invitations.

Despite serious woodcock population declines in recent years, due more to loss of habitat than hunting pressure, this delightful bird remains rather common in this region. It is so rarely seen simply because of its shy and reclusive habits — except, that is, in April.

30. American Ambassadors

Shortly after graduating from the University at Buffalo Jajean Rose-Burney and his wife Ana Hernández Balzac joined the Peace Corps. They were assigned to Puebla, Mexico, a city whose metropolitan population is 2.6 million. During their thirty-month stay there, Jajean and Ana helped change the direction of urban sprawl, reinterpreted the highly polluted 90 square mile Valsequillo Reservoir from a "dead" lake to an important wildlife region, nominated the area as an international Important Bird Area, established it as a Ramsar Convention wetland of global importance, and gained state park status for part of the region, in the process gaining recognition for the work from Felipe Calderon, then president of Mexico, and winning the American Planning Association's Pierre L'Enfant International Planning Award.

Wow! And that's not all. During that same period they also established a regional society of bird watchers, led trips to birding sites throughout central Mexico and wrote, edited and published two bird books.

Anyone who has reservations about our young men and women today has only to look at these accomplishments to be encouraged. We can only hope that Jajean can continue them in his new role as development coordinator for the Western New York Land Conservancy.

How did all this come about?

When the Peace Corps assigned the couple to a government planning office in Puebla, Jajean was not at all enthusiastic. A birdwatcher by avocation, mentored by local senior ornithologists Dave Junkin and Bob Andrle, he had hoped to be assigned to a tropical forest rich in bird species. Instead the couple was sent to work in urban Puebla where they would lead environmental education projects, prepare a temporary employment program for rural communities and design a training center for low-tech sustainable technologies.

Checking a map of the region around Puebla looking for birding opportunities, Jajean noticed the eleven square mile Valsequillo Reservoir. When he asked about it, however, he was warned that it was "too polluted to drink from, swim in, or even boat on. No fish and no birds. The reservoir is nothing more than a smelly, toxic mudhole."

But Jajean visited the reservoir anyway. What he found surprised him: "Yes, the water is used as a dump for nearby industry. Yes, the fifth largest city in Mexico pumps its untreated sewage into the reservoir. Yes, half of the reservoir is covered with invasive water hyacinth. Still, the water was clear and blue. Huge rafts of ducks were floating on its surface. Flocks of herons were wading in its shallows. Fishermen were pulling in the day's catch. Farmers were collecting the last of the season's harvest along its shores. No, the reservoir wasn't dead; it was teeming with life."

Excited by this discovery, the couple convinced their boss that they could submit the reservoir area as a Ramsar conservation site and Jajean went to work collecting data about the plants and animals of the area. His own year-long survey listed 169 birds, eight of them protected or threatened and twenty particular to that region. He gained support from Benemérita Universidad Autónoma de Puebla biologists and their students to inventory reptiles and amphibians and colleagues to do the same for plants. His final 20-page Ramsar Wetland proposal in Spanish was for a 96 square mile area — twice the size of Buffalo.

In doing this he helped head off plans to develop urban Puebla to the shore of the reservoir. Working with the federal environmental agency and Valsequillo area zoo director Amy Camacho, who fortunately had been appointed state environmental director, they gained support for the designation of part of the Valsequillo borderlands as a state park, thus changing the vision for the area from urban development to an ecologically sustainable region.

Building upon the interests of university students who had helped with the bird inventory, Jajean and Ana then organized a club that sponsored monthly field trips throughout the state of Puebla and promoted Puebla birding. And with local colleagues they prepared an identification guidebook, *Las Aves del Municipio de Puebla*, which includes information in Spanish about 80 of the most common birds of the state.

Jajean, Ana and others also prepared the guide, *The Birdwatching Hotspots of the State of Puebla, Mexico*. Remarkably, both of these exceptional books are available for free download from the web.

31. Gnatcatcher

I am always impressed with our small birds. Of course, the ruby-throated hummingbird is far and away the champion among our tiniest, but we have a number of others that aren't too much larger.

For a weight comparison consider a pat of butter, what you get when you scrape that 1/6-ounce out of its foil cover. A robin weighs in at over 16 of those pats, a bluebird over 6; and then among our small birds: house wren and chickadee 2.3 pats, kinglets and gnatcatcher 1.3 pats and finally hummingbird .7. Just imagine, that feisty little hummingbird that beats its wings at a spectacular 20 to 30 times per second weighs only 2/3 as much as a pat of butter. (And the brain that drives those wings weighs only 1/500 of a pat.) I hope you find those sizes as impressive as I do.

I will consider in this essay the bird on that list of diminutive characters that is almost certainly least known to you. It is among my favorites of all birds: the blue-gray gnatcatcher. It partly makes up in name-length what it lacks in weight.

To identify a gnatcatcher, simply look for a small, quite slim bird, gray above and white below with a long and constantly flitting black and white tail. Or, if you know what a mockingbird looks like, shrink its dimensions in half and take away the white patches in the wings.

I don't see gnatcatchers all that often because they generally remain high in trees and are usually located by their distinctive call notes. Francis Weston, who wrote the Bent Life History of this species, describes those notes as "scarcely louder than a whisper." Those thin buzzing calls with many *spee*-like sounds are too high for my aging ears to pick up. I did, however, find a pair recently along the Swallow Hollow Nature Trail off Knowlesville Road in the Iroquois National Wildlife Refuge. They were flitting about the branches of a cottonwood next to the boardwalk about a hundred yards south of the main trail entrance.

They are great fun to watch. Weston tells us, "The gnatcatcher is a little bird of intense activity; active, not with the methodical continuity of the brown creeper, but with an irrepressible vivacity of its own in all phases of its life cycle – feeding, nesting, care of its young – at all times, in fact, except during the enforced inertia of incubation."

Like chickadees, nuthatches, kinglets and creepers, gnatcatchers feed on the tiny insects they find in their constant search of tree limbs and leaves. But gnatcatchers don't deviate from this diet. Those other species will take seeds from your feeders; the gnatcatchers stick exclusively to arthropods. Thus they are very beneficial birds.

Although gnatcatchers do not overwinter here, they appear among the early passerine migrants each year, arriving in mid-April. After a week or two of courtship each pair sets out to build a new nest. I say new because, if there is one left over from the previous year, they won't use it but will instead tear it apart and use the materials for this year's home.

I've only seen one gnatcatcher nest and it certainly impressed me. It was a slightly larger version of a hummingbird nest. Hold the tip of your index finger against the end of your thumb and those fingers would have enclosed its approximate area. It was really small.

Located on top of a horizontal limb about 20 feet high it was beautifully constructed: gray, cup-shaped and compact. The materials they use to make their nests include plant down and fiber, lichens, oak catkins, feathers and bark. All of these ingredients are held together by spider web and insect silk, like that of the tent caterpillar.

Gnatcatchers' 4 to 5 eggs are scarcely larger than peas. They are pale blue with reddish-brown spots.

Unfortunately, they are far too often victimized by cowbirds. One observer found over 83% of their nests stuffed with cowbird eggs or young. The results are inevitable: tiny gnatcatchers feeding greedy immature cowbirds more than twice their size, their own offspring unable to compete. This may be the major reason why gnatcatchers are so uncommon.

32. Oology

An article in the July 22, 2013 *New Yorker* brought back memories of my early days of birding. The essay by Julian Rubenstein is titled "Operation Easter", but all it has to do with that religious holiday is its association with Easter eggs. The subtitle makes this clear: "The hunt for illegal egg collectors".

Although the article is about criminal egg collecting in Great Britain, the practice is just as unlawful here. There is an international law, the Migratory Bird Treaty Act, which makes it unlawful without a waiver "to pursue, hunt, take, capture, kill or sell" 800 species of migratory birds or any bird parts including feathers, eggs and nests. Game birds are excepted with the Fish and Wildlife Service and state agencies establishing hunting seasons for them.

But waivers, mostly for scientific collecting, are issued. Those permits are very difficult to obtain today but, when I was young, permits to collect eggs were easier to get. In fact oology, the study and collecting of birds' eggs was then still a respected practice. There was even an international journal, *The Oologist*.

Three of my friends were participants in this activity and so too was Dudley DeGroot, the coach at the time of the University of Rochester football team. An All-American as a Stanford undergraduate, he later coached the Washington Redskins.

Don Spitz, one of the Rochester collectors, gave a talk to the

Genesee Ornithological Society about his oological experiences. I already knew Don as a daredevil who climbed trees without hesitation, but I was floored when he told of his visit with DeGroot to Yosemite, where he climbed a Sequoia. He wore leg irons but he couldn't use a climbing rope as the tree circumference was too great. He had to grasp the bark to inch his way up several hundred feet.

But his worst experience was, he told us, climbing a sand bank to get an egg from a kingfisher's burrow. Just as he reached to nest hole, the bird emerged, vomiting half-digested fish in Don's face as it dashed past him.

I asked which eggs he thought were most attractive. Without hesitation he responded, "Blue jay," and he showed us one. It was blue-green like a robin's egg but it was beautifully freckled on one end with dark spots.

One reason I never participated in this activity was the skill required in handling the eggs. No one wants a collection of rotten eggs so their innards had to be removed. Don showed us how he did this by first drilling a small hole in a robin's egg using a dentist's drill. Then he carefully held a thin tube close to the hole and blew at it. The pressure this created inside the egg forced the albumen and yolk out, finally leaving the egg empty.

And very delicate. Don's collections were protected in glass-covered trays seated inside in cottonbatten.

Some collectors took eggs shortly before they were hatched, in those cases with an almost fully-formed bird inside. They would leave the eggs in a tray of maggots which would devour the embryos. Don did not approve of that gruesome practice.

He justified taking eggs from birds' nests by the fact that the female would simply produce replacements. Unfortunately, there is more to the story than this. Just as bird watchers are more interested in observing rare birds, egg collectors are more interested in collecting rare bird eggs. And many collectors were — and are, for the activity continues illegally — interested in having complete clutches of eggs. One of the reasons given for the extermination of the passenger pigeon was the collection of their eggs when the bird became rare.

Rubenstein describes how British law-enforcement officials are trying to protect birds from collectors, some of whom are so uncontrollably driven that they cannot stop.

Here at one time a California condor egg was sold for $350 and a single collector bragged about gathering over 700 peregrine falcon eggs. Those days may be gone, but I am certain that the practice continues here as it does in Britain.

If you take home an egg, nest or feather, rarely will a federal agent pound on your door. But you still should not do so.

33. Eskimo Curlew

If you were asked to identify one of this continent's extinct birds, the name that almost certainly would occur to you is the passenger pigeon, the species whose numbers declined from an estimated three to five billion when Europeans first arrived in North America to a final individual named Martha that died in the Cincinnati Zoo in 1914.

A few of you might suggest others: the Carolina parakeet, last seen in 1913; the heath hen, 1932; the Labrador duck, 1870; and the great auk, 1844. You might even include the ivory-billed woodpecker, despite the remote possibility that a few are still around.

There is, however, a lesser-known species whose demise in many ways paralleled that of the passenger pigeon: the Eskimo curlew. Like the passenger pigeon its population dropped from millions to zero in a very short period of time.

The Eskimo curlew was a large shorebird. Its name curlew derives from its inch and a half long de-curved bill. There are other species in the curlew's *Numenius* genus: one that is occasionally seen here is the whimbrel.

Arthur Cleveland Bent tells us, "The story of the Eskimo curlew is just one more pitiful tale of the slaughter of the innocents. It is a sad fact that the countless swarms of this fine bird and the passenger pigeon, which once swept across our land on migrations, are gone forever, sacrificed to the insatiable greed of man."

If this shorebird had been able to remain through the year on its nesting grounds, it would almost certainly be with us today, for it summered in the extreme northwestern strands of Alaska and possibly nearby Russia along the coast of the Arctic Ocean. Unfortunately, each fall it migrated south down through the eastern Canadian provinces and United States all the way to Patagonia, returning in spring up through the

Mississippi valley. Guns were trained on it all along that route.

Bent describes this problem: "The gunner's name for the Eskimo curlew was doughbird, for it was so fat when it reached us in the fall that its breast would often burst open when it fell to the ground, and the thick layer of fat was so soft that it felt like a ball of dough. It is no wonder that it was so popular as a game bird, for it must have made a delicious morsel for the table."

He goes on to say, "It was so tame and unsuspicious and it flew in such dense flocks that it was easily killed in large numbers. On the Labrador coasts and in Newfoundland the inhabitants killed all they could and preserved them for winter use."

Bent's comments apply to the fall migration. Even more were killed in spring as they flew back north through the mid-continent.

Myron Swenk, who wrote a monograph for the Smithsonian Institution about the Eskimo curlew, described the out-of-control behavior of market hunters during the spring migration: "During such flights the slaughter of these poor birds was appalling and almost unbelievable. Hunters would drive out from Omaha and shoot the birds without mercy until they had literally slaughtered a wagonload of them. Sometimes when the flight was unusually heavy and the hunters were well supplied with ammunition their wagons were too quickly and easily filled, so whole loads of the birds would be dumped on the prairie, their bodies forming piles as large as a couple of tons of coal, where they would be allowed to rot while the hunters proceeded to fill their wagons with fresh victims."

Swenk goes on to describe how easily the birds were killed: "The compact flocks and tameness of the birds made this slaughter possible, and at each shot usually dozens of birds would fall. In one specific instance a single shot from an old muzzle-loading shotgun into a flock of these curlews as they veered by the hunter brought down 28 birds at once."

This appalling behavior shows mankind at its worst. No one, including every hunter I know, would justify it. The result was predictable. The birds were almost gone by the end of the 19th century. A few remained, but the last confirmed sighting of the Eskimo curlew was in 1963.

34. Juncos

Along with their brown sparrow relatives, some mostly gray birds regularly visit bird feeders. Although they do occasionally eat at trays, more often they are to be seen with doves and other birds feeding on the ground under the feeders.

These birds are dark-eyed juncos and the subspecies that occurs here almost exclusively is the slate-colored junco. Local checklists record them by that subspecies name.

They aren't entirely gray-plumaged. Their belly is white and, when they fly, they flash white outer tail feathers. If you look closely, you'll also see that their bill is slightly pinkish as are their legs.

Most birders welcome these juncos to their feeding stations because they represent an additional visitor. But they don't have the charisma of many of the other birds. Their neutral coloration doesn't have the flash of the cardinal or oriole. They don't dash about like chickadees or head down trees like nuthatches. They aren't tiny like kinglets or feisty like those hummingbirds that chased each other away from your sugar-water tubes all summer.

Birders think of juncos as wintering birds here even though a few do remain to breed, mostly in the higher elevations of the Southern Tier or the depths of the Genesee gorge at Letchworth. In fact they are often called snowbirds, a name shared with the entirely different appearing snow buntings. I receive great pleasure watching a group of juncos, often together with a few tree sparrows, popping up from a snowdrift individually like untimed pistons to pick seeds from winter weeds.

Several years ago I spent a week in the western states where I came across another subspecies of the dark-eyed junco called the Oregon junco. When I first saw the bird, I almost mistook it for a towhee as it had a black hood. It turns out that this and other junco subspecies occasionally appear here. Not much attention is paid to them, however, as birders — and those who keep species lists in particular -- don't "count" subspecies.

I should insert here that a species is defined as a group of individuals capable of interbreeding and producing fertile offspring. A subspecies is a group within a species with differing characteristics (like those black hoods or in their genetic make-up) but that can interbreed with other subspecies. That they do not do so is usually due to the fact that those subspecies do not occur in the same region.
It happens that these little juncos who visit your feeders have been serving for about a hundred years as a perfect model for studying subspecies differences and their evolution. Those of you with computers have a wonderful opportunity to learn about that history. Indiana University's Center for the Integrated Study of Animal Behavior has produced with National Science Foundation support 1½ hours of film titled *Ordinary Extraordinary Junco* to which you can gain free access at www.juncoproject.org.

The film follows the activities of an international team of scientists as they study these birds. They extend the work of Alden Miller, who spent the 1930s trapping 11,774 juncos across North and Central America to determine their differences. He identified 21 distinct groups, 15 in the United States and Canada. Since Miller's time those United States groups have been reduced to the six subspecies of the dark-eyed junco. Additional subspecies south of the U.S.-Mexico border belong to another junco species: the appropriately named yellow-eyed junco.

Every birder should watch at least the two chapters of this extraordinary film that cover junco diversification. They describe those subspecies and employ genetic analysis to determine how and approximately when they split apart over millennia. Captured by these chapters, you will probably go on to the others for they are equally interesting.

At the end of the film the many participants review the wide range of subjects that are being explored through working with juncos: how birds live in an urban environment, speciation, adaptation, climate change, the brain, hybridization, violence, how genes affect behavior, reproduction, mate choice, evolution, gene expression, range expansion, communication, maternal care, geographic variation, hormones, gonads, monogamy, sex, food, death, sensory systems, prey selection, disease ecology, olfaction, and beauty in nature.

Watching this film I gained a great deal of respect for these little gray birds. I'm sure you will too.

35. Booby

Mike Gelsinger's call came just before 10:00 p.m. on Friday, November 1, 2013. I remembered Mike from earlier email exchanges. On the phone he was quite excited: "There's a brown booby in the front yard at my cottage," he told me.

I get calls like this rather often and they always raise questions. Non-birders occasionally mistake common birds for rarities. One I recall confused a catbird for a Clark's nutcracker. Another reported an ivory-billed woodpecker at his feeder.

But Mike went on to give me some details. Although he admits readily that he is not a birder, his description of this one fit; he had compared what he was seeing with his field guide. Also, his cottage is at Mohawk Point on the north shore of Lake Erie and that day south and southwest winds of up to 60 miles per hour could have driven this bird onto land.

Under normal circumstances I would have been hard put to accept any report of a brown booby in this region. This is a species of the tropical ocean. Birders travel to the Dry Tortugas, miles south of Key West, to see them. Recently, however, a booby had made its way to Buffalo, where it had been seen off and on for several weeks mixing with the cormorants near the Small Boat Harbor. When this species was first reported there by Jim Pawlicki, senior regional ornithologist Kayo Roy told him, "This is the rarest bird reported in this region in modern times." Kayo said that his restriction to modern times was only because birds like the now extinct passenger pigeon had once occurred here.

I was in fact one of those who climbed to the tower and spent hours looking for this bird. When it was finally pointed out to me by Rochester birder Kim Hartquist, it was a quarter mile off, seated on the concrete corner of the old lighthouse base. I could barely make out the bird to say nothing of its field marks. All I could note was the fact that it was shaped differently from the nearby cormorants and gulls. Thankfully

Kim and others with better telescopes and better eyes picked up the species' characteristics: general brown color, a light bill, yellowish feet and a white belly. Then a final clue: when it raised its wings, it showed their white undersides.

In any case on that Friday night I accepted Mike's judgment and the following day set out before dawn to visit his cottage.

When I arrived just after 7:00 a.m., it was still quite dark, but I spent the next half hour looking for the bird. I checked the cottage lawn, the beachfront and the line of rocks next to the road. No luck.

Now dawn was upon me and I saw my first bird flying along the shore. Was it the booby? I ran out onto the beach, only to see that it was instead a herring gull. But then, just as I returned to the road, a truck pulled up and Dan Hill asked me if I had seen the booby. When I told him that I hadn't, he got out and pointed; "There it is," he said.

And indeed, there crouched a brown booby, shivering and with its head under its wing. I had nearly stepped on it when I climbed over the rocks to get to the beach.

After a time the booby briefly brought out its head to look at us and it stood up, exposing those bright yellow duck feet.

Soon Canadian birders Kayo Roy, Blayne and Jean Farnan and Bill Curry arrived and we discussed the possibility of carrying the apparently moribund bird to a rehabilitator. But before they had a chance to so the bird waddled to the top of a rock and flew west out over the lake.

On the way home at the Peace Bridge I was asked the reason for my trip to Canada. When I told the agent that I was a bird watcher and my visit was to see a rare brown booby, he responded, "Last week I saw a dozen of them birds from the Maid of the Mist." Eager to move on, I didn't respond.

36. Bluebirds

It is difficult to imagine a bird more attractive than the male Eastern bluebird. Other male birds have more striking colors like our cardinal, Baltimore oriole, indigo bunting and scarlet tanager or more delicate markings like the warblers and kinglets, but I know no other bird with color as rich as the blue of our bluebird.

I say our bluebird because there are three bluebird species in North America. Both of those other bluebirds are handsome, but the mountain bluebird's blue is not nearly as rich as ours; it is a more subdued, grayer blue. The Western bluebird is very similar to its eastern cousin, but to me it is not nearly as well patterned.

And there is a kind of all-American quality to our bluebird: it is red, white and blue. Well, not quite. Its throat, chest and the sides of its belly are a rusty red that is as rich as its blue. That's at least a red relative. And its belly and under tail coverts are white.

My own favorite bluebird quality does not reside in its coloration. It is its soft, mellow, almost mournful *chur-lee* song, which some record most appropriately as "spring's here."

What I always find surprising about this beautiful bird is that you often fail to notice it. Until you focus on it, even that bright male is simply a gray silhouette. I think that is the main reason why, when I write a column like this, I get so many calls from people who say they have never seen a bluebird.

The best way to see bluebirds is to drive into the countryside and look for a birdhouse (or more often as I will describe two birdhouses close together) near an open meadow. Odds suggest that almost half of those birdhouses will be homes to bluebirds.

Why the two houses close together? Another attractive bird, the tree swallow, likes those same birdhouses and most tree swallows arrive in spring before the bluebirds to take over the nesting sites. Fortunately, tree swallows will not tolerate another tree swallow nesting nearby. They will, however, be happy to have a bluebird neighbor.

If you seek a particular place to find bluebirds, I suggest Knox Farm State Park in East Aurora.

Bluebirds are shy birds and are easily displaced from their nest by snakes, raccoons and those three infamous "house" species: house wren, house sparrow and house finch. Sixty years ago their populations were at a low point. In this regard consider some local data. The Buffalo Ornithological Society May Counts that include all of western New York and nearby Ontario found only an average of 65 bluebirds each year through the 1950s and 1960s. Since 2000 that average has risen to 240. That recovery has been due to the intervention of dozens of volunteers locally and thousands nationally who set out nest boxes for them. Although many individuals did so, it has been mostly New York State Bluebird Society here and the North American Bluebird Society members internationally who have established and maintained them. And not just a few boxes apiece. One of my local heroes, Carl Zenger, recently monitored over 150, but even his number is eclipsed by Oswego bluebirder John Rogers' who set out and cares for over 400. I agree with the North American Bluebird Society's claim that these folks and their comrades continent-wide have indeed "brought back the bluebirds."

You too can contribute to the welfare of this species by building, setting out and maintaining bluebird boxes. A simple house plan calls for two boards and about three dozen galvanized siding or aluminum nails. Ten saw cuts, two holes drilled, some nails pounded and you have an assembled box. No painting necessary. Full plans are given at nabluebirdsociety.org/nestboxes/eastwestbox.htm and at many other websites. The house should be set out as early in the year as possible as bluebirds begin to establish territories in early March.

Unfortunately for most of you city and suburb dwellers, bluebirds shy away from your area. Instead they are truly country birds. They like open areas with a few trees and, since they often find insects on the ground, short cropped vegetation. You find these conditions in pastures, golf courses, parks, cemeteries and near homes with large lawns. Those are sites where you should ask permission to place nest boxes. Here are some caveats about care for those boxes:

* Place a box in an open area away from buildings and especially away from woods where house wrens lurk.
* Place the box on a post four to six feet above the ground with a guard to deter raccoons, snakes and other predators from reaching the box.
* Face the box east away from the prevailing west wind.
* If you place two boxes back to back you may attract a bluebird in one and a tree swallow in the other as I have suggested.
* Leave 100 yards between nest sites. (Note that this suggests that Rogers' route, even with pairs of houses erected, is over ten miles in length.)
* Even if you have followed these rules, consider moving any box unused for several years.
* Okay, now you have one or more boxes erected. Your job has only started. You should check your boxes about once a week. Remove the nests of unwanted birds or mice. Replace any nesting material that has harbored blowflies. (Even if this requires handling young birds, songbirds have little sense of smell so this will not bother them.)
* Finally clean out and disinfect your boxes each season.
* And if you wish to join others who care for bluebirds, you can seek information on the web about those two societies I have mentioned.

Bluebirds are, of course, not the only birds that utilize nest boxes. There are other cavity-nesting species that you can support by building and setting out such artificial homes.

Fall or winter is the time to build or buy appropriate boxes for cavity nesting birds and to locate them for possible occupancy later in spring. It is usually too late in April or May to set out birdhouses.

Nest boxes are simple to make and there are few rules to follow. Their construction is a perfect parent-child activity. Use untreated 3/4-inch lumber. Make the roof extend well out over the entrance hole. Provide additional small holes for ventilation and drainage. Hinge a front or side wall so that it will bend out for cleaning and for quick peeks at the birds in their nest. If you shop for birdhouses, look for these features also. House size is related to the species you hope to attract. The following dimensions are for interior width, length, height and hole diameter, all in inches; and placement height in feet. Chickadee: 4 x 4 x 9, 1 1/8, 5-15. Nuthatch, titmouse, bluebird, downy woodpecker: 4 x 4 x 12, 1 1/2, 5-10. Hairy and red-bellied woodpeckers: 6 x 6 x 14, 2, 8-20. Flicker: 7 x 7 x 18, 2 1/2, 10-20. Screech-owl and kestrel: 9 x 9 x 18, 3, 12-20. Wood duck and hooded merganser: 12 x 12 x 24, 4, 5-20. Barn owl: 12 x 36 x 16, 7, 15-30. Of course locating houses appropriately is important. There is, for example, little possibility that a barn owl box in an urban or suburban setting would attract the desired occupants. Normally this species nests in barns near extensive open fields. (However, strange things do happen. Barn owls once nested in Yankee Stadium.)

About a quarter of our local breeding birds are cavity nesters. In earlier times these birds found homes in hollow trees, but such sites are becoming less available as dead and dying trees are removed from yards and parks and as the ubiquitous starling takes over the few remaining holes. Nest boxes then provide an admirable substitute. They have made a big difference in the welfare of many native species. In particular wood ducks have made spectacular comebacks. Since the 1960s when observers worried about their disappearance from this region, their numbers have tripled.

Some of you will wish to learn more about birdhouses. A respected friend, Scott Shalaway, has written a delightful little pamphlet called *A Guide to Bird Homes*.

Now I have a confession to make.

Despite my affection for bluebirds, many years ago I was a participant in a failed palace revolt. I joined a group that sought to have the bluebird displaced by the kingbird as our New York State bird. It seemed to us that the regal kingbird was a more appropriate choice to represent the Empire State. And the bluebird was not unique to New York. We share it as state bird with Missouri and the closely related mountain bluebird represents Idaho and Nevada.

Of course our insurrection was immediately quashed and the lovely Eastern bluebird continues to represent us to this day. There were many arguments in its favor, but I recall only one of the telling criticisms of our candidate. A discerning opponent felt that the kingbird represented one aspect of what he termed "our state personality" too well: our belligerence.

As punishment for that aberrant conduct, I have recalled that embarrassing episode every time since then that I have seen or heard a bluebird. Tarnished to this date is the exquisite pleasure of observing that soft blue back as a male flies off down a fence row, or hearing that distinctive mellow call across springtime fields.

37. Redstart

It is finally mid-May, that delightful time we thought would never arrive — especially through that long cold April. Woodlands are flooded with white and red trilliums, Virginia bluebells and yellow adder's tongues. Fruit trees, magnolias and shadbushes are awash in pink or white. And unfolding leaves hide winter browns with summer greens.

Even against this sumptuous backdrop, if you look carefully, you can pick out May's richest jewels: the warblers. More than two dozen species of these delicate chickadee-sized migrants pass through this region on their way to Canadian forests. Only a few remain here for the summer.

For this brief period they are widely distributed through the area. My favorite place to look for warblers is around Mirror Lake in Forest Lawn Cemetery. There you can often see them at close range flitting among the fruit tree blossoms.

Yellow is the predominant color of most warblers. For this reason Cubans call them mariposas — butterflies. But among their mariposas, the Cubans rightly single out one non-yellow species for the name candelita — the little torch. That name is assigned to the American redstart.

If you are a neophyte warbler watcher, the redstart is easy to learn first. Unlike any other warbler, the male redstart is all black except for bright orange patches in its wings and tail. Females and juveniles are less striking: olive grays and white replace the male's black. But they are easily recognized by their yellow patches where the males show orange.

The redstart offers more than its spectacular coloration. Frank Chapman says of the male: "*Ching, ching, chee; ser-wee, swee, swee-e-e* he sings, and with wings and tail outspread whirls about, dancing from limb to limb, darting upward, floating downward, blown hither and thither like a leaf in the breeze. But the gnats dancing in the sunlight and the caterpillars feeding in the shade of the leaves know to their sorrow that his erratic course is guided by a purpose."

Happily for us, redstarts are among our most common warblers during migration and also among those that remain here to nest. In both seasons they are only outnumbered by yellow warblers and common yellowthroats and in migration by yellow-rumped warblers as well. That doesn't mean that you will find them in your backyard. That is more often the reserve of the yellow warbler. The redstart and the yellow-rumped warbler are forest dwellers. The yellowthroat is a bird of the swamps.

Last summer in a Machias glen, I stopped at the base of a sawed-off tree to play taped tanager songs. Immediately a pair of redstarts announced their displeasure at my intrusion. While the male chattered at me, his mate struggled along the ground feigning a broken wing. I soon discovered the reason for their antagonism: my foot was inches from their nest. The tiny bowl was well hidden between fern fronds and the stump.

Before I retreated I looked at their four creamy white eggs. Brown speckles gathered into a wreath around their larger end, giving them too much the appearance of my own mostly bald head. That redstart family was fortunate: no cowbird had yet discovered their hiding place.

In his report on the relation of birds to New York State forests, W. L. McAtee says, "Busy at all times in the pursuit of insect prey, the redstart...must account for vast numbers of the forms injurious to trees." Rarely do they eat plant food, but Aretas Saunders found one eating Juneberries in Allegany State Park. Clearly this is a very beneficial species.

The black onyx among the warbler jewels, the American redstart is one of the richest treasures of May on the Niagara Frontier.

38. Bird Surnames

We often meet birds in surnames. There was a television program about the Partridge family. The story of King Arthur always includes the magician, Merlin. Some of us recall from our reading the school teacher, Miss Dove, or from the movies the actors, Peter Finch, Walter Pidgeon and Christopher Reeve. (The reeve is the female of the ruff, a snipe-like shorebird, an odd name assignment for the actor who portrayed Superman.)

Those are literary or stage names, but there are "real" ornithological surnames that have come down to us through the genealogical history of our families. They include, for example, the architect, Christopher Wren, who redesigned London after the 1666 fire and Florence Nightingale, the founder of modern nursing. Today I have friends named Tony Cardinale, Ron Raven, Al Starling and Bill Swift.

These considerations lead to two questions. Where did the names come from and what is the most common avian surname? I invite you to consider the second question while I address the first.

At least a dozen books in the University at Buffalo library discuss the source of our largely English surnames. They tell essentially the same story. Before we had hereditary names, individuals were known by personally descriptive names like Armstrong that died with them. But then between the Battles of Hastings and Agincourt — 1066 and 1415 — the practice of passing names from father to child became institutionalized.

The hereditary names derived from four sources: parentage (Johnson), places (Churchill), occupations (Carpenter) and the more general category of nicknames. In this last group are those given names that formerly didn't last beyond one generation. Some of the characteristics of those now-frozen nicknames were birdlike. C. M. Matthews suggests: "A small man might become Wren.... The Jay was a gaudy overdressed fellow...; a Starling noisy and a blabber of secrets, according to Chaucer; the Woodcock was foolish and so was the Quayle...." Authors do not agree on such things: P. H. Reaney knows the "Quale [by] its supposed amorous disposition and timidity." (Both those quotations predated recent political history.)

Some names were modified in this process of assignment. Sparrowhawk was shortened to Sparks. Owl was lengthened to Howell or Howlett, Hawk to Hawkins, making this last name an unusual combination of a fierce source pacified by a diminutive suffix.

Tracing sources is not an exact science. Another quite different surname route to Hawkins, for example, passes through the parent name Halkin referring to a relative named Hal. Similarly the name Drake might derive from a male waterfowl or from draco, a dragon. Names also came from other languages: Speight or Peck, for example, from German words for woodpecker.

Obviously avian surnames designate a very small fraction of our neighbors. We can gain some sense of how many through the interesting investigation of Charles W. Cook of Duke University. Professor Cook checked the over 100 million national phone listings for bird names — not by endlessly paging through directories but by a computer search.

He answers that second question. The most common bird surname he found is Martin (206,541 listings), well ahead of second place Crane (12,947). Next in order follow Finch, Crow, Swift, Swan and Peacock, each with over 6500 listings. Cook's catalogue is a long one with about a hundred species, his counts running down to 19 Hummingbirds and one Tanager. Interestingly even larger family groups like Bird itself (11,421) don't match up to Martin.

We have to wonder, why Martin? Was it some similarity to this bird's communal life style, its purple color or its dining preference for flying insects that provoked name assignment?

39. Winter Wren

The winter wren was singing when we first arrived at our cabin in the Minnesota Boundary Waters and a week later it was still serenading us as we packed up to leave.

The song is impossible to describe. To say that it is a long series of unexpectedly loud warbles and tinkles and trills, its notes higher than the highest on a piano, is like describing the painting of an old master by naming its colors. Maine author Cordelia Stanwood describes it as a babbling brook come to life and I agree with her that it is the Spirit of the Woods. To my ear this is the most beautiful bird song.

This was the second time this year I was serenaded by a winter wren. On our May hike on the Finger Lakes Trail in Chemung County, Jim DeWan and I were sung to sleep one evening and awakened the next morning by that lovely sound.

How one of our tiniest birds can sing so lustily is a mystery. The winter wren is not even as big as a house wren. I seldom see them because they are so shy. Mouse-like they usually frequent the undergrowth. But once I followed a song to its source deep in a wooded glen where I found the diminutive, dark brown wren, tail up and constantly bobbing, searching for insects among mushrooms, moss and exposed tree roots. At my approach its song quieted to a near whisper, but after several minutes the little wren ignored me and suddenly burst forth. I have never seen a bird's mouth so wide open. Its upper and lower bills were in a straight line. If it had faced me, I am sure I could have seen down into those ballooning lungs. And the resulting glorious song encompassed me.

Years ago when bird song was first being recorded, Paul Kellogg invited me to name a bird I would like to hear. Paul, a retired acoustical engineer, had joined ornithologist Arthur Allen at Cornell University to pursue his hobby of birding.

There he started one of the world's finest collections of bird and other animal sounds. I knew Paul as a fellow officer of the then newly formed Federation of New York State Bird Clubs (today the New York State Ornithological Association) and his offer came after a board meeting of that organization.

No contest. I chose winter wren.

Paul took down a tape spool, carefully placed it on his desk-sized sound apparatus and turned on the speaker. The room was immediately filled with that wonderful song.

We timed successive bursts. Each one continued for six to eight seconds, quite unusual when you consider that a song sparrow's seemingly lengthy chatter lasts less than three.

Next Paul reran the tape at half speed. This not only slowed the song so that we could begin to separate trills and warbles, it also lowered the pitch an octave. But the notes still came so fast that we could not distinguish them. Only when Paul slowed the tape to one-eighth speed — in the process reducing the little wren's soprano tinkle to a baritone burping — were we able to count them. Remarkably, there were over a hundred in each series.

The male winter wren, unlike house and marsh wrens, is a family man who takes his responsibilities seriously. He carries food — almost exclusively insects — to his mate on their nest and continues with her to feed their four to seven offspring until they fledge. In another year some of those youngsters will add to the forest chorus.

My friend Paul Kellogg died some years ago. I hope that his particular heaven rings with a winter wren's delightful melodies.

40. Cormorant Massacre

Recently 800 cormorants were massacred on Little Galoo Island in Henderson Harbor near Watertown. Department of Environmental Conservation Commissioner John Cahill called it "an act of savage brutality."

Among the dead and dying birds conservation officers found hundreds of shotgun shells. Evidence suggests that the cormorants were killed by locals who either fish themselves or charter boats for others in eastern Lake Ontario where the sport fish population has plummeted. DEC staff and the police are currently investigating this violation of the International Migratory Bird Treaty Act.

No one should defend this crime but it is reasonable, I believe, to consider the underlying very serious conservation problem. My own experience may help to place it in perspective.

For several years during the 1940s I joined a team of bird banders to ring gull nestlings on Little Galoo Island. We motored out to an island encompassing several acres, which at that time was still covered with wildflowers, shrubs and trees. But over those few years I witnessed a decline in this vegetation due to the excrement of thousands of gulls. Also the island tern colony was eradicated by the last year I worked there. The last tern I found there had been killed by a single peck in its back.

During my final year we were excited to observe cormorants nesting on a nearby islet, the first Lake Ontario breeding record for this seabird.

Today, fifty years later, Little Galoo and many other uninhabited islands of the St. Lawrence River and Lake Champlain regions are wastelands, foul smelling guano fields completely taken over by cormorants. Their Great Lakes population has risen exponentially. For example, from less than a dozen birds on the Niagara Frontier in October 1986, regional Buffalo Ornithological Society census takers counted over 900 just ten years later.

The impact of these birds on fish is being debated. The fishing community cites the crash of game fish numbers that correlates with the increase in cormorant numbers. Ron Ditch, a Henderson Harbor charter boat operator, supports this observation with his film of cormorants consuming hundreds of trout fingerlings just after they were stocked in Lake Ontario. On the other hand, the few available biological studies suggest that cormorants consume a meager diet of game fish — less than two percent of what they ate in one study. Necessary additional studies take time; meanwhile local guides losing their livelihoods are increasingly frustrated.

So we have another wildlife population dilemma. And this wanton act has arrayed most conservationists against the fishing community. I do not join them.

Of course the felons who broke the law should be found and prosecuted, but the underlying situation demands a reasonable solution. And the cormorant issue represents just one of these overpopulation emergencies that are not yet being addressed. With them belong gulls, crows, Canada geese, mallards and, of course, among mammals white-tailed deer and house cats.

What many animal preservationists fail to take into account is that these problems go beyond the species level. Often they affect us: jobs are lost and personal property is damaged. An underlying concern is whether non-human animals should receive equal status with humans. At least as important, these species also affect the overall ecological community. Urban crows have already eliminated our regional nighthawk population; deer are everywhere obliterating rare wildflowers; where gulls and cormorants nest they destroy virtually all the vegetation.

Through our past actions we have certainly contributed to our wildlife problems, but I don't believe that means we should now adopt the animal rights philosophy: "Let nature take its course."

These are serious matters that we exacerbate by our failure to address them — not just in Henderson Harbor but in western New York as well.

41. Bald Songbirds

The first call came in mid-August.

"Are there any songbirds that have no feathers on their heads? "

Over the years I have fielded so many inquiries that most now are repeats. But this was something new to me. A bald songbird?

There are, of course, birds with no head feathers: our turkey vulture is one. The black vulture, a southern species rarely seen here, is another. So too is the California condor, now recovering from near extinction in the far west with the assistance of zoo-bred and released birds.

But no bald songbirds.

"We have one coming to our feeder. He's out there now. He looks just like a male cardinal except for the head, which is completely bare. "

I was stumped. All I could do was promise to look into the matter.

Within minutes Noreen Olek called. Noreen and her husband Mike are two of our finest regional animal rehabilitators. They had received a similar inquiry, but this time it concerned three bald birds at the same feeder: another cardinal, a blue jay and an unidentified blackbird. Mike forwarded a picture of the cardinal, its purple head so ugly I could hardly look at it.

I called Art Clark, vertebrate zoology curator at the Buffalo Museum of Science. This was unusual for him as well. He and I both searched the literature but found little help there.

The four of us — Art, Mike, Noreen and I — came up with possible causes of this aberration. Unfortunately, each had shortcomings.

(1) Something wrong in the molting process. John Terres in *The Encyclopedia of North American Birds* points out that molts usually replace feathers in waves so that bare spots rarely appear. This process might have malfunctioned. But many birds at once?

(2) Disease. We found none with this characteristic.

(3) Feather mites. Why then are only the heads affected?

(4) Feather-picking. Some birds, especially crows, peck head feathers from others. But they usually attack their own species.

(5) A feeder entrance rubbing off head feathers. None was found nearby.

Until recently, that is where the matter would have ended. However, today we have an effective new resource — the Internet. I posted a description of our dilemma together with a request for assistance on the Internet mail group, Birdchat. Through this medium our message was carried to over 7000 ornithologists around the world.

Among the many responses, most told of personal experiences with this phenomenon. For example, Julie Stielstra of Illinois wrote, "This time every year this comes up. I've been laughing at a totally bald blue jay, a mutant-punk grackle with a Mohawk and a very pathetic looking cardinal with a little plume on a bald head at my feeder. " Note the remarkable coincidence of her species with those reported to the Oleks.

But two respondents gave us our answer. Mark Monroe,

biologist at Hawk Mountain Sanctuary in Pennsylvania, wrote that it was indeed a mite infection and that it would not affect the next molt. And Susan Thuener — quite appropriately of Mohawk, New York — wrote, "The head is the one vulnerable spot on the bird that it cannot reach to preen. "

And so our mystery is solved. Seasonally, a few birds are attacked by feather mites, tiny arthropods whose feeding destroys feather shafts. Normally, the birds would divest themselves of these mites by preening, but birds cannot effectively preen their own heads. Once the mites have destroyed their food source on the birds' heads, they must either move on to a new victim or place themselves in jeopardy on another area of their host's body.

We close our file on The Case of the Bald Birds.

42. Kirtland's Warbler

Jared Potter Kirtland was an 18th century Ohio physician whose biological avocations earned him several natural history honors. *Kirtlandia*, the journal of the Cleveland Museum of Natural History is named for him as are two species, Kirtland's water snake and Kirtland's warbler.

Spencer Baird of the Smithsonian Institution named the warbler based on specimens collected by Dr. Kirtland near his Ohio home. Sadly the species is long gone from that area and it became one of our most endangered birds, its breeding range restricted to a few square miles.

In mid-June Mike Hamilton and I drove to Grayling, Michigan to see this rare bird. There we joined a tour of the jack pine plantations that are carefully managed to support this warbler as part of a program sponsored by the U. S. Fish and Wildlife Service, the U. S. Forest Service, the Michigan Department of Natural Resources and the Michigan Audubon Society. Our excellent guide was F&WS officer Tammy Giroux.

There were about twenty birders in our group. Much to our surprise, seven of them turned out to be members of Rainbow Country Birders of Niagara County.

Before we ventured out into the plantations, we were provided some background. We learned that the number of Kirtland's warbler pairs dropped from almost 600 in 1961 to 201 in 1971, biologists identifying two causes for this precipitous decline. First, cowbirds laying their eggs in warbler nests and crowding out the warbler chicks; the second, loss of habitat. And second, these warblers require very specific breeding grounds and the pines here were growing too tall.

The first problem has been solved by trapping and removing thousands of cowbirds over the years. The second, more difficult problem, has required a carefully managed tree harvesting cycle.

Nature originally managed this forest through lightning-ignited fires that destroyed trees when they grew too tall and at the same time burst their tightly sealed cones to provide new seedlings. Now, with fires strictly controlled, the 210 square miles of plantations go through a three stage management cycle, each year only one-third providing the required habitat for the warbler.

Given that excellent introduction, our caravan now proceeded out into a beautiful day, clear blue skies over the rich green of the pines. No sooner had we parked and started down a trail into a plantation than we heard the loud song of our target bird. Within minutes we had binoculars and telescopes focused on the handsome gray and yellow songster and we could watch him proudly proclaiming his home territory.

There was other wildlife as well. A hermit thrush provided an organ background to the warbler's refrain and a thirteen-lined ground squirrel — a chipmunk look-alike — bustled about in the thick undergrowth. I knew this little rodent from summers at Notre Dame in Indiana and I whistled this one in close for others to see.

Ms. Giroux showed us one of the cowbird traps. In it several well-fed birds play the role of Judas goats. Attracted by them, other cowbirds fly in through holes in the trap roof and are unable to fly out. Each day several are removed.

This management has been successful. Today there are about 800 pairs of Kirtland's Warblers and the birds have even established a new breeding area on the Michigan northern peninsula. An individual was even recorded recently in Hamlin State Park. When they reach 1000 pairs biologists will remove them from the endangered species list.

To some this may seem like a large investment to protect one little warbler. Don't tell that to local residents whose economy benefits from the many tourism dollars spent by those who come to see this rare bird. And all of us should support this program for its ecological, historical, educational and esthetic values.

43. Ivory-billed Woodpecker

"The ivory-billed woodpecker, long suspected to be extinct, has been rediscovered in the 'Big Woods' region of eastern Arkansas."

That initial sentence appearing in *Science* in 2005 and the associated official announcement at the United States Department of the Interior on April 28 that year struck a unique chord in the birding world. To both amateur birders and professional scientists this recovery from near-extinction represented the biggest ornithological news in the past half century.

The most recent earlier accepted record of the ivory-billed woodpecker was in 1944, sixty years before the April 25, 2004 video-supported observation on which this announcement is based.

It is hard to think of news that would be more extraordinary in the birding world. A passenger pigeon joining mourning doves at your feeder after a 90-year absence, perhaps, or a dodo showing up on Mauritius Island in the Indian Ocean after an absence of 340 years. Even in human terms 60 years is a lifetime, a remarkable period for a bird species not to be observed in a country with an estimated 20 million active birdwatchers, several hundred of whom are professional ornithologists.

And this is no tiny wren-sized bird. The ivory-billed woodpecker is as big as a crow and the flashing white of its wings and back makes it look still larger. It is even bigger than the pileated woodpecker, an uncommon resident in western New York that occasionally visits rural suet feeders. Like the pileated, the adult male ivory-bill also sports a bright red Woody Woodpecker crest, but the pileated woodpecker's bill is a dirty gray.

Here is the story of the discovery, mostly drawn from central character Tim Gallagher's timely new book, *The Grail Bird*.

What may have been this bird was first sighted by Gene Sparling on February 11, 2004 while he was kayaking in the Cache River National Wildlife Refuge in eastern Arkansas. Sparling posted an account of his trip on a canoe club listserve only adding a brief description of his ivory-bill observation as a kind of footnote. Hearing of this, Gallagher and Bobby Harrison separately called Sparling and were soon convinced that this could be an ivory-bill. They traveled to Arkansas and entered the swamp with Sparling.

Here is Gallagher's account shortly after they paddled their canoe near a road and with Sparling well ahead: "As we paddled along, we talked and joked about floating through the trackless swamp. Then Bobby started to grouse that we were being way too noisy to see any ivory-bills.

"'We don't need to worry about that,' I said. 'The road's so loud they'll never hear us coming. And who knows, maybe Gene will chase one back to us.'

"And then it happened. Less than eighty feet away, a large black-and-white bird that had been flying toward us from a side channel of the bayou to the right came out into the sunshine and flew across the open stretch of water directly in front of us. It started to bank, giving us a superb view of its back and both wings for a moment as it pulled up, as if it were going to land on a tree trunk. 'Look at all the white on its wings!' I yelled. Hearing my voice, it veered away from the tree and continued to fly to the left. We both cried out simultaneously, 'Ivory-bill!'"

The three looked for several days without further sightings before Gallagher returned to Ithaca where he edits *Living Bird* for the Cornell Laboratory of Ornithology. There he faced intensive interrogations from his colleagues.

They were convinced, however, and a week later an expedition was back in Arkansas. No luck.

Shortly after this a team of Cornell birders converged on the swamp. Again nothing. In early April a third team headed south. Finally some results.

On April 5, Jim Fitzpatrick saw an ivory-bill. Here is Gallagher's account: "He was fumbling around in his daypack when he happened to take a look north up the lake. At that instant a large bird appeared, coming right at him, flying above the trees. 'I just thought to myself, that's a really big pileated,' he said.

"When it cleared the tree, I finally realized that the wing pattern was all wrong for a pileated,' he said. 'I was seeing white on the downbeat as well as on the upbeat — and not that little star shape like a pileated; it was a full-blown patch of white.' And the bird didn't fly like a pileated woodpecker. 'There was no undulation in its flight,' he said. 'It was flapping briskly and strongly, like a loon. The flight seemed exquisitely efficient. He didn't waste a lot of body movement. He just cooked right along. That's when I realized, holy shit! That's not a pileated!'"

The next day Ron Rohrbaugh and David Bonter also had a brief look at what they took to be an ivory-bill.

April 10: Mindy LaBranche "spotted a large black-and-white bird flying from west to east above the forest canopy.... 'I kept seeing the top of the wing and the white trailing edge of the wing,' she said.... She slowly lowered her binoculars and sat there repeating over and over, 'The trailing edge was white, the trailing edge was white, the trailing edge was white... This can't be a pileated.'"

April 11: Melanie Driscoll added an eight second observation.

A total of five observations but no acceptable evidence for a bird thought to be extinct.

Then, two weeks later on April 25, David Luneau and Robert Driscoll got that evidence. Their boat had a mounted camcorder running continuously. Here is Gallagher's account: "It happened just after 3:30 in the afternoon.... [A] large black-and-white woodpecker burst from the other side of a tupelo, just a couple of feet above the water, and flew straight away from them. With the paddle in his hands, David didn't have time to grab the camcorder but he swung the canoe to the left, trying to keep the bird in view.

"'What was that?' he asked.

"'I don't know,' said Robert. 'I sure wish I could see it again.'

"David looked down at the camcorder in front of him. It had been pointing in exactly the direction the bird had flown, and it was running. The entry he jotted down in his field notes for 3:40 p.m. reads, 'Saw B&W Wp fly away. Never caught anything but a rear-end look. Right at camera T2. Caught it on video briefly.' You would never know from that matter-of-fact note that he had just nailed the first videotape of our feathered phantom."

Gallagher adds: "David told me later that he would never have mentioned the sighting if not for the videotape. 'I just didn't get a good enough look,' he said."

That videotape has satisfied some but far from all ornithologists that the ivory-billed woodpecker is not extinct.

One more sighting was added on February 14, 2005 by Casey Taylor, but about two dozen birders continuing to search the area.

The failure to find this bird earlier had not been for lack of effort. In 2002, for example, after a turkey hunter reported seeing ivory-bills in the swamps of northeastern Louisiana, a team armed with all kinds of technological equipment spent months searching the area without success.

I knew several of the observers who saw the ivory-bill during the 1930s and 1940s. One of the latest accounts was Roger Tory Peterson's. His observation was in Louisiana in 1942. Here is his narrative from *Birds over America*: "We had gone a half mile from the road when Kuhn [a local woodsman acting as their guide] stopped short. He had caught a note on the edge of his sphere of hearing. I thought I heard it, but it could have been a versatile chat. We had been told to listen for a voice that sounded something like a nuthatch. But there were plenty of nuthatches in these woods, too, to confound us. We found ourselves starting at strange unfamiliar notes that turned out to be squirrels and red-bellied woodpeckers. Kuhn assured us that when we heard the ivory-bill we would know it all right. 'Nothing in the whole woods sounds like it.'"

The next morning they set out again. "By noon we were back at the spot, down the road, where we had seen so many diggings the day before. We would make another sortie before throwing in the sponge. Hardly had we gone a hundred yards when [I heard] an indescribable tooting note, musical in a staccato sort of way. For a moment it did not click, but then I knew — it was the ivory bill! I had expected it to sound more like a nuthatch; it was much more like the 'toy tin trumpet' described by Alexander Wilson or the 'clarinet' of Audubon. Breathlessly we stalked the insistent toots, stepping carefully, stealthily, so that no twig would crack. With our hearts pounding we tried to keep cool, hardly daring to believe that this was it — that this was what we had come fifteen hundred miles to see. Straining our eyes, we discovered the first bird, half hidden by the leafage, and in a moment it leaped upward into the full sunlight. This was no puny pileated; this was a whacking big bird, with great white patches on its wings and a gleaming white bill. By its long recurved crest of blackish jet we knew it was a female.

Tossing its hammer-like head to right and left, it tested the diseased trunk with a whack or two as it jerked upward. Lurching out to the end of a broken-off branch, it pitched off on a straight line, like a duck, its wings making a wooden sound."

On an earlier 1935 expedition to Louisiana Arthur Allen photographed and Paul Kellogg recorded the calls of ivory-bills at their nest. Paul told me later that they set up camp and patrolled the swamps searching for several days only to find that the shy birds were nesting just yards from their tents.

The final sighting accepted before the current rediscovery was that of the fine bird artist, Donald Eckelberry, in April 1944. He told of the logging going on nearby that was destroying the rare bird's habitat. The logging company employed German prisoners of war who, according to Eckelberry, "were incredulous at the waste — only the best wood taken, the rest left in wreckage."

Of course early ornithologists like Mark Catesby and John James Audubon — his ivory-bill painting is in volume 4 — were familiar with the ivory-billed woodpecker, but even Audubon noted its decline. Perhaps the most interesting account is that of Alexander Wilson (Wilson 1811), who describes his experience trying to keep a pet ivory-bill. It tore up his room at an inn and then, when Wilson attached its leg to a mahogany desk leg by a string, proceeded to tear apart the desk.

Buffalo has an unusual connection to this species. Jerome Jackson, author in 2004 of *In Search of the Ivory-billed Woodpecker* and of the *Birds of America* species account, visited the Buffalo Museum of Science to measure and photograph the museum's mounted pair. Recently he told former museum ornithology curator Art Clark that the local pair had the only red glass replacement eyes he had ever seen, the normal coloration being yellow. But Jackson also pointed out that the famous artist George Sutton had painted this species with red eyes. Thus Sutton almost certainly worked from these specimens somewhere prior to their being acquired by the Buffalo museum.

In addition to the literature I have cited, a number of additional resources are available. Perhaps the most important historical account is James Tanner's doctoral thesis, which remains in print. A recent account that does not include the rediscovery is Phillip House's *The Race to Save the Lord God Bird*. For an account together with those for other vanished species, see Christopher Cokinos' *Hope Is the Thing with Feathers*. There is also a YouTube program titled "Rediscovery of the Ivory-billed Woodpecker," that includes the Fitzpatrick photographic evidence.

It is important to note that, despite serious further efforts to find an ivory-bill and produce acceptable evidence for it, including installation of recording devices that run continuously, none has been forthcoming and the American Ornithologists Union continues to list this species as extinct.

44. *The Profanatory*

The Buffalo Ornithological Society celebrated its 70th anniversary with a dinner at the Protocol Restaurant in Cheektowaga. Continuing a long-standing tradition at these banquets held every five years, an issue of *The Profanetary*, a tongue-in-cheek take-off on the society's regular monthly journal, *The Prothonotary*, was distributed. With the permission of the anonymous editors of that broadsheet, I share two of its articles with you.

Under the title "Bird Flocks": "There are already odd names for bird groups that appear on that long list of proposed aggregations along with a pride of lions and a pod of whales. Two on that list that come to mind are a murder of crows and a murmuration of starlings. But given those two unusual names, birders have felt challenged to come up with additional references for flocks of the various avian species.

"Here are some for a few of our local birds: a college of cardinals, a cord of wood ducks, a chain of bobolinks, a dynasty of kinglets, a barrel of woodcocks, an awning of canvasbacks, an earful of waxwings, a grain of sanderlings, a harassment of harriers, a wake of mourning doves, a treasury of goldfinches, a tyranny of kingbirds, a cone of pine warblers, a Gallup of redpolls, a foreclosure of bank swallows, a guttering of flickers, a dean of martins, a show of peeps, a pint of bitterns, an RSVP (or perhaps SVP) of egrets, a graveyard of shovelers, a little house of prairie warblers, a motor of scoters, a curmudgeon of coots, for golfers an iron of chipping sparrows, a realm of kingfishers, a complaint of grouse, a reading of palm warblers, and (our favorite) a dribble of pewee.

"Going somewhat farther afield we have: a gallon of petrels, an embarrassment of red-faced cormorants, a moustache of whiskered terns, a strop of razorbills, a fanfare of trumpeter swans, a gang of masked ducks, a cotillion of elegant terns, a bowl of spoonbills, a family of partridges, an audience of clapper rails, a collar of ruffs, a prayer of godwits, a range of mountain plovers, a bunch of bananaquits, a guffaw of laughing gulls, a blush of scarlet ibis, an exile of Bonaparte's gulls, an easel of painted buntings, a stampede of cattle egrets, a Gordion of knots, a shish kebab of skuas, a ladle of dippers and an orphanage of anis.

"As one contributor to the list concluded: 'I'm going to retire now — to an asylum of cuckoos.'"

Another article is titled "Ornithological Bias": "The American Ornithologists Union is currently considering renaming the oldsquaw, the duck well known for the almost constant gossiping calls exchanged by these birds when they gather in winter flocks on our rivers and lakes. The proposed change is to long-tailed duck, the name already assigned this species in Europe. The reason for the change is, however, not simply to bring us into line with the Old Country: in this single current species name, oldsquaw, we have what has been deemed insensitivity to sex, race and age, something of a record for a single word.

"But the proposed change has not met with universal approval. One critic has suggested some additional species that might cause disquiet among various minorities: the common loon which offends those in psychological therapy; the bald eagle, those with thinning hair; the hermit thrush, those who have chosen to live alone; the grosbeak, those with large noses; the coot, our elderly; and the vulture, our lawyers. The sapsucker and the booby he claims need no characterization."

We await — with some trepidation — the next issue of this unusual journal.

45. An Adventure with a Raven

There is, I am told, a National Raven Week.

I have no idea who comes up with these designations and, in fact, I suspect that this particular week is somehow designed to be self-serving. That it just happened to come up shortly after the publication of Bernd Heinrich's wonderful book, *The Mind of the Raven*, may have something to do with it.

Whatever the reason, National Raven Week gives me the opportunity to tell about my raven encounter.

Before I share that story, however, I note here that autumn is the time of year when, according to retired St. Bonaventure ornithologist Steve Eaton, ravens are most often seen in Western New York. At this season these normally reclusive birds occasionally venture out of their usual deep woods isolation in Allegany State Park to scavenge the remains of butchered deer carcasses left by hunters.

Back to my raven adventure.

Many years ago my wife and I joined my brother and our children for a family reunion in the Rocky Mountains west of Denver. We spent a week in a mountain lodge at Keystone. It was a week almost exclusively devoted to cooking, eating and screaming grandchildren. I avoided two of those three activities — you can easily guess which — by wandering out on my own to look for birds.

Most of those hikes provided me with pleasant experiences in unfamiliar country. I added several birds to my North American list: among them a dipper, that remarkable semi-aquatic bird that dashes in and out of turbulent streams (remarkably I had seen one in England) and a lesser goldfinch, an even more beautiful, miniature cousin of our eastern species.

I was particularly interested in seeking out those rare grouse of the high mountains — ptarmigans. They are indeed a tough find. In winter they are almost pure white to match the snow and in summer they molt into plumage so similar to that of the thin vegetation of the high country that they are nearly impossible to pick out.

A guide to the region indicated that the 12,000 foot Loveland Pass was a good place to look for ptarmigans so I drove there early one morning in hopes of spotting them.

I parked at the pass and hiked up a steep trail. There were no trees and the views in the early morning sunlight were spectacular, but I spent most of my time focusing binoculars on the low shrubbery looking for ptarmigan.

Suddenly I was startled by the hoarse *cruck* of a raven. I turned and there he was, almost within reach. He was easily distinguished from his crow cousins by his call, his larger size and his even more outsized bill. How remarkable, I remember thinking. I have never, before or after that time, seen a raven other than in the distance, yet here was this big bird strutting among the rocks a dozen feet away.

I watched him for several minutes. All that time he circled around me maintaining that same minimum distance. What in the world was he doing?

After enjoying several minutes of this odd two-step I climbed on up the trail to continue my fruitless search for those mountain grouse. Not only did I have no luck but I found as I turned back toward the car that I had lost my glasses. I searched everywhere for them and I even went back to the lodge, gathered the family and returned to have them help me scour that hillside. No luck.

Finally I realized where those glasses went.

Somewhere high in the Rockies is a raven's nest adorned with bifocal picture windows.

46. Shrike

I first catch sight of the bird as it flies low over the Iroquois National Wildlife Refuge marsh. It's robin-sized, gray, and it flashes white patches in its dark wings as it beats purposefully over the reeds and a broad snow covered pond. My first thought is mockingbird. But when it reaches the line of tall trees and swoops effortlessly up, up, up to perch on the tip of the highest branch, I know that this is my first Northern shrike of the winter.

Excited to find this uncommon visitor from the spruce forests of northern Labrador, I focus my binoculars on it. It has black wings and tail, a soft gray back and crown, and a finely barred white breast. But most noticeable are its black mask and the hooked raptorial bill that identifies this songbird as a predator.

As I watch, the shrike bends its head to look in my direction. Sighting something, it sails steeply down to a dogwood bush only twenty feet from me. Oblivious to my presence it stares at the ground where the fickle wind has cleared snow from a small area.

Suddenly the shrike drops to the ground and I can see it grasp something brown at the edge of the snowdrift. It beats its wings several times to provide the leverage to drag a big meadow vole out into the open.

But the exposed field mouse quickly breaks out of the clutches of the shrike and turns on its assailant. This is not an unequal battle as the mouse is bigger than the torso of the shrike and clearly outweighs its opponent. Fierce and aggressive, it springs at the shrike several times. The bird retreats before each of these onslaughts, but it fends off the mouse's thrusts with sharp blows from its hawk-like bill.

For a time the outcome appears uncertain, but then the mouse seems to tire and it stops its attacks. The combatants face each other for a long moment, but the shrike stares down its opponent and the mouse turns to dash for safety under the snow.

It doesn't make it! In a flash the shrike springs to the mouse's back and digs its bill deep into the rodent's neck. All is over quickly. The mouse twitches twice and then is still.

The shrike now grasps the big mouse with its bill and feet and takes off toward the woods. I continue to watch it until it disappears behind the trees. All that are left behind are a few drops of blood rapidly congealing on the snow.

Only now do I realize that I have been standing perfectly still through this entire drama. A chill sweeps up my back and the aching of my cold fingers becomes apparent. I must move on to prevent hypothermia in the biting cold. I trudge ahead, my snowshoes sinking into the very light snow with that squeak, squeak, squeak familiar to winter hikers.

But the episode is not quite complete. The trail along the levee leads to a patch of woods. There a single honeylocust still retains a few of its long seedpods. However, that is not what captures my attention. Impaled on one of the honey-locust's big thorns is the body of the vole. On another is a junco. The shrike has cached its victims here for later feeding and has flown off in search of other prey. This behavior — hanging its victims like carcasses in a butcher's shop — gives the shrike another name: butcherbird.

Now to my surprise a tiny chickadee flies up and begins to peck at the vole's stiffening carcass. Obviously any food source is to be utilized in the frigid temperatures of this winter.

47. Mockingbird

My wife's father, James Theodore Copeland, a lifelong teetotaler, knows the mockingbird's song by a bit of doggerel, designed, I am sure, to shock his wife and daughter:

> *Theo, Theo, Theo:*
> *Get dressed, get dressed, get dressed;*
> *Go to town, go to town, go to town;*
> *Get drunk, get drunk, get drunk;*
> *Puke, puke, puke.*

In his rich southern accents that line is drawled into *pea-uke, pea-uke, pea-uke*. And the verse ends:

> *Shame, shame, shame.*

I can think of no more charming way to remember the mockingbird's thrice repeated phrasing, but no rhyme can convey the full repertoire of this versatile songster.

As I write this I sit on the open porch of my in-laws' home in north Alabama listening to a mockingbird sing into silent awe several brown thrashers who share its territory.

Mockingbirds mimic a wide range of the songs of other birds. Some of their copies are so close that electronic analysis cannot distinguish them from the original. One was recorded at the Cornell Laboratory of Ornithology imitating 30 species. On the Niagara Frontier Willy D'Anna, Patrick O'Donnell, and Betsy Potter found one mimicking 27 species. But the all-time record seems to have been established in 1924 when C. W. Townsend reported a mockingbird that mimicked 55 species in one hour!

My Alabama bird sticks to its neighbors. It occasionally mixes in variations on the notes of oriole, pewee, red-eyed vireo, and towhee, but three it has down pat and imitates often. They are the Carolina wren's *teakettle, teakettle, teakettle;* the crested flycatcher's *whirr, whirr, whirr;* and the tufted titmouse's *peter, peter, peter.*

A light rain falls. Bob-whites, meadowlarks, and a cardinal call in the distance. A loggerhead shrike, a threatened species in New York State, hawks the field from a dead tree across the country lane. Four attractive birds of varying shades of blue are to be seen within a few yards of the house: blue jay, eastern bluebird, indigo bunting, and blue grosbeak.

But the mockingbird remains center stage.

For a time he sat on the highest snag of a woodpile in a neighbor's yard, but now he sings while perched motionless on a phone wire a few yards from the bluebird. He could command attention with the flashes of white in his wings and tail as he flies or displays, but he doesn't need that now. His voice carries full effect.

Nesting territories have long been established so this bird can hardly be announcing his domain. Rather, I believe, he is simply singing for enjoyment. He has been at it all day and he even sang at intervals before dawn this morning.

Another mockingbird feeds now perhaps 50 feet away in a recently mown field. I have seen only the reddish egret use a similar technique. The mockingbird fans out its wings showing their contrasting dark and white areas, watching intently as it does so. The motion and the shadow it produces evidently frightens insects into moving, because the bird follows these displays by refolding its wings, hopping forward, and picking insects from the tufts of grass.

Starlings feed nearby. They drill deeply into the sandy soil possibly for Japanese beetle larvae. Even though they share the restaurant, the two species evidently read from different pages of the menu.

Listed as a rare visitor by Beardslee and Mitchell on the Niagara Frontier in 1965, mockingbirds are still uncommon here; however, their numbers have increased through the recent spell of mild winters, especially along the Ontario plain west of the Niagara River. One or more mockingbirds were found regularly for several years in the hedges above the public boat landing in Lewiston. When those hedges were removed recently, the birds simply moved to nearby yards. Like the cardinal before it and now with the Carolina wren and the tufted titmouse, their northward spread is supported by those who provide food for birds through the winter. And now, of course, climate change.

Plant berry bushes or add apple slices to your feeder and you might attract one of these delightful birds.

48. Pennsylvania Expedition

In mid-July I tagged along with Chris Hollister on his visit to sparrow country south of Clarion in western Pennsylvania.

Sparrow country? Your first reaction, like that of my wife, might be that we have more than enough sparrows here. Sparrows by the dozen crowd out more interesting birds from local feeders. Who needs to get up at 2:30 a.m. and drive 200 miles to see still more of them? I'll have to admit that I gave quite a bit of thought to that inquiry myself as I struggled out of bed that morning.

There are several things about that question that non-birders fail to understand. First, many of those so-called sparrows that infest your hedges and bird feeders are not even true sparrows: those house sparrows belong to a separate category of weaver finch. And, of course, they are aliens. They were among those species introduced to this country in a misguided program that sought to import to North America all the birds that occur in Shakespeare. (That program brought starlings as well.)

Our true sparrows are far less aggressive. Most common are the song and chipping sparrows, each of which adds to the ambience of suburban and country yards. Other species also come to our feeders in winter and during migration: those are the tree, white-throated and white-crowned sparrows and the dark-eyed junco. Almost all of them move on to breed in the far north. A few birds of another species are found here year around: the swamp sparrow, appropriately named for its habitat.

But none of those were the birds we were looking for. We sought grassland sparrows, many of which are increasingly difficult to find. The numbers of field, savannah, grasshopper and vesper sparrows have declined, some precipitously, in recent years and the Henslow's sparrow, named for James Henslow, a friend of Audubon, has now apparently winked out from here on the Niagara Frontier. None have been reported on the Niagara Frontier for several years.

Chris had monitored reports of some of these uncommon sparrows from three interesting areas all within a few miles and we set out to visit them, maps and commentaries in hand.

He timed our excursion just right as we arrived at the first site, an area called Piney Tract, just at dawn, the time when birds are most active. The area appeared to be about a square mile of open grassland spotted with widely separated shrubs, mostly honeysuckle, that gave the area its special character. The pines from which the area took its name were in a few groves around the edge of the fields.

We no sooner arrived when Chris heard a vesper sparrow. It turned out to be the only one we would find that day. But then we began to hear the distinctive *chepick* chirp of Henslow's sparrows, one of our target species. We were shocked to find it the most common bird in the area. We were to find at least an amazing two dozen.

Now came the drum rolls of field sparrows and the buzzing notes of grasshopper and savannah sparrows. Then another of our target birds piped up: a pair of clay-colored sparrows, a mid-continent species only rarely recorded on the Niagara

Frontier.

These were not the only birds we found, of course. Among the others were towhees, indigo buntings, meadowlark, a beautiful prairie warbler, a few late bobolinks and an orchard oriole.

Now we moved on to a second area designated the Curllsville Strips, which we found to be quite similar to the Piney Tract. More Henslow's and clay-colored sparrows. And a new species checked in: a dickcissel. This is a sparrow-like midwestern species that occasionally strays east. Its odd name is onomatopoetic: the song one or two *dick*s followed by a short series of *cisse*s. Once we heard its song, we trained our binoculars on the bush from which it was singing and finally picked it out. It is a handsome sparrow-like bird with a yellow eye-line and malar stripe, chestnut shoulders and a black bib over a yellow chest. Its coloring is suggestive of a meadow-lark.

Already nearly sated with interesting species we headed for our last stop: the Armstrong Trail along the Allegany River. No sooner had we left the car when we heard the squeeze toy-like *flee-slip* of an Acadian flycatcher. A half hour search then picked up our final target species: a pair of worm-eating warblers.

So ended a quite remarkable day in the field.

49. Escape

Linda Markle's cockatiel, Becca, escaped from her home in North Buffalo. The bird slipped past Mrs. Markle's husband when he opened an outside door. On its first opportunity to soar, an adrenaline rush sent it flapping higher and higher into the sky until, despite Mr. Markle's frantic whistles, it disappeared from sight. Thus began a futile search for their pet.

Cockatiels are robin-sized Australian parrots. Most, like Becca, are gray with a yellow head and an attractive crest, but a few are all white. According to Mrs. Markle, who is physically handicapped, they make splendid pets. Becca had been with them for seven years and Mrs. Markle says that the bird gave her more pleasure than any of her previous pets. Cockatiels are companionable and not jealous like the larger macaws. When guests visited the Markles, for example, Becca flew to greet each of them in turn. Their bird only chattered and whistled but some learn many human phrases.

The Markles knew that Becca would be unable to find its way back to them, but they also knew that it was imprinted on people and would approach them when it became tired or hungry. So they initiated a campaign to retrieve their bird.

They contacted the SPCA, every pet store in the area, several groups of cage bird fanciers and the Buffalo Zoo. They placed advertisements in *The Buffalo News* and other newspapers. They made up fliers which Mr. Markle posted and distributed at events like yard sales. And they offered a generous reward for Becca's return.

The response to these efforts was quite remarkable. Ten people called to report cockatiels found after the Markle's bird escaped. All but one made it clear that they would retain and care for "their" bird if its original owner was not located. Unfortunately none of these birds turned out to be the Markles' beloved Becca.

One of the ten cockatiels reported was white; another had a

banded leg; a third had clipped wings. Two others the Markles even took home, hoping that, once the birds recovered from their traumatic episodes, one would turn out to be their pet. No luck. They returned the cockatiels to the people who had found them.

The only unwanted bird was captured in an Amherst warehouse. The workers who caught it called Mrs. Markle. Even though it was evident this was not theirs, the Markles took it home. Contact with the SPCA identified a possible owner. When Linda phoned him, the man told her how distressed his ten-year-old daughter was about loss of their family pet. He also informed Mrs. Markle that their bird would respond to the phrase, "Hello Robin." The cockatiel wouldn't answer Mrs. Markle, but when the man arrived and spoke the same phrase, the bird immediately raised its crest and perfectly mimicked his voice. When the man left with his cockatiel, Mrs. Markle could see tears of joy in his eyes.

The Markles — and I — were amazed that so many of these birds were lost in such a brief time period and we were astounded that no one came forward to claim any of these other birds. They are valuable pets, several of which were very well trained.

Clearly Becca had great sentimental value to Linda Markle and it was sad that there was no happy conclusion to the search for their pet.

50. Black Birds

Three blackbirds are common to the Niagara Frontier during our summers. They are the brown-headed cowbird, the red-winged blackbird and the common grackle. A fourth species, the rusty blackbird, passes through the region as a spring and fall migrant on its way between states south of New York and the boreal forests of Canada.

The rusty blackbird has shown what the Migratory Bird Center of the Smithsonian National Zoological Park identifies as "chronic long-term and acute short-term population declines, based both on breeding season and wintering ground surveys." Moreover, the Center indicates: "The decline, although one of the most profound for any North American species, is poorly understood." For that reason Center members formed the International Rusty Blackbird Technical Working Group to study this species and seek understanding of its decline. They feel that the information they gather may have implications for many other species as well.

As one part of the Group's study, it is asking birders across North America to report observations of this species. For more information about this visit rustyblackbird.org.

There is a problem associated with this reporting. It is easy to confuse rusty blackbirds with other blackbirds. For that reason I offer some identification suggestions for black birds.

European starling. In all seasons this species is easily separated from true blackbirds by its short tail. In breeding plumage males also have a long yellow bill. Females and juveniles are grayer. Introduced to this country in 1890, it is now by far our most common bird.

Red-winged blackbird. Adult males are black except for their red-over-yellow shoulders which they spread when they sing that standard of our marshes: *kong-ka-reee*. Females are brown striped birds. Be careful, however. Some males show much less shoulder color and are often confused with rusty blackbirds.

Brown-headed cowbird. Males are small blackbirds with, as the name suggests, brown heads. Females are plain brown.

Common grackle. Our largest black bird with a long wedge-like tail. In bright light the black is iridescent with purple highlights. Males and females are similar.

Bobolink. Like the starling, this is not a true blackbird, but most of its body is black. Breeding males are easily distinguished by the white of their backs and the pale yellow of the backs of their heads. Females look like large sparrows.

With that background I turn to the species of concern here, the rusty blackbird. Breeding males are very similar to red-winged blackbirds but they are all black. Remember, however, that some red-wings do not show those shoulder epaulettes either. Female rusties are plain brown with a narrow black eye-line. There are two ways to distinguish this species: by its pale eyes and by its call from which its name is derived. Grackles are the only other species of this group that have this pale eye, but they differ in size and tail length. The rusty blackbirds song sounds like a rusty gate opening, a gurgling start followed by a high pitched squeek.

Rusty blackbirds are most common here in April and October. They often accompany the large flocks of migrating red-winged blackbirds that occur at this time as well. Both species are most often associated with wetlands. Although they can appear anywhere during migration, including occasionally at bird feeders, I have found them most often along Sour Springs Road in the Iroquois National Wildlife Refuge and in the marshes along River Road in North Tonawanda.

Here is what Arthur Cleveland Bent said about rusty blackbirds in 1958: "The spring migration of the rusty blackbirds is spectacular, noisy, and ubiquitous; the birds may be seen in enormous numbers almost anywhere, following the plowman as he cultivates his land, blackening the stubble or grain fields, filling the air in passing clouds, or gathering to sing in the leafless treetops along the roadsides or in the swampy woods and roosting at night in the swamps and sloughs."

Those numbers are long gone. In many areas the thousands of fifty years ago are down to dozens today.

51. Kestrel

Recently Peter Ciotta contacted me to tell me how Solar, a Jacksonville, Mississippi subsidiary of Buffalo's Gibraltar Industries, is contributing 100 rural mailboxes to be converted to provide nesting sites for kestrels, another of those species whose population is in serious decline. Their contribution supports a project of New Hampshire's Squam Lakes Natural Science Center.

When I was a youngster, this raptor was called a sparrow hawk. But then the remarkable Roger Tory Peterson, who revolutionized birding in the 1940s with his first field guide, assigned to it the name of its European cousin and the sparrow hawk became the American kestrel. (At the same time Peterson changed the name of pigeon hawk to merlin and duck hawk to peregrine falcon, thus in all three cases giving these falcons names that avoided their less attractive side at a time when hawks were too often shot as vermin.)

The American kestrel is our smallest hawk. At nine inches in length, it is even smaller than a robin's ten inches. I most often see kestrels perched on telephone lines where I find it easy to mistake them for mourning doves. This is due to their posture and shape because the doves are nearly twice their size.

Observed in this way only in silhouette the kestrel's beauty is missed. Both males and females are very attractive when seen in good light. Both have bright rufous backs and tails and what David Sibley calls "boldly patterned heads." Vertical grey lines on each side of their eyes give them a helmeted appearance, somewhat like that of the peregrine falcon. The rufous coloration of the back is carried over to the wings of the female, but the male's wings are grey. The female's throat, breast and stomach are also rufous streaked on white while the male's white underparts are only lightly spotted with grey.

It is interesting to watch kestrels hovering thirty to forty feet high over an open field looking for prey in the grass below. In spring when they depart from their usual solitary habits to mate, the pair often communicate with each other with high-pitched screams of *killy-killy-killy* or *klee-klee-klee* that are similar to the *killdee* calls of the killdeer. (I once embarrassed myself by pointing out a killdeer to Harold Axtell that he gently informed me was a kestrel. My only excuse: the killdeer also has an orange lower back which I took for the kestrel's rufous.)

All falcons are designed for fast flight. Unlike the sharp-shinned and Cooper's hawks, their wings are sharply pointed and, except when they hover, the falcons dash about in a great hurry while those accipiters usually flap and glide.

But the kestrel is still a carnivore. With that former name in mind we should consider its food. In summer most of its diet is grasshoppers, dragonflies, lizards, mice and voles. But in winter, while they continue to feed on small mammals, they also take birds, indeed mostly sparrows.

Maryland birders Richard and Diane Van Vleck even set out mice during three periods of stress for their local kestrels: when they have young, when local fields are sprayed with pesticides and during severe winter storms.

My own observations suggest that these tiny falcons are far less common today than when I was a youngster and counts at migration stations confirm this. They indicate that the kestrel population has declined by more than half over the past forty years.

Thus kestrels do need our help and I recommend that country dwellers put out nest boxes. Kestrels are cavity nesters and take well to such boxes. You too could convert one of those metal mailboxes to this purpose, but wooden boxes also serve. In *Your Backyard Wildlife Garden* Marcus Schneck recommends an 11″ by 11″ base by 12″ high box with a 3″ by 4″ hole. Mount the box 20-30 feet above the ground in an open area.

One such nest box is located behind the administration building at Iroquois National Wildlife Refuge. A camera in its top records the lives of the kestrel family and plays them inside the building.

I salute Gibraltar for its contribution to the welfare of this threatened species.

52. Steve Eaton

Earlier this year Stephen W. Eaton and his wife Betty moved from their home near Olean to southern Pennsylvania to be near their children. To me this represented the end of the important Eaton era in New York State ornithology for Steve and before him his father, Elon Howard Eaton, represented the best of this field. I will write about the author of the first Birds of New York State in another column, but I salute Steve Eaton in this one.

I have known Steve Eaton since the mid-1950s when Harold Mitchell introduced us. That was at the time when I took over from him editing the state journal, *The Kingbird*, a task about which he was very helpful. Interestingly, many years later he passed on another task from which he was retiring: editing regional reports for that same journal.

We met only occasionally over the years but I spent a wonderful day with him in March 1992. In a column about that day when he showed me how he made maple syrup, I described him as, "a retired St. Bonaventure University biology professor who remains active on his Shadbush Farm east of Salamanca. There he tends a dozen beehives, raises blueberries, and manages a maple woodlot of 540 trees."

This past April the Cattaraugus County Bird Club, of which he was a founding member, held a dinner honoring Steve and Betty Eaton for their lifetime of devotion to the natural history, the local history and the community of Cattaraugus County. Dr. Eaton also received a lifetime achievement award from the New York State Department of Conservation for his work in preserving the Wild Turkey in New York State.

Eaton was an outstanding botanist as well. With Edith Schrott he wrote the definitive *Vascular Plants of Cattaraugus County*, a book reviewed as "one of the finest and most comprehensive of its kind."

Those achievements clearly identify Steve Eaton as important to this region, but he had a national reputation as well. He contributed important papers on turkeys, goshawks, Northern and Louisana waterthrushes, other wood warblers and yellow-billed cuckoos, and he studied and wrote about the birds of Cuba; Kwangsi, China; and Tamaulipas, Mexico.

My favorite of his papers served as the lead article in the July 1948 issue of *The Auk*, the professional journal of American ornithologists. In it Eaton described his Canadian bird study expedition. Here is a paraphrase of his trip description:

Starting on June 15, 1940, H. O. Palmer of Geneva and I traveled by canoe and later raft 600 miles from Peace River, Alberta to Fort Resolution, Northwest Territories. We averaged about 50 miles a day, camping under the spruce trees along the riverbank at night. To run the Peace River required about two weeks and we made our first camp on the Slave River on July 1. After three days traveling and several more camping on the Slave River, we cached our canoe and hiked ten miles from Grand Detour to the Little Buffalo River. There we constructed a raft of dead spruce, which carried us 100 miles downstream to Great Slave Lake. From the mouth of the Little Buffalo River we hiked 16 miles along the lakeshore to Fort Resolution. From there we took passage on a diesel ship back to Fort Smith, stopping to pick up our canoe on the way. After portaging our canoe again around the Smith Rapids, we boarded another diesel ship and rode it to McMurray, several hundred miles south on the Athabaska River, arriving there on July 23.

I find two interesting features of this report. One is the fact that birds were not "collected", that is, shot for identification. Only a few years earlier such an article would not have been accepted by an ornithological journal. The other is that 50 miles per day. To me that represents a major paddling achievement.

Former president of state birders Tim Baird has spoken for all of us: "I never had a formal class with Steve, but every time I enjoyed talking with him or trying to keep up with him in the field, my knowledge of the natural world vastly improved. Both Steve and Betty are gracious, gentle people who will be sorely missed."

53. Elon Howard Eaton

For many years I had been after my friend Steve Eaton to talk about his famous father and finally Steve did so at the 2007 meeting of the New York State Ornithological Association. He has also given me permission to quote from his biographical talk and I will devote this essay to the life of one of the state's foremost ornithologists.

Elon Howard Eaton was born October 8, 1866, in a farmhouse on the Zoar Valley Road about a mile west of the village of Springville. He began school there but he fainted in school one day and his father and mother decided to homeschool their son. After his lessons he was allowed to roam the fields and woods and he soon taught himself most of the native birds. He also enrolled in a Buffalo taxidermy course.

Eaton graduated from Griffith Institute in 1885 and entered the University of Rochester. After his junior year there he left to teach at Canandaigua Union School, probably to help support his mother and father on the farm and to raise money for himself, but he returned in 1889 to complete his classical education. He also played tackle on the university's first football team.

In 1890 Eaton graduated with a Phi Beta Kappa key and returned to Canandaigua Union School where he was appointed vice principle and science instructor. He established at this time The Eaton and Wilber Taxidermy Studio, which mounted birds and mammals. They even mounted the skeleton of a mastodon for Vassar College. In 1895 he left Canandaigua Union School to teach at the Bradstreet School in Rochester. There he taught chemistry, physics and natural science, including ornithology and botany.

In 1899 he took a leave of absence from Bradstreet School to attend Columbia University, taking courses in paleontology from Henry Fairfield Osborn, who also did much to establish the acceptance of Darwinian evolution; Bashford Dean, the famous ichthyologist; and E. L. Thorndike, who helped to establish modern animal psychology.

He returned to Bradstreet School in the fall of 1900 and the next year his *Birds of Western New York* was published by the Rochester Academy of Science. In 1901 Eaton and Howard Bradstreet, the school founder, built a slab-sided cabin on the west shore of Canandaigua Lake just north of the present Bristol Harbor. This was where much of the *Birds of New York* was written.

On September 13, 1902, Eaton saw his last passenger pigeon flying over the village of Canandaigua. As a teenager and later he had shot them around Springville. One immature he shot was used as the model for the immature illustrated in the famous bird artist Louis Agassiz Fuertes' passenger pigeon plate. Fuertes returned the specimen to the Eaton home in Geneva in 1926. Steve remembers the incident well. His brother — four years older and bolder — asked Fuertes if he would draw him a ring-necked pheasant. Paper was provided and in five minutes a beautiful sketch materialized.

In 1904, John Clark, Director of the New York State Museum, authorized Eaton to edit a new *Birds of New York* to replace the earlier version written by James E. Dekay in 1844. After accepting the task one of Eaton's first acts was to invite Fuertes to supply the book's plates.

By March 5, 1908 Eaton had finished text for *Birds of New York* Volume 1 and had written the preface. It was published by the State Museum in 1910. A circular sent out by the museum announced Volume 1 Water Birds with 42 colored plates, $3.00. Volume 2 Land Birds with 60 colored plates was later sold for $4.00. Today on the Internet they sell for up to $100 a volume.

That fall Eaton was hired to develop the Biology Department at the newly established Hobart and William Smith College. He was also given the title of Curator of the Museum of Natural History. He became a very charismatic teacher of biology at Hobart where he was famous for one-liners. For example, when a student asked one day in class if it is possible to contract a venereal disease from a toilet seat, Eaton responded, "That's a hell of a place to take a lady."

This first is my favorite of the final two volumes. It includes, before the individual species accounts: summaries of New York birds by season, maps of breeding ranges of selected species, charts of bird occurrence in various life zones, a commentary on changes in bird populations, suggestions for bird students including how to keep notes, several field trip lists, a lengthy compilation of county migration records, and a narrative of a forty day midsummer trip Eaton and several of his Hobart students took to the Mount Marcy region. It is impossible to read these sections without unearthing gems of information. Among them: the complete absence at that time of cardinals, tufted titmice and Carolina wrens from western New York.

The pressure of full-time teaching, his studies of the limnology of the Finger Lakes — taking all their temperatures from the surface to 50 meters from 1911 to 1918 — his marriage in 1909 and the start of his family, and a major heart attack in 1913, all slowed production of the text for the second volume, but it was finally issued in 1914. Ornithologist

William Brewster described it as "a truly monumental work, alike to him who wrote it and to the broadminded generosity of the state authorities who have sanctioned what must have been the very heavy expense of publishing and distributing so sumptuous and handsomely illustrated a book."

After *Birds of New York* became available Eaton received hundreds of letters from state birders. One that stands out came from a Jamestown teenager, part of which reads: "Dear Mr. Eaton; I have found a Pileated Woodpecker's nest in the swampy woods bordering the Outlet of Chautauqua Lake, about a mile from town. I would like to know if this is very unusual, for I always thought that it never nested in this section. I found the hole about May 10th. I resolved to keep tabs. The hole was placed near the top of a tall dead elm stub, about 50 feet from the ground. The other day I returned and the female was at the mouth of the hole. I watched her for two hours from a neighboring tree but she did not leave; in fact, she didn't seem to mind my presence. Occasionally she would call to her mate from the hole, and the male came to the nest twice, to see if things were going all right. I took one picture of the male at the hole as I stood below the stub. The picture was extremely sharp but the image of the bird was only about 3/16" long, so I am going to try to get a good enlargement of it. I will send you a copy. There is a second pair of these birds down farther in this woods, because sometimes when this pair would call to each other, a third bird would chime in in the distance. Yours truly, Roger T. Peterson".

After Eaton's death in 1934, one of his colleagues wrote in a college publication entitled, "As we were": "Professor Eaton, who was particularly my friend, possessed more varied knowledge than any man whom I have ever known. Not only did he appear to know everything in his own domain of living things, but all the natural objects of the universe seemed to talk to him. He was well acquainted with everything in the outside world from the atom to the galaxy, while his tolerant and humorous comprehension of human nature was as profound as it was delightful. To his training in the sciences, he added the culture of a classical education; to his wide knowledge of the liberal arts, he added those of the vintner and the chef. He was an enthusiastic sportsman and an excellent shot; and those who have enjoyed the game he killed, the wine he made, and the excellent meals he cooked have something to look back upon."

The Eaton Bird Club honors the name of this ornithologist.

54. Ross's Gull

The Ross's gull is at once the most beautiful and the rarest gull that occurs in North America. It is small for a gull, dove-sized. Adults appear all white, but their breasts are suffused with the delicate pink that makes them so attractive. In breeding plumage a fine black necklace circles the throat and rises over the back of the head; this is replaced at this time of year by a dark smudge behind the eye. And there is one other black characteristic: a narrow line along the leading edge of the wing that is obscured when the bird is at rest.

I have before me a chart of Ross's gull distribution in *Sea-Birds*, the definitive North Atlantic reference by Fisher and Lockley. The map is centered on the North Pole and the dots representing sight records are almost all within the Arctic Circle.

The restricted Siberian breeding ground is also north of the Arctic Circle. These delicate gulls nest at the farthest northward reach of vegetation: on the ground under stunted alder and willow thickets. There they brood eggs and raise young just inches above the permafrost.

Little is known about where Ross's gulls spend the remainder of their year. They don't migrate south like most birds but instead apparently move around the pole probably to the edge of the ice pack. They are seen regularly during these migrations along the north coast of Alaska. The only records in southern Canada or the United States of which I am aware were single birds seen in Illinois and Massachusetts in the 1970s.

So you can imagine the great excitement on December 18, 1994 when word was spread that an adult Ross's gull was sighted with a group of Bonaparte's gulls over the Welland Canal that passes between Lakes Ontario and Erie in Canada, within a quarter mile of where another rare bird, an ancient murrelet, had appeared a month earlier. Discovered on the St. Catharines Christmas Bird Count, it would almost certainly represent the outstanding species on all of the North American counts taken that season.

The hot-line announced that the bird had been observed for several hours and was floating in the canal at dusk.

Bob Andrle, Bob Brock and I drove over early the next morning confident that we would find the gull. When we arrived at 8:00 a.m., we joined a hundred birders already anxiously awaiting the bird's appearance.

But it did not show up. All I could think was, "I have jinxed these folks again: like the murrelet, this bird left when it heard that Rising was coming."

Word spread that the Ross's gull had left the water after dark and, when last seen, was roosting in the grass on the far side of the canal. Mary Ellen Hebb and several other Ontario birders drove several miles back along the canal to across a bridge and drive down the other side to investigate. We saw them arrive across from us.

The man standing next to me followed them with his telescope.

"She's pointing," he called out. "They see it." Then: "She's making neck-slicing movements. She's signaling that..., that...," and finally he blurted it out: "Oh my, she's telling us that it's dead."

The shock that went through the crowd was palpable. I could hear the intake of breath and several unprintable comments were voiced. Rapidly the disconsolate birders began to disburse.

We waited until the investigators returned. The identification evidence they brought was compelling: many pink feathers and two black-lined primaries.

Claw prints in the dirt indicted a great horned owl as the killer. That owl gourmet had picked the Ross's gull out of hundreds of nearby ducks and gulls. It not only thwarted our once-in-a-lifetime observation, but it also set a new low for regional hospitality.

In preparing my report of this sad episode I came across some interesting history. As should be expected of this bird of the Arctic, its story is intimately associated with exploration of that region.

The Ross's gull is named for James Clark Ross, who first sailed to the far north in 1818 with his uncle, John Ross, in search of the elusive Northwest Passage over North America. The younger Ross was at that time only 18. Accompanying them was Edward Sabine, for whom another gull is named.

After that unsuccessful voyage Ross joined William Parry for two further Arctic explorations and it was on the second of these in 1823 that he collected the gull later to be assigned his name. He found it on the Melville Peninsula at the north end of Hudson's Bay.

Ross's life was exciting and often unbelievably arduous. He joined eight expeditions to the Arctic: on one in 1833 traveling by dog sled to the North Magnetic Pole. On that trip his ship was locked in the ice for three winters! Finally abandoning it in desperation, Ross and other crew members struggled 500 miles over the ice to Baffin Bay where by good fortune they were picked up by a whaling ship.

He then turned his interest to the Antarctic, sailing there

with the botanist, Joseph Hooker. That expedition is commemorated in the names Ross Sea, Ross Ice Shelf and Ross Island. (Ross's goose, on the other hand, is named for Bernard Ross of the Hudson's Bay Company.)

James Ross returned to the Arctic only once more, that time in search of the missing explorer, John Franklin, after whom still another gull is named. It was later discovered that Franklin and all of his men had perished. Although he fell a few miles short, Franklin is credited with discovery of the Northwest Passage.

The Ross's gull originally honored James Ross in its scientific name, *Larus rossii*, as well; but it turned out that. William MacGillivray had published another name in 1824. (Although his sighting was after Ross's, publication precedence rules in systematics.) The Latin name MacGillivray assigned and by which we now know this gull, *Rhodostethia rosea*, relates in both genus and species to the rosy plumage of the adult birds.

For 82 years after its discovery Ross's gull breeding grounds were unknown. Few of the gulls were even seen through this period. After one naturalist, R. L. Newcomb, collected several in 1879, his ship foundered and the survivors had to travel by small boat to the Siberian mainland, suffering horribly on the voyage, their captain dying. Through this ordeal Newcomb carried three Ross's gull skins protected under his shirt.

Finally in 1905 a Russian explorer, Sergius Buturlin, found a colony of these birds nesting along the Kolyma River delta on the Arctic coast of eastern Siberia. Locating the nests was not easy as a passage from Buturlin's log attests: "A little low island in a lake is usually selected...and this made the nests very difficult of access, as...a boat can only be used near the banks and must be then dragged over the ice. [This] is exceedingly slippery and generally unsafe...as I found to my cost." He added that "a long and heavy" late June snowstorm interrupted his observations of the breeding of these delicate birds.

Until then as elusive as Lewis Carroll's snark, the Ross's gull had finally been tracked down by naturalist explorers.

I cannot resist adding a less serious footnote to this commentary. I have always found the word Ross's a favorite because it represents a rare instance of the same letter appearing in a word three times in a row.

55. Roger Tory Peterson

When in 1996 we returned to Sawbill Landing after six days away from civilization canoeing the Minnesota Boundary Waters, the first news we heard was the death of Roger Tory Peterson, the world renowned naturalist, artist, and author. We learned that even before we were told about the Atlanta Olympics pipe bombing.

Indeed, this loss of the world's leading advocate for nature was significant news. Roger Peterson was a very important person, to my mind second only to Rachel Carson in his influence on our attitudes toward the environment. Of course, Rachel Carson addressed environmental concerns and in particular pesticides directly in her landmark book *Silent Spring*. Peterson, on the other hand, seldom spoke to environmental issues. He got us there indirectly.

Peterson was born in Jamestown, New York, where he spent his youth studying the insects, birds, flowers, and mammals of southwestern New York State.

As a boy Peterson had read Ernest Thompson Seton's *Two Little Savages*, in which one of the boys found mounted ducks in a museum and drew their silhouettes, distinguishing them through the use of arrows pointing to their unique features. Peterson remembered this and, when he wrote his bird guide, combined this technique with his own superb talents as an illustrator to produce what has come to be known as the Peterson identification method.

When I was a beginning birder my first resource was the Reed field guide which provided no such assistance and I found my first "Peterson" — the name by which his bird guide is universally known — to be a godsend. So too did first hundreds, then thousands and today millions of bird watchers.

Today this method has been applied in over forty books in the Peterson series to everything from mammals to mushrooms, reptiles to rocks, and shells to stars. And every other field guide today has been influenced by Peterson's approach, even including military manuals for distinguishing aircraft and ships.

Now with little effort amateurs can identify most of the natural objects about them. As a result interest in natural history has burgeoned and the secondary effect of this increased interest in conservation has been widely recognized. Today's world would be measurably different were it not for Roger Tory Peterson.

Most naturalists think of Peterson only as an illustrator and fail to realize how good he was as artist, writer and teacher. The text of his books is equal in quality to his illustrations. In less than a hundred words he describes a bird at rest and in flight, special features that separate it from similar species, different plumages, voice, range, and habitat. If you think that is easy, try it yourself on a familiar species like a song sparrow.

When the 19-year old Peterson boarded the train from Jamestown to New York City to study art in 1927, few outside his family knew him by any other name but "Nuts." He was a shy loner. He had obtained permission directly from the police chief to stay out to collect moths past the strict town curfew for teenagers. He didn't date. With one or two friends he had wandered the countryside in search of wildlife. "Nuts" was a suitable name, the townspeople thought, for this other-worldly young man.

But 50 years later when he was approached by Lorimer Moe, Clarence Beal, Carl Hammerstrom, and a few others to assign his archives to Jamestown, "Nuts" Peterson remained loyal to this community. The Smithsonian Institution had held these archives temporarily and now placed a strong bid to retain them. Yale University offered a building already available on campus. Even against the cogent arguments of his wife Virginia, a Connecticut Yankee who supported the Yale offer, Peterson stood firm for Jamestown. And so the Roger Tory Peterson Institute was built there.

This native Western New Yorker is easily the best-known naturalist in the world today. He was even chosen by the citizens of his home town (but by just one vote over Lucille Ball) "as the most famous person to have ever come from Jamestown."

I was fortunate to have several opportunities to interact with Roger Peterson personally. For several years in the 1950s Alan and Sandy Klonick and I joined Roger for breakfast at Joe Taylor's Rochester home whenever he was in town to give an Audubon lecture. It was at one of those breakfasts that I committed one of those terrible social errors for which I am unfortunately well known.

At about that time Peterson had drawn the plates for *The Birds of Newfoundland*, a book whose publication was timed to coincide with an annual meeting of the American Ornithologists' Union, the major organization for scientific bird study. The dust jacket of the book repeated Peterson's portrait of three-toed woodpeckers. And in that painting, unnoticed until the books were on display at the meeting, he had portrayed those birds with four toes.

My mistake was to ask about that episode. Peterson

mumbled something and for a few moments the breakfast degenerated into silence. I had clearly touched a nerve. Finally Helen Taylor turned the conversation to a more acceptable topic and I gratefully faded into the background. For all his success, it seemed that Roger Peterson wanted to be known as a bird artist as well as an illustrator and that event had seriously bruised his substantial, but well-earned, self-esteem.

My last observation of Peterson speaks more directly to his commitment to his colleagues. With his wife he sat for over four hours signing books for a seemingly interminable line of birders at a Federation of New York State Bird Clubs meeting. Insisting on attending every admirer, he made himself late to the banquet at which he was the major speaker.

Roger Tory Peterson's life work is a unique legacy.

56. WANTED! ALIVE!
**Killer may be found lurking
in a barn loft or silo,
appearing at dusk to wander silently
over open meadows in search of victims.
Do not approach.
If you observe this perpetrator,
contact this writer immediately!**

Of course this killer is a killer of mice and rats, not people. Armed only with talons and beak, it is definitely not dangerous. It is the barn owl, a.k.a. monkey-faced owl, golden owl, and, as I will suggest, other colloquial names. Formerly rather common in this region, it is now very difficult to find here.

We western New York birders have searched for barn owls for years. Often when we have seen barns or silos with openings that would allow these owls access, we have asked the owners if they have such a tenant. So far, no luck. In a few cases their response has begun, "A few years ago..." or even "Last year...," but never a simple yes.

Now Charles Rosenburg, who studied barn owls in Virginia for his master's degree in zoology, has moved to this area. He and his brother John have stepped up the pace of the search. I will pass on to them any information communicated to me.

As part of his study Chuck examined owl pellets, the masses of indigestible matter that all owls regurgitate. Occasionally he found feathers of small birds, but 80 to 100 per cent of these owls' food, he says, is meadow voles and short-tailed shrews.

The barn owl is easy to identify. It is about 18 inches in length with a wingspan of 42 inches. Seen flying from below it appears white: thus the names ghost owl and spirit owl. Its back is tawny or golden. But its most prominent feature is its heart-shaped white face, quite unlike that of any other owl.

It makes a wide range of sounds, most discordant. Its alarm cry is a shriek that is quite frightening when heard coming unexpectedly from the dark. Other calls include snarls, rattles, hisses, and most often clicking sounds that some observers believe are designed to communicate with nearby owls.

Only rarely would other owls be seen in or near farm buildings. Barn owls nest there but elsewhere as well: in tree hollows, church steeples, water towers, and even underground in abandoned woodchuck burrows. The young are voracious eaters: a month old bird fed nine mice was hungry again just three hours later. You can imagine from this the inroads on the local mouse population made by a family of these predators.

I once climbed to a nest high up in a huge barn in Scottsville. I won't do that soon again. The smell alone nearly knocked me off the ladder. There in their own filth, hissing and snapping their bills, stood three young owls, spindle-legged and knock-kneed. Their only attractive features were their cream colored faces. They could have served as object lessons for youngsters who won't clean their rooms.

Barn owls are found on every continent except Antarctica, but we live at the northern edge of their western hemisphere range. They appear to be retreating from this area. Chuck's research indicates that they need to forage over 200 acres or more of open grassland, a requirement that is fulfilled throughout this region, so that cannot be the problem. We simply need more information.

That column was written in 1992. The following column appeared two years later.

As we drove down Route 219 into the Southern Tier, my thoughts turned to a verse in Lewis Carroll's *The Hunting of the Snark*:

> *They sought it with thimbles, they sought it with care;*
> *They pursued it with forks and hope;*
> *They threatened its life with a railway-share;*

They charmed it with smiles and soap.

It seemed to me that we had about as much chance of seeing a barn owl, the bird we were looking for, as the Snark hunters did of capturing their invisible prey with "smiles and soap." I hadn't seen a barn owl for 35 years.

The goal of the team I accompanied, Chuck and John Rosenburg and Mike Galas, was not even to see a barn owl; instead it was to install a nest box in a barn where this species had been reported. If we saw the owl, that would be an extravagant bonus.

Under Chuck's leadership we had been looking for barn owls intensively for two years. We had received a number of reports of recent visits and at several sites found pellets, egg-shaped masses of regurgitated fur and bones, but no birds. Often inquiry responses began, "Just a few years ago...."

Our host greeted us between his charming country home and the old barn in his backyard. He helped us unload our 2' x 2' x 5' nest box with its outsize entrance hole near one end. An enlargement of a normal birdhouse, it would be mounted sidewise rather than erect. Together we hoisted the heavy box into the barn loft and leaned an extension ladder against the beams another 30 feet overhead.

From the top of the ladder Chuck mounted a pulley on the barn roof and with it we hoisted the box up to him. Then by a remarkable series of body contortions worthy of a circus performer, he worked the box into position and bolted it securely to a crossbeam. This had to be done just right as improper placement would mean inevitable predation by those wily foragers, raccoons.

This was the 25th box that the Rosenburgs had mounted in western New York. Boxes were placed in barns or silos near extensive open grasslands, the kind of foraging area that these owls patrol.

Farmers welcomed the boxes and well they should. In one

year a single monitored barn owl consumed 1407 mice, 143 rats, 5 rabbits, 375 house sparrows and 23 starlings. For an average owl family of six to nine birds those numbers would multiply.

With the box mounted and the tools replaced, we stood in the yard with our host, his porch light dimly illuminating extensive gardens. A small bat fluttered by: a myotis or pipistrelle.

Mike played a tape of barn owl calls: shrieks that sound like cars skidding.

Was that an answering scream?

Then it happened. Suddenly a barn owl drifted overhead at the edge of the light: white, silent, ghostly, its dark eyes probing for the source of the taped calls. You cannot imagine our excitement. As soon as it disappeared, there were high fives all around.

Since our visit, two barn owls have been heard in that loft calling to each other. One was even seen standing in the nest box. Unfortunately few sightings have been reported since then.

57. Osprey Return

The bird flapped steadily toward us from far down Kioskokwi Lake. As Al Chestnut and I watched its approach, it seemed to grow in size. I found myself going through a series of identification trials based on this growth: crow, raven, red-tailed hawk and finally eagle.

It was indeed an eagle: a fish eagle or osprey. Soon we could make out its dark forward thrusting shoulders and, when it finally reached our end of the lake and sailed above us, we could easily see the white body and head markings.

Now the osprey put on a show. It soared directly over our canoe perhaps a hundred feet above us, so close that I could see it tip its head and look down at us with an intense yellow eye. A few yards on it suddenly veered into a stall, did a wingover and plummeted straight down, hitting the water with a tremendous splash just yards away.

That act was so close, abrupt and unexpected that I felt as though the bird had dived at us and missed. It was soon apparent that this was wrong for the osprey now rose from the water, awkwardly and straining at first, but soon regaining its graceful flight. In one fist it carried a big lake trout.

It flew a few hundred yards back down the lake to a tall white pine. There we could see it land on a big stick nest partially hidden in the green foliage.

When this unforgettable experience happened in Algonquin Park in 1970, it had a somber aspect. We thought that we might be seeing one of the last of this species. Pesticide residues had been making their way up the food chain from water plants through aquatic worms and insects, crustaceans and amphibians, fish and finally to this beautiful bird. As a result almost all osprey eggs were then either sterile or had such thin shells that the adults broke them while brooding.

We could see no young on the nest in the pine.

Fortunately the publication of Rachel Carson's *Silent Spring* in 1962 contributed to the demise of DDT a decade later and to subsequent tighter limitations on some of the other pesticides with long-term toxicity. Those restrictions saved the osprey. As evidence of its recovery, Buffalo Ornithological Society May and October censuses show migrating osprey numbers double from their low in the 1960s to the 1980s and double again in the 1990s. In the Tonawanda-Iroquois-Oak Orchard wildlife refuge complex and along the Niagara River, you can now see osprey nests on platforms erected for their use.

To initiate the return of breeding ospreys to western New York, for two years in the early 1990s osprey chicks were brought from Long Island to the Oak Orchard Wildlife Refuge where they were hacked — that is, raised with as little human contact as possible. I played a very minor role in that project.

My most recent baby-sitting had been years ago when I took a four-year-old to the Buffalo Zoo. When the boy's attention flagged, I got him one of those nippled sugar water bottles and set him to feeding the goats and deer in the petting area. He seemed content and my attention strayed. The next thing I knew, the little boy was fending off the animals while he sucked on the nipple himself.

Needless to say, I didn't tell the boy's mother and I also didn't share this episode with Gail Seaman when he gave me my baby-sitting assignment for the five ospreys at Oak Orchard Wildlife Reserve. He might have had second thoughts if I had.

And so on a sunny afternoon I drove in the lane just south of Goose Pond. A great blue heron rose from the road ahead and flapped off slowly and a hummingbird buzzed across just over the car hood.

At the observation post 200 yards from the osprey cages, Barb and Rev Newton, who had already taken several shifts there, showed me the simple procedures. All I had to do was scan with my telescope every few minutes to see that the five birds were in no difficulty. They had just been fed their afternoon fish and we could see them tearing at the carcasses or occasionally testing their wings with five-foot flights across their cages. It was clear that they were almost ready for release. There wasn't much that could go wrong the Newtons assured me before they drove off.

They were right. I spent a pleasant evening alternately sitting in my lawn chair and wandering about the nearby fields. Near the lake edge I squeaked up a black-masked male yellowthroat. A few paces further and three snipe exploded from the wet field and zigzagged off.

At every step a half dozen leopard frogs leaped across my path to get to the deeper weeds. It is lucky for them that their bodies are so supple. One hit a sweet clover stem in mid-flight, performed an unplanned aerial cartwheel, and landed on its back. It rolled over and, evidently disoriented, jumped directly toward me. Later I watched one of these frogs through my scope. The species is surely a model for our military camouflage clothing with its black spots against khaki green. But the amphibian adds a trick that has not yet been copied. It also has body length yellow lines that make it still harder to pick out from the slanted grass twigs of its habitat.

As evening progressed I sat keying some of the flowers around me: the dark brown curled dock, nightshade with its odd shaped leaves and its delicate purple florets from which extend outsized yellow noses, jaunty black-eyed Susans, spikes of mullein already losing their yellow blossoms, and several kinds of goldenrod. A movement in the undergrowth almost at my feet disclosed a skulking Virginia rail. I could just see its long decurved bill but its black eye reflected the slanting light. Quickly as it came, it melted into the background.

Jeanne Hickey, my DEC boss, arrived. We climbed up to the cages to record how much the ospreys had eaten and to give one an antibiotic. Holding this beautiful bird, I could feel its heart beat wildly in distress and I was glad to set it back on its perch.

After Ms. Hickey left darkness came fast. I could barely make out skeins of Canada geese flying in, but I could hear them splash down in the pond and call to each other. The ospreys were resting quietly.

I wished my charges well as I drove off.

58. Passenger Pigeon

There is a reason we heard so much about passenger pigeons in 2014. That year marked the hundredth anniversary of the demise of that species. On September 1, 1914, the final individual named Martha died in the Cincinnati Zoo. Martha had outlived two male companions by several years.

Among the recent books devoted to this remarkable species is *A Feathered River across the Sky* by Joel Greenberg. Greenberg spoke at the Buffalo Ornithological Society's quinquennial banquet that year.

Of course sooner or later every nature writer has something to say about the demise of the passenger pigeon, a story easily oversimplified as many to none. But of all the writing about these doomed birds, I found Edward Kanze's prize-winning "In Search of Something Lost" far and away the most compelling. It appears in his book, *Over the Mountains and Home Again*.

Kanze talked his friend Bill Schoch into climbing a mountain in the Adirondacks to visit a summit where passenger pigeons once roosted by the thousands. And here is how this graceful essay continues: "Right from the start, I'm feeling like a Don Quixote who has pressed Bill into the precarious shoes of Sancho Panza. The idea for the hike borders on crazy. For three years, in all seasons, I gazed out across the wilderness from our house near Bloomingdale. Time and again, my eyes found greatest interest not on Whiteface Mountain, rising like a ziggurat on the eastern horizon, nor on Moose Mountain, nearer and wearing a landslide like a crooked necktie, but on a low, little-known peak, forested all the way to the top, named Pigeon Roost."

From there Kanze balances the story of their difficult bushwhack with the sad record of the birds that we wiped out in the early 20th century for Pigeon Roost was one of the pigeon's final enclaves. I urge you to read his essay.

The story of the passenger pigeon is more than an account of an extinction; it is the story of the removal of the most numerous bird species in our country's and probably the whole world's history within a period of a few decades.

Recently I reported on large flights of purple martins and starlings. Although starling flocks are occasionally estimated to include tens of thousands of birds, those numbers are dwarfed by the flights of passenger pigeons. Here is some of the testimony to their numbers:

John James Audubon reported pigeons "in greater numbers than I thought I had ever seen them before. The air was literally filled with pigeons: the light of noonday was obscured as by an eclipse, the dung fell in spots, not unlike melting flakes of snow; and the continued buzz of wings had a tendency to lull my senses to repose." This flight continued for three days.

Greenberg tells about an episode in Columbus, Ohio. "One warm spring morning in 1855 the people of that city were going about their usual routines when they first noticed 'a low-pitched hum' that slowly engulfed them. It grew louder, as horses and dogs began fidgeting. Then just within the limits of vision wispy clouds appeared on the southern horizon: As the watchers stared, the hum increased to a mighty throbbing. Now everyone was out of the houses and stores, looking apprehensively at the growing cloud, which was blotting out the rays of the sun. Children screamed and ran for home Women gathered their long skirts and hurried for the shelter of stores. Horses bolted. A few people mumbled frightened words about the approach of the millennium, and several dropped on their knees and prayed. Suddenly a great cry arose from the south end of High Street. 'It's the passenger pigeons! It's the pigeons!' And then the dark cloud was over the city. Day was turned to dusk. The thunder of wings made shouting necessary for human communication. When the flock had finally passed almost two hours later, the town looked ghostly in the now-bright sunlight that illuminated a world plated with pigeon ejecta."

Finally, Alexander Wilson estimated the size of "an almost inconceivable multitude" that spanned a mile wide and extended for some 240 miles, consisting no fewer than three pigeons per cubic yard of sky. He calculated this single flock to include over 2.2 billion birds. (To gain some sense of that number, consider this arithmetic result: at 14 inches each and placed end to end, that number of pigeons would stretch over 520,000 miles, a distance greater than a round trip to the moon.) Yet that was just one flock.

So indeed there were many pigeons. How could that many birds be completely wiped out in such a short time?

Passenger pigeons had always been easy to kill. In pre-Columbian times Native Americans, including the Neutrals who lived in western New York, had visited their massive roosts to harvest squabs and eggs by thousands. One such roost was near the Genesee River, another in Warren County, just across the border in Pennsylvania. But these harvests had virtually no effect on the overall population.

That came later as another host spread over the land — us.

Marshlands and forests that had served as breeding areas were drained and cut. And market hunters killed the birds and shipped them to cities in full barrels. From just two areas in Pennsylvania almost a million birds were harvested in one season. The species could not withstand this decimation.

The decline locally is recorded in Beardsley and Mitchell's *Birds of the Niagara Frontier Region*. In 1828 and 1846 huge flocks were recorded in Rochester and Fredonia but the sightings wink out with a final entry: "September 28, 1899: Flock of 20 seen by F. J. Sager."

59. Birding Baghdad

The recently coined word "blog" represents "a shared on-line journal where people can post diary entries about their personal experiences and hobbies." Thousands of them now appear on the Internet.

One blog I found most attractive and recommend to you is titled Birding Babylon at birdingbabylon.blogspot.com. It is maintained by an American soldier who identifies himself only as Jonathan. Although this soldier's duty tours were in 2004-2005 and 2009-2010, his blog remains accessible at the time of this writing.

His first posting read: "I'm a soldier in Iraq. I've been mobilized for up to 18 months, which includes a definite 12 months in Iraq and Kuwait. I've been birding since I was 12, which makes it 24 years now. I serve in a New England medical unit. I plan to write about my nature observations during my time here, both birds and other critters. Birding on base doesn't usually elicit any undo attention from the MPs. I think everyone thinks I'm doing security work when I'm looking into the distance with binoculars. I'm not sure what they think when I'm looking up in a tree."

What is so stirring about his postings is their "life goes on" character. There is no question whatsoever that this soldier is representing his country in an extremely dangerous region, but he refuses to reduce his life to conflict. I am certain that, when he returns safely, he will not be one of those whose lives are compromised by post-traumatic stress disorder.

"On our convoy up from Kuwait we had to stop because one of the humvees had a flat. We all piled out of the vehicles and set up a defensive perimeter with our weapons pointing out. It was a surreal scene because, as I'm lying on the ground with my eye on some guy racing around in a pickup truck wondering if he's going to take a potshot at us (which would have been suicidal), a pair of crested larks were not even ten feet from me with the male displaying and dancing around."

"Easter Sunday I was up at 0530 to meet one of our doctors for a little early morning birding. We've had a lot of rocket and mortar attacks in the last few days. One day we had eight or nine hit inside the wire. As a result we need to go everywhere in body armor and helmet. So it was a day for birding in 'full battle rattle', weapon included of course."

Sometimes the conditions are not good: "It was 115 degrees and my gear adds 5 degrees. I was completely exhausted after about a 4-mile walk. It would be easy to get heatstroke here."

But even crossing the barren lands Saddam had drained "to destroy the traditional home of the Marsh Arabs," he continues his hobby: "I haven't had so many life birds in a day since being in Indonesia in 1990. Birds were everywhere, waterbirds and shorebirds in the pools, landbirds flying by or sitting on fences. Their number was in stark contrast to the dearth of birds in Kuwait. The pools had so many shorebirds that I could only identify the large and distinctive ones as we whizzed by. There were lots of black-winged stilts, avocets, red-wattled plover and black-headed gulls. Lots of hooded crows and rooks."

Birds are not his only interest: "Today I caught a brown and black colored skink that ran under the air conditioner unit. When I picked up the lizard, it promptly dropped its tail in an attempt to get away from me." In one of Saddam's former palaces he finds tomb bats and a strange insect. It "revealed itself to be a webspinner. Though some members of this order are found in the warmer parts of the US, I've never seen one. I brought it inside and made quite a fuss about it. The people left in the clinic thought I was crazy."

A single late-July break makes his experiences even more poignant: "I've taken a 6200 mile change in venue for a few weeks. I'm back in the northeast US for R and R. My kids and I took a drive yesterday and stopped by a large field to watch a coyote padding around. We hiked in the woods a few days ago and found Indian pipes. We collected a big variety of mushrooms and brought them home to make spore prints. The goldenrod have started to flower, a sure sign that summer is half over. I'll be back in Iraq soon enough."

I am certain that readers join me in praying for the permanent safe return of this soldier and all of his comrades.

60. Rock Pigeon

Few birdwatchers pay any attention to rock pigeons, those downtown birds that come readily, often in groups, to feed at your feet on scraps of discarded -- or too often proffered -- food. They are especially unattractive to clean-up crews, their messy feces strewn along window ledges and on bridge supports.

There appear to be dozens of different kinds of birds among them, their neutral colors extending from pure white to almost pure black, but those are simply variations on the species' basic plumage: light gray body, darker gray head, breast and tail and two black stripes on each wing.

These feral pigeons are easily distinguished from similar sized birds when in flight. Unlike most other species, they sail with their wings held in a high V.

I will never feel the same about these birds after reading Courtney Humphries' book *Superdove: How the Pigeon Took Manhattan...and the World* (Collins). Now when I see pigeons sailing among city skyscrapers, I will think how they first inhabited rocky cliffs — and still do in a few remote areas. Humphries had to travel all the way to Sardinia in the Mediterranean to find such wild forbearers of our city birds.

Much happened to pigeons over the more than 5000 years since they were first domesticated and later escaped to become today's urban squatters.

The earliest records have the Egyptian Pharoah Ramses II sacrificing 57,000 pigeons. Then and later they were captured and kept in dovecotes to serve two purposes: food — squab remains a delicacy today — and fertilizer — their leavings serving farmers before the discovery of tropical guano deposits and the advent of the chemicals we use today.

Then two things changed pigeon history. Pigeon-keepers allowed their birds to feed in farm fields and their depredations turned farmers against them. So rural pigeon-keeping largely ended and the birds reverted to the wild where we still see them today around barns. At the same time urban areas began to develop, providing new food sources for these birds already acclimated to humans.

But pigeons were not finished with their association with humans. First, they were raised as show birds, much as dogs are today. They were bred by pigeon fanciers into over 400 varieties with all kinds of strange names. Charles Darwin supported his theory of evolution in the first chapter of *On the Origin of Species* with examples drawn from this breeding. His own pigeons included fantails, pouters, runts, Jacobins, barbs, dragons, swallows and almond tumblers. Today breeders continue to exhibit their birds at fairs and special pigeon competitions.

Fanciers also trained homing pigeons, birds that would return from hundreds of miles to their home dovecote. Humphries tells the story of Cher Ami, "a British-trained bird that was credited with saving nearly 200 American lives in World War I." Surrounded by enemy troops, the 'Lost Battalion' sent its pigeons for help. All but Cher Ami were shot down. Despite being wounded by shrapnel, it still carried its message.

Pigeon racing continues today with pigeons trucked off to be released at distant locations carrying sophisticated timing devices that are stopped when the pigeon reenters its nest.

But perhaps the most interesting use of pigeons was by psychologist B. F. Skinner, who trained them to respond to immediate stimuli. Skinner's initial idea was to have pigeons guide World War II missiles. In a kind of preview of modern guidance systems, his pigeons would peck at a target on a television screen to cause the guidance system to maneuver the rocket.

He trained pigeons to do this by providing them with immediate rewards (food seeds) for small motion improvements that quickly accumulated. Although his proposals during World War II were rejected, this line of experimentation on pigeons and other animals, technically called operant conditioning, contributed to the development of behavioral psychology, which had a profound impact on teaching. Many educators believed that all instruction could be carried out in a series of tiny steps like these. Like so many panaceas, this one was severely limited.

61. *Niagara Birds*

A major ornithological event took place on October 16, 2010: John Black and Kayo Roy's book, *Niagara Birds*, was introduced to the public. This 702-page volume is about the 368 species of birds that occur in the nearby Niagara region of Canada.

In one sense *Niagara Birds* relates only to a tightly restricted enclave: the Niagara Regional Municipality of Ontario. That region extends from the Canadian side of the Niagara River as far west as the townships of South Grimsby along Lake Ontario and Wainfleet along Lake Erie. That's an area of just over 720 square miles compared with the 1227 square miles of Erie County here in New York. Clearly that would be scarcely more than a dot on any map of the vast areas of Canada and the United States.

Don't be fooled. First, to ornithologists of this region on both sides of the Niagara River this is an important publication. The *Niagara Birds* coverage is nearly contiguous with the western half of the region surveyed by the Buffalo Ornithological Society and it updates that section since the publication of Clark Beardslee and Harold Mitchell's *Birds of the Niagara Frontier Region* in 1965 and the supplement to that book by Mitchell and Robert Andrle in 1970. Farther west, it incorporates and updates records gathered by Roy Sheppard of Hamilton, Ontario.

Many stateside birders contributed to this book. Mike Hamilton, Bob DeLeon and Richard Stockton were among the 25 authors who wrote chapters and Mike Morgante and others wrote species accounts. Dozens more United States birders reviewed materials and, of course, even more provided records. BOS "Hotline" monitor and record keeper Dave Suggs and BOS statisticians Andrle, Fran Rew, Tim Baird and Morgante are singled out by the authors for special praise.

Clearly, every serious birder of this region will want a copy of this book.

But remarkably, that is not all. I have read *Niagara Birds* and I find it a book that should be in the home of everyone who loves birds in particular or the out-of-doors in general. I have reviewed hundreds of natural history books and consider this among the finest.

What is truly exceptional about *Niagara Birds* is its artwork. From that lovely cover painting of the Ross's gull flying over the Niagara River with New York State that dim blur in the background to the brilliant goldfinch photograph that is the last of the over 500 color photos that grace this book, the artwork is spectacular.

Canadian photographers and artists stepped forward to contribute their work to this all-volunteer project. I find it very difficult to pick out a favorite. There is the calling red-necked grebe taken by Raymond Barlow; Brandon Holden's snowy owl winging toward you through a snowstorm just inches above the ground; Harold Stiver's tiny blue-gray gnatcatcher singing up another kind of storm; an alert spotted sandpiper perched on a water-soaked log by Barry Cherriere; Jukka Jantunen's radiant blackburnian warbler; and many many more.

Every photograph and painting speaks to the quality of

these professionals, but they are extremely well served by designer Judie Shore, who has worked them seamlessly into each page. Jean Black and Arleane Ralph's copyediting contributes as well.

Of course this book has species accounts and you will learn much from them, but it has much else. Among the essays is a history of regional ornithology (including Audubon's painting of passenger pigeons and another painting of early settlers shooting these now extinct birds), a description of this interesting region and information about its natural history clubs. There are other essays about Kay McKeever's Owl Foundation together with its problems with the devastating West Nile disease, about the problems with birds in the region's vineyards, about hawk migration and peregrine falcon hacking, about radar-tracking of birds, about the wintering gulls in the Niagara River gorge, about the April, May, October and Christmas bird counts in the region and about where to look for birds.

62. Bobolink

Most of our grassland birds are in serious trouble. The populations of field, grasshopper and savannah sparrows have declined precipitously and Henslow's sparrows are no longer to be found. Meanwhile, that lovely whistle of the meadowlark, *teyou toowee*, and their flight chatter, both formerly heard from open fields, are now only rare treats.

Few people realize that grasslands need conservation as well as woodlands. Unless they are cared for, succession takes over. It takes only a few years for the meadow to disappear, replaced first by bushes, then by trees. To retain a meadow, the land must be plowed every year or two.

Of course, grain crops like wheat or oats are also grasslands, but harvesting schedules, especially for winter wheat can destroy nests. We need wild meadows.

Despite these problems, however, one species, the bobolink, is doing quite well.

I joined Paul Kielich for a pleasant walk around Knox Farm State Park a few days ago and we came across at least a dozen bobolinks. Aside from the many swallows, bobolinks were the most common birds we found on our hike. Their bubbling *spink-spank spink-spank* calls, often given in flight, resounded across the fields. Their name evidently arises from their song, rather than from some human connection.

The male bobolink is easily identified. It is our only eastern bird whose back is lighter than its underside. Its base color is solid black: this is the color of its head, breast, belly, tail feathers and even its eyes. Its back, however, is mostly white and buff colored.

This is an anomaly among birds. Almost all birds have lighter breasts than backs. There is an evolutionary value to this dark-above-light-below coloration. Camouflage is important to birds: it can serve them as a defense against raptors or hunters.

There is a simple experiment that shows the possible value of this normal color pattern. Hold a ping pong ball or golf ball under a lamp. Notice how it is light above and dark below because the bottom is shadowed. Only if you darken the top side does the difference in coloration disappear and the two blend in.

The bobolink breaks that general rule. Its topside exaggerates the color difference making it a very striking bird. Why is this? Your guess is as good as mine.

Female bobolinks (should they be called robertalinks or bobbilinks?) fit the normal pattern. They are drab brownish birds — slightly darker above — that look like female house sparrows.

As are most meadow birds, bobolinks are ground nesters. Their nests are woven grass, sometimes with a canopy. They are very difficult to find because the females, rather than flying to perches near the nest, instead drop into the grass some distance away and creep to it through the undergrowth. This is probably one reason their nests are rarely parasitized with cowbird eggs. The bobolinks' own four to seven eggs are cinnamon or gray, usually heavily spotted with brown.

Stomach analyses of bobolinks indicate that their diet when they arrive in the north in early May is almost 90% insects with over the summer months increasing amounts of plant food as those plants mature, a mix of weeds like dock and grain crops. Those results were obtained before winter wheat was widely planted, however, and the proportion of grain probably makes up more of their early summer diet today. In any case, by September when they depart, their diet is 80% grain.

Depart indeed. Bobolinks fly south 6,000 miles to Argentina, Bolivia and Paraguay to spend the winter, some traveling as much as 1000 miles in one night.

Their southern excursion is not altogether pleasant. In

Jamaica they are known as butterbirds because of the fat they gained for migration. There they are often harvested for food. And when they get to their southern destination, where they are called ricebirds, they are shot as crop destroyers.

Bobolinks go through two complete molts each year, the males and females similar when they are in South America. When the males molt back into their bright color, new feather ends cover these colors completely. Only when that feather rust wears off do they become the handsome birds we know.

63. Birding Movie

Reviews of the film *The Big Year* are in and nationally it did not fare well. A number of reviewers hated it, the *Buffalo News* assigning it one star with an accompanying vitriolic review that focuses on the film credits and its lack of belly laughs. The reviewer even walked out before it was finished. Overall it did only slightly better, averaging only middling ratings, a few positive, many negative.

I was out of town when the film opened and returned to find my mailbox filled with complaints about that *News* review. One of the mildest read: "I am wondering if you saw the really nasty Jeff Simon review of the new film *The Big Year*. I think someone like you needs to see the movie and answer his attack. There have been other reviews (*USA Today*, Oct 14, 2011) that have been favorable. I have been to see the film and I did enjoy it. I do not understand why Simon was so against it."

I hadn't been in a movie theater for several years, but after reading the Simon review I took those messages as an assignment and located the film locally. I plunked down my $7.50 and joined just four others in the theater — I assume non-review readers — to watch it.

An hour and a half later I left the theater with a very different impression from those who disliked this film. I felt that I had received full value from my ticket. It was clear from the details in his review that Simon and I had seen the same movie, but beyond that our reactions were very different.

The film is about three birdwatchers who seek the North American record for the number of species seen in one year. As those familiar with this kind of listing know, this involves dashing around the continent from Key West to Attu and even far out to sea on small yachts off the California and New England coasts. To give some sense of the number of species involved, my life list is just short of 450; these birders compete at over 700 in one year. So much for my puny achievement.

Okay, that's the technical stuff and indeed, there is much racing about in cars, trains and airplanes to find those birds. But this is a movie whose real focus is on obsession and friendship. The birds simply provide a base from which to explore those concepts.

Bird watchers are far from the only obsessed people in this modern world. Substitute golf, shopping, televised sports, work, housekeeping or politics and you can find obsessed people, but birding allows this kind of compulsive behavior to be nicely encapsulated into a single year.

During *The Big Year* a marriage disintegrates and a betrothal is undone but another marriage is further solidified, a new relationship begun, and two of the competitors and a father and son work their way through their differences. These are each well portrayed in this low-key movie.

Jack Black plays the central character in the film. His is the Kenn Kaufman role, the poor guy competing against others who can afford the major expenses involved. Steve Martin plays against type as he did in *Planes, Trains and Automobiles* as one of those wealthy opponents. And Owen Wilson plays the villain of the piece, another rich migrant for whom I finally felt empathy.

There is indeed one point in the film when others feel that Wilson's character is cheating, recording birds he has not really seen or heard. But in an episode that is easily missed he shows his opponents that this is not one of his faults.

Three quick notes all relating to local birding: Buffalo gets a brief mention as a locale for snowy owls; in winter we see in the Niagara River thousands of the buffleheads marked in the film as rare finds on Attu; and observers occasionally witness the film's courting eagles displaying with talons locked in flight at the Iroquois Refuge.

I join Mary Pols, whose *Time* review calls this "an unexpectedly sweet comedy" and adds, "It's like an Easter egg hunt for adults, joyous and sweet. *The Big Year* competition may be fierce, but the movie is as soft as a bunny."

64. Horned Lark

We all have our favorites in the animal kingdom. I can, for example, imagine no more attractive non-human mammal than a flying squirrel. Birders too have their favorites. Some like colorful birds like scarlet tanagers or bluebirds; others, majestic birds like the bald eagle or osprey; still others, delicate birds like hummingbirds.

One of my favorite birds I doubt would make the list of many of my fellow birders. It isn't colorful, it isn't majestic, and it certainly cannot match any of the hummingbirds for delicacy.

It is the horned lark.

I was reminded of my preference for this species when we saw a number of them along Ledge Road on a Oak Orchard Christmas Bird Count. Across the now open cornfields around us the wind was whistling and blowing snow swirls into the air to add to the new snow finally falling in this so long delayed winter.

There were a dozen or so of these sparrow-sized birds braving the weather to feed among the sheared off corn stalks and occasionally flying up to the road itself to pick up the fine gravel necessary to their digestion. Birds are, of course, toothless and in their gizzard the grit grinds otherwise indigestible food into fine particles to be processed.

Unless you look at them closely, you won't be able to distinguish horned larks from sparrows. They have brown streaked backs and plain bellies. Only some intricate markings around the head are different. There is a black killdeer-like band across the throat, a black cheek mark that looks to me like a teardrop and a thin black line above the eye. There is some light color on the face as well, an eye stripe that circles down and around the back of that teardrop.

You have to look still more closely to see their so-called horns: tiny feather tufts that rise from the back of that black eye line. It has always seemed to me that using the word horned for these nearly invisible tufts is wrong. Horns are big rough features on deer, cows and rhinos. These eighth-inch feathers don't deserve that designation. How much better is the name for this species' European relative, the sky lark, which has now been introduced in a few areas in western Washington and British Columbia.

It is almost impossible to see those small colorful features when the birds are flying, but birders can identify horned larks in flight by a particular characteristic: they don't usually flap and sail with wings always spread; instead, between each flap they completely close their wings to their bodies before flapping again.

Most of these horned larks are winter visitors here. Only a few stay to breed. As winter deepens those resident birds are joined in fields by other birds retreating from the far north including not only other horned larks but snow buntings and Lapland longspurs as well.

There is a similarity between the nesting behavior of those northern birds and the larks that stay with us. The buntings, longspurs and some of these larks will leave to fly so far north that they will nest near melting snow in late May and even June. But the horned larks that stay will nest here much earlier when we too have snow on the ground. They are our earliest nesting songbirds with eggs sometimes laid in March. You can imagine the additional stress this places on the adults of all these species, caring for their eggs and young through sub-freezing times.

Do our horned larks build sturdy nests to protect their

young from those elements? Hardly. They build no nest at all and even prefer to lay their three or four egg clutches on patches of flat open ground. It seems as though they seek out the worst possible conditions for nesting.

What I find most attractive about these hardy little birds is their lovely song, a kind of tinkling that we begin to hear in mid-February as they initiate their courtship. The sound has none of the strident quality of sleigh bells; rather, it is the sound of tiny wind chimes in a soft breeze.

65. Blogger

Sue Barth is a website developer who works at her Orchard Park home. From where she sits at her computer she has an excellent view of her attractive yard and several bird feeders.

Always interested in nature, Sue decided in 2010 to formalize that interest. Drawing on her computer skills, she developed a blog (a sequential series of recorded observations posted on the web) titled, *Chirps and Cheeps*. And she began to keep a life list of the birds she saw, photographing them as well.

I first was led to her website a few days ago and have been captivated. I'll draw upon her writing to introduce it — and incidentally to let Sue write this essay.

An interesting feature of Sue's blog is its progression as she becomes a more confident birder. Here are two of her first entries:

> October 8, 2010: I ventured off to Tifft Nature Preserve today. It's been about fifteen years since I've been there. It's still a terrific place to view nature in its untouched form, although there are a few indications of man's intervention — all for the good of the preserve.
>
> I hadn't even gotten into the park when I spied my

first warbler, and I mean my very first, life list warbler. As an examination of my photos later showed, this guy was a yellow-rumped warbler. He was perched up in a pine tree near the entrance of the park, flitting from branch to branch. I'm thrilled I got at least one identifiable photo.

November 16, 2010: What a treat today brought. I've been preparing my bird friends to eat from my hand by leaving a gardener's glove of seed out on our deck railing. It's close to the feeders and eventually, birds began to accept that purple glove as a regular deck accent and pick at the seeds in its palm. (This was all my son Tom's idea.)

So the next step was to try enticing the birds to eat from my hand with the glove on. But today, impatient as I am, I just went ahead and skipped that step, anxious to see if they would comply. Sure enough, a little male red-breasted nuthatch obliged — and not only once, but he came back to my bare hand several times. I had expected a chickadee to be first.

And here are two more recent entries:

June 14, 2012: Joe Mitchell reported a pair of red-headed woodpeckers at Como Park the other day. I decided to take advantage of the late daylight and head out there this evening to see if I could find them. I was rewarded with some lovely views of the pair. They were just where he said they'd be, near the sledding hill. Thanks, Joe.

September 3: How to get these little guys to come to me? They're not seedeaters, so what can I offer them?

I had an inspiration: water. It's been such a hot summer, why not provide a little sprinkler action and a makeshift pool? So the next day I got the hose and sprinkler, a big pan lid, and some stones to make my little bird 'pool'. I also set up my photo blind close by and sat down to watch what would happen.

Wow, I hadn't sat for more than ten minutes when the first warbler showed up: a young Wilson's warbler — a lifer. Soon to follow was a black-throated green warbler, and then another life list addition, a Philadelphia vireo. What fun.

One of the great pleasures senior birders have is watching beginners develop their life lists. In doing so we can replay our own early experiences. We can see this in Sue's posted commentary. Like many beginners she started with a number of birds she already knew like robin, Baltimore oriole and crow. But the third species she added, starling, identified her as a beginning list keeper. As this is written in 2016, Sue's life list is a remarkable 439.

Sue's enthusiasm is infectious. She has interested a number of her family members: her children, Tom and Kate, and now even her young grandchildren, Josh and Will, are "into birding."

Visit Sue's blog at www.chirpsandcheeps.com. But beginners beware: she'll soon have you compiling your own life list.

66. Snow Geese

Have you ever seen a flight of snow geese? Probably not here in western New York, because only a few dozen normally appear here each spring when they join our thousands of Canada geese.

I think that it was in about 1995 when a group of us saw a line of twenty of these geese flying high overhead. They were beautiful white birds with black primary wing feathers seen against a backdrop of blue sky. It was a thrilling sight, the best of a great day of birding. And I recall thinking: wouldn't it be great if we could see more of these birds.

In fact snow geese were rare everywhere in about 1970, so uncommon in fact that hunting seasons were closed.

So much for the past. Today the situation is very different. Any year you can travel east to Cayuga and Seneca Lakes or to the Montezuma National Wildlife Preserve to see tens of thousands of these birds. Resting on the water, they literally fill in extensive sections of those lakes.

But the spectacular view is when they rise like a snowstorm to fill the sky.

The migration of snow geese that brings those numbers in spring and fall is only about a hundred miles from us yet we normally see few of those birds. And even in Rochester they are seldom seen in such numbers. The flyway that takes them from Chesapeake Bay and Atlantic shorelines to the northern border of Laborador and beyond is usually very narrow and, except for a few individuals, misses us entirely.

But not this year. Reports have been coming in from the fields along Lake Ontario in Orleans and Niagara Counties of snow geese in the hundreds of thousands with one estimate of a million birds. Among them are dozens of blue geese, the dark color morph of the snow goose. And we thought we had too many Canada geese. They are far outnumbered this year by these newcomers.

Birders from all over the region are rushing to those areas to see this spectacular show.

Why has this remarkable event happened? As Bob Spahn of Rochester says, "Looking at bird distribution questions is one of the fascinating, open-ended opportunities in bird observation and study," and he goes on to speculate: "With the snow geese, clearly a major factor in all that we are seeing now is the huge population explosion."

Since we normally see so few of these geese, it may seem strange to learn about that population explosion for indeed snow geese numbers have been increasing exponentially. Their population has doubled many times since that 1970 low.

As a result of this population explosion today those far northern breeding grounds are being devastated. In some areas over 8000 pairs nest in each square mile. Jody Gienow and Louis-René Sénéchal record the result in just one area: "At McConnell River, on the west coast of Hudson Bay, a colony of about 200,000 breeding geese has denuded the original nesting area of edible vegetation so that little more than bare soil remains." A photograph of one nesting area with small parcels fenced off shows a fenced area that excludes the geese covered with green vegetation, the rest lifeless earth. In fact observers tell of the soil depleted down to the gravel underneath.

This kind of thing is happening across vast areas of the far north all the way to the Pacific coast.

Okay, so one reason for the occurrence of these geese here could be their increased numbers. But there is another aspect of their appearance as well. Although the range of their migration dates is wide, normally these birds appear each spring in mid-April. This year they have showed up at the beginning of February.

A suggestion if you go to see the snow geese: They have a black "grin" mark on their bill that gives them an ugly appearance up close. They are far more attractive seen from a distance.

That desire I expressed at the beginning of this essay — to see more snow geese — is another example of my failure to be careful what I wish for.

67. Cowbirds

A scene in the film *Dances with Wolves* initiated a train of thought that led me finally to the subject of endangered birds.

It was quite a stretch, so let me make the connections.

In the motion picture the Indians reach a hillcrest and observe a wide path of barren ground where the bison they follow have torn up and obliterated the prairie vegetation. I had never before thought of this effect of the great herds. In some ways they were like a plague, their millions leaving only destruction behind them, sterile lands to be replenished only over time. I could imagine, for example, how a farm or village might be wiped out by stampeding buffalo.

Clearly these vast buffalo hordes defined their own ecosystem, their own environmental community. One member of that community was the cowbird, a small iridescent brown-headed blackbird now common across the contiguous United States and southern Canada.

Cowbirds followed the buffalo in order to feed on insects from the beasts' backs and incompletely digested seeds from their offal. But this role created a problem for them. Very likely their ancestors had been nest builders like their cousins, red-winged blackbirds; however, the nomadic ways of the bison made this difficult to accomplish. If the cowbirds stayed in one spot to raise a brood, their food source would soon be far away. To accommodate, cowbirds adopted the European cuckoo's way of life: they lay their eggs in other birds' nests and left rearing their young to those parasitized species while they moved on with the bison.

This turned out to be a highly adaptive way of life for this species and unfortunately today, with the sixty million buffalo reduced to a few thousand, the cowbird has not modified this behavior. The female cowbird observes the nest building of a target species, most often a bird smaller than itself. When the nest is complete and the host species is ready to incubate, the cowbird quickly moves in to lay its own egg, often removing and eating a host bird's egg at the same time. An individual female may parasitize one nest several times or several nests. For example, Herbert Friedman observed a cowbird laying its first egg in the nest of a chestnut-sided warbler, its second in a veery's nest, its third in another veery's nest and its fourth and fifth in the nest of a redstart.

Cowbird eggs have a short incubation period, giving the hatching chick a head start on its nest mates. Its adoptive parents, driven by instinct, stuff food into the most demanding mouth. Too often as a result pairs of tiny warblers or flycatchers feed a giant nestling already larger then themselves while beneath it lie their own dead offspring.

John Terborgh claims in a recent *Scientific American* article that this cowbird parasitism is a major factor contributing to what he calls the "steep decline" of populations of many of our favorite forest-nesting songbirds. We have too glibly assigned this problem to tropical deforestation when we in the North are at least as responsible. By breaking up extensive forests into smaller woodlots we have provided greater access to the parasitic cowbirds of more open country. At the same time we have set out our garbage pails to feed the exploding numbers of predatory raccoons and opossums, crows and jays.

Terborgh suggests that we can do little to stop this degradation of suburban habitat but that, among other actions, we should support consolidation and expansion of our largest tracts of forest including those of the Adirondacks and Appalachians rather than subsidizing clear-cutting of these same woodlands.

Those huge buffalo herds are long gone. It is remarkable to note that our careless destruction of their numbers is returning through this circuitous route to haunt us by contributing to our future silent springs.

68. Niagara River Gulls

We crossed the Rainbow Bridge into Canada and headed south down the broad empty parkway along the Niagara River. At seven-thirty on this bitterly cold and windy Sunday morning there was not a soul at Horseshoe Falls. But when we reached the Engineerium a few hundred yards to the south, we began to see them. The small parking lot at that building was full and a dozen people crowded the small observation area. More stood along the fence upstream.

The biggest crowd was another half mile south at the water control barrier. Along the lookout above this structure there were already perhaps fifty cars. I noted license plates from New Jersey, Michigan, Ohio, Pennsylvania, Massachusetts, Ontario, Quebec, one van even from Missouri. Hundreds of people crowded the rail peering down at the breakwall with binoculars and tripod-mounted telescopes.

A passing jogger was forced to dodge through the mass of people. As I got out of the car I inadvertently shouldered into him. He responded to my apology with an angry, "What the hell are you doing here?"

Hoping he meant that "you" in the plural, I responded, "We're looking at gulls."

He shook his head as he trotted off.

"Looking at gulls" did indeed draw several thousand people to the length of the Niagara River over the past several weeks, not an insignificant number for the local tourist industry. Many, including visitors from as far away as Scandinavia, stay at local motels, eat at local restaurants and in the evenings frequent local theaters and nightspots. This is our Niagara Frontier component of what has become a national occupation: catering to bird watchers.

To place this in perspective, consider the many areas that cater to hunters. Today birders outnumber hunters and in fact they outnumber participants in most other outdoor recreational activities as well. Alert promoters respond to this new clientele. You can send to many Chambers of Commerce — to Brownsville, Texas, for example — to obtain beautifully designed and printed brochures describing local birds and where exactly to go to find them. Imagine filling Buffalo and Niagara Falls motel rooms at what most consider the worst time of year for tourism.

What brings out these birders? Not the tens of thousands of ring-billed gulls, the thousands of herring and Bonaparte's gulls or the hundreds of great black-backed gulls, but rarer varieties that must be separated with great care from the mob.

Every winter a few white-winged gulls appear: big glaucous gulls and smaller Iceland gulls. Old World visitors called little gulls have become annual visitors. Early in the season you can often find Franklin's and even Sabine's gulls. Still rarer possibilities include Thayer's, lesser black-backed and laughing gulls, black-legged kittiwake and the irritatingly misnamed common black-headed gull, a beautiful little red-billed gull that I have found especially elusive.

Those are enough to bring hundreds to this area, but this year is special. Three species that have never been recorded along the river before have miraculously appeared: a mew gull, a California gull and a slaty-backed gull.

The California gull is the species the Mormons honor for attacking their locust plague and Utah is at the eastern edge of its normal range. The mew gull is also a western species.

But most remarkable is the slaty-backed gull, a bird of northern Asia rarely seen even in Alaska. When word spread about this occurrence, bird listers flew in from across the country to look for it here.

Our all day pursuit of these rare species was not rewarded. We and hundreds of other birding enthusiasts (many would use a different word) will return to search again.

69. Turkey

One summer morning recently my wife and I had an experience that is becoming increasingly common in Western New York. I had just come into the kitchen for breakfast when Doris frantically motioned me over to the window. She whispered, "There's a turkey in our backyard."

Sure enough, just as I got to the window a big gobbler noisily flapped up over our juniper hedge, its beard barely clearing the top branches. It maneuvered close under our electric lines and continued on, in its awkward but powerful flight narrowly missing trees, telephone poles and our neighbors' homes.

I remain amazed at that event. When we moved here over 25 years ago, there were open fields behind us and occasionally ring-necked pheasants strutted through our back gate. But then a new road was built and houses filled in those fields. Now home lots extend off in all directions and the pheasants are long gone.

That turkey probably wandered from open country into the ever narrower confines of Baehre Swamp a quarter mile from us and, when something flushed it from its nighttime roost on a low tree limb, it tried its luck in our direction. Of course, flying is not an easy task for a turkey. Its big, un-streamlined body must be difficult to lift on its relatively small wings. When I flush them in the woods, they rarely fly more than a hundred yards. So, soon exhausted, this one had dropped down next to our sheltering hedge.

Our region has a special attachment to the wild turkey. Steve Eaton, retired St. Bonaventure University biologist, wrote its life history for the new *Birds of North America*, the only account for that project produced by a Western New Yorker.

Remarkably the turkey many of us will share on

Thanksgiving is the same species that wanders our fields and forests and that serves as a favorite for hunters. It is one of only two Western Hemisphere birds that have been domesticated worldwide. The other is the homely Muscovy duck of Central and South America that is occasionally seen in area barnyards.

A Schmoo-like Bird

The resourceful cartoonist Al Capp, whose "Li'l Abner" comic strip appeared in newspapers for many years before he died, created unusual fictional creatures he called shmoos. Shmoos were perfectly designed to serve humankind: they were extraordinarily tame and prolific, they required nothing to be raised, when cooked they tasted like steak and they practically jumped into your frying pan.

Capp was a difficult man. Among other things he was a crudely artful male chauvinist and deeply reactionary in his politics, but he was often able to touch our nerves in instructive ways. His shmoos served as a metaphor for our interface with wildlife.

Over the history of civilization there have been a number of real shmoos. We don't have to go to the Island of Mauritius in the Indian Ocean where the dodo was doomed or the Galapagos Islands where ships' holds were filled with giant turtles to find shmoo-like animals and birds. We had several in North America as well.

The penguin-like and equally flightless great auk, whose bodies served fishermen as food and bait and whose feathers stuffed pillows, was last taken from Iceland in 1844 and Martha, the last passenger pigeon, died in the Cincinnati Zoo in 1914. During the 1870s 25,000 passenger pigeons were netted daily and shipped to posh city restaurants in overstuffed railroad boxcars.

One bird that seemed destined to follow these species from abundance into extinction because of its human-serving qualities was the wild turkey. Ornithologists estimate that there were ten million in North America when Europeans first reached these shores. In 1641 at Fort Orange (now Albany) a minister reported "so many turkeys that they came to the houses and hog pens to feed." Another author designated it "one of the commonest birds in New England." This was fortunate as those turkeys served as a diet staple for early settlers who were carving a meager existence out of a hostile wilderness.

Here again uncontrolled harvesting finally took its toll. The last New York State 19th century wild turkey was reported from Allegany County in 1844 and the species was extirpated from all of New England a few years later.

Providentially a few reservoirs of wild turkey populations remained in the extensive forests of the southern Appalachians. Nearest to us were a few birds in Clearfield County in central Pennsylvania. Even these were threatened by the loss in the early 20th century of their favorite food crop — the American chestnut — and by diseases that were traded back and forth with domesticated turkeys. (The barnyard birds are the same species, now bred into waddling but heavy-bosomed relics of their majestic ancestors.)

The lesson was finally learned and hunting regulations were established. It was not too late and the populations slowly grew. Unlike shmoos that never learned, turkeys modified their behavior. They become wary birds better equipped to withstand hunting pressure. They adapted to new areas and spread down out of the deep forests to open country. Thriving, their numbers expanded northward, finally crossing our Pennsylvania border into Allegany State Park around 1950.

Buffalo Ornithological Society regional counts reflect the repopulation of this biggest game bird. The first returnee was reported in May 1951. By the 1960s there were an average of 11 each year. That rose rapidly to 60 for the 70s, 92 for the 80s and 212 for this decade. In 1995 alone almost 700 were recorded.

Shmoo it's not. Rather the wild turkey is today not only a symbol of our heritage but also of our willingness to learn from one of our mistakes.

And a Franklin Favorite

By 1784 Benjamin Franklin was an elderly man. He had served in France as ambassador for the past six years and during part of that time he had participated in the protracted peace negotiations with England. Early that year he wrote a long letter to his daughter, Sarah, now the wife of Richard Bache, who had followed Franklin as U. S. Postmaster General.

Like so much of what Franklin wrote, it is a charming letter, full of insights and leavened with humor. Its main context is an argument against hereditary nobility for our new country. Some of the flavor of his argument is contained in his comment on the Chinese, among whom "honor does not descend, but ascends. If a man from his learning, his wisdom, or his valor, is promoted by the Emperor to the rank of Mandarin, his parents are immediately entitled to all the same ceremonies of respect...on the supposition that it must have been owing to the education, instruction, and good example afforded him...."

But the section of the letter of interest to naturalists contains his comments comparing the eagle and the turkey. Some, he says, "object to the bald eagle [portrayed on a medal] as looking too much like a dindon, or turkey. For my own part, I wish the bald eagle had not been chosen as the representative of our country; he is a bird of bad moral character; he does not get his living honestly; you may have seen him perched on some dead tree, where, too lazy to fish for himself, he watches the labor of the fishing-hawk; and, when that diligent bird has at length taken a fish, and is bearing it to his nest for the support of his mate and young ones, the bald eagle pursues him, and takes it from him. With all this injustice he is never in good case; but, like those among men who live by sharping and robbing, he is generally poor, and often very lousy. Besides, he is a rank coward; the little kingbird, not bigger than a sparrow, attacks him boldly and drives him out of the district. He is therefore by no means a proper emblem for the brave and honest Cincinnati of America, who have driven all the kingbirds from our country....

"I am, on this account, not displeased that the figure is not known as a bald eagle, but looks more like a turkey. For in truth, the turkey is in comparison a much more respectable bird, and withal a true original native of America. Eagles have been found in all countries, but the turkey was peculiar to ours; the first of the species seen in Europe, being brought to France by the Jesuits from Canada, and served up at the wedding table of Charles the Ninth. He is, besides (though a little vain and silly, it is true, but not the worse emblem for that) a bird of courage, and would not hesitate to attack a grenadier of the British guards, who should presume to invade his farmyard with a red coat on."

There is, of course, still more to argue for the wild turkey as a representative of this country. For example, turkey was a staple, together with venison, corn and pumpkin, at those harvest feasts shared by the Massasoits and Wampanoags and Pilgrims in the Massachusetts Bay Colony of the 1620s.

It is interesting that both the bald eagle and the wild turkey were nearly extirpated from this country, the eagle by pesticides and the turkey by market hunting. That both have so successfully repopulated our land adds to our list of things we appreciate at Thanksgiving time.

70. Winter Trip North

It was in early February when Mike Hamilton, Gail Seaman and I ventured north on a two-day, thousand mile driving trip that took us to Algonquin Park and Sudbury in Ontario. The main goal of our adventure was to see a rare visitor from the Rocky Mountains: a gray-crowned rosy-finch that had been regularly appearing at a feeder near Sudbury.

By setting out at 2:30 a.m. we were able to beat the terrible Toronto commuting traffic. At daybreak we were driving around Lake Simcoe looking for the great gray owls that had been reported in the area. Thank goodness the weather had warmed from the thirty below temperatures of the previous week, but it was still a brisk morning with thermometers registering teens.

Near the lake we were encased in dense fog and could see only a few yards into the haze. As it lifted, we found ourselves surrounded by ice-covered trees twinkling in the filtered light.

Dozens of owls had been reported from along these roads, but we began to think that they had departed. Finally we sighted one, however; then another, two within a few yards, and still more until we counted 13 of these spectacular birds. Coming as they do from the far north, they show no fear and we were able to photograph one sitting on a fencepost no more than ten feet from our car.

They were very big owls but what most impressed us about them was how they could perch atop the tiniest of branches. The reason: their great volume is almost all fluffed-out feathers and these emaciated individuals probably weigh little more than two pounds. We could just imagine the high insulation R-value of that plumage.

When we were finally satiated with owls, we headed for Algonquin. There we hoped to see boreal chickadees, a species that Mike, whose life list is more than twice mine, had not yet observed in Ontario. No luck, but we did find plenty of ravens and a number of other northern species. The croaking of ravens was one of the few sounds that broke the silence of the woods.

In the park we walked along the unplowed road toward Opeongo Lake followed by a group of inquisitive gray jays. Each time we stopped they approached, evidently hoping for another handout of sunflower seeds. I always enjoy the company of these big chickadee look-alikes that have earned the colloquial name camp robber.

Suddenly a flock of white-winged crossbills flew overhead to perch in the highest branches of nearby spruce trees where they began to use their strange bills that are crossed x-like to pry open cones. The males are especially attractive, their torsos washed with soft pink.

On another trail we found two black-backed woodpeckers quietly pecking at the bases of conifers. Unlike our other eastern woodpeckers, males of this species sport yellow instead of red caps. Later as we drove back out of the park two pileated woodpeckers flew across the road ahead of us.

Our trip to Sudbury was not uneventful. Driving at night I suddenly came upon a big deer carcass in the road. I managed only to straddle it. That wasn't enough, however, and a bang announced a broken tailpipe. For the remainder of the trip our presence was announced by a drum roll.

Early the next morning we drove to the house at whose feeder in Chelmsford the rosy-finch had been seen every day for weeks. We placed bets on the first species that would appear. A black-capped chickadee won for Gail. Then two others appeared that I rarely see: pine grosbeaks and redpolls.

The plumage of the male pine grosbeak is a lovely pink and gray. In the females the pink is replaced by soft yellow. There must have been at least thirty of these handsome birds feeding on an only partly snow-covered lawn.

Redpolls always make me think of the old "Call for Philip

Morris" page boy of advertisements, because these small, sparrow-like birds have red caps on their foreheads and also sport a black chin strap. Among them were two almost white hoary redpolls.

The rosy-finch didn't turn up. The only other species we saw at the feeders was a single evening grosbeak, like an outsized goldfinch stuffing itself on sunflower seeds.

But we were not done yet. A few yards from where we pulled off the highway to change drivers, atop a small tree sat still another owl. We thought at first that it was a great gray but it turned out to be a hawk owl, another rare winter visitor.

We missed our target species; however, we returned happy with the many birds we had seen.

71. Sapsucker

What's in a name indeed.

I urge the nomenclature committee of the American Ornithologists Union to consider changing the name of one of our attractive eastern woodpeckers.

Here's why. Picture one of those movie western sheriffs. He pushes aside the swinging doors to enter the town saloon and, seeing the outlaw he's after, announces, "Get ready to draw, you yellow-bellied sapsucker!"

Okay, you're unimpressed with that. Consider then at least that "yellow-bellied" designation, a reference that has come to mean cowardly. Surely this is not a cowardly bird. And although there is some yellow around its black bib, the belly of this species is actually white. In fact, in no way does their yellow differentiate this species from its western cousins; they have yellow underparts as well.

Since its breeding range extends west as far as the Rocky Mountains only in Canada, surely Eastern sapsucker would suffice. I would go further: call it the Eastern sapdrinker. In any case give these birds a break.

All sapsuckers, the western species as well, split the size difference between downy and hairy woodpeckers and are easily differentiated from them by the broad white bar that runs down their side like spilled milk. Once you see that mark you can pick out the other differences in our eastern species. Those woodpeckers have white throats and breasts. Both of our male and female sapsuckers instead have a black bib, the male's with red spilled onto its throat. Also the red on the head of both male and female sapsuckers covers the forepart of their crown, whereas the red on the male downies and hairies is only a spot on the back of that crown.

Another way to identify our sapsucker is to listen for their distinctive drumming: a burst of four to six taps followed by a slowing series of single and double taps.

They may not be as flashy as red-headed woodpeckers or as startling as the pileated, but I find these sapsuckers very handsome birds and a welcome sight when they appear in numbers each spring. A few are residents mostly in the Southern Tier but they are far more common across this region from mid-April to mid-May after which most of them will have moved farther north to reappear again between mid-September and mid-October.

Winsor Marrett Tyler comments on this spring appearance: "At this season the sapsucker is light-hearted and jaunty compared to the sober, quiet bird that visited us the autumn before. The breeding season is near at hand, and if two birds meet they often engage in a sort of game, a precursory courtship, wherein one bird flies at the other in a playful attack; the other eludes the rush of the oncoming bird by a sudden, last minute retreat — winding around the branch on which it rests, or sliding off into the air. They do not appear to impel themselves by strength of wing alone, but, especially in their slanting descents, they let the force of gravity pull them swiftly along, and then, by the impetus of the speed attained, glide upward to a perch. They seem to swing from branch to branch with little effort, slowly opening and closing their wings to guide them on their way. As we watch them we are reminded of trapeze artists in the circus."

And of course you don't have to see or hear this species to know that they have been around. They leave those lines of holes in tree trunks. The holes serve as sap reservoirs to which the sapsucker returns to drink as the flow continues. In fact so too do other birds. I once photographed hummingbirds drinking from those wells after the feisty little birds drove off two sapsuckers.

C. E. Bendire offers an interesting commentary on the sapsucker's diet: "That it should be fond of the sweet sap of trees does not surprise me, as this contains considerable nourishment, and likewise attracts a good many insects which the birds eat; but it is not so easy to account for its especial predilection for the sap of the mountain ash, which has a decidedly bitter taste, and I believe possesses intoxicating properties, unless it be taken for the latter purpose; and the fact that after drinking freely of the sap of this tree it may often be seen clinging to the trunk for hours at a time, as if stupefied, seems to confirm this view. It is well known that some of our birds indulge in such disreputable practices, and possibly this species must be included in the number, as there are sots among birds as well as among the genus *Homo*."

Does that drilling damage trees? According to a 1969 Forest Service publication, *Sapsucker Damage Varies with Species and Seasons* by Francis M. Rushmore, it does indeed. Rushmore observed sap feeding on 23 tree species, damage on 51, with significant tree mortality on three: gray birch 67%, paper birch 51% and red maple 40%. He noted extensive feeding on hemlock and red spruce among conifers and red oak among hardwoods. And as his essay title indicates, he found differences by season: for example, serviceberry was visited only in fall after birch sap had become scarce. It has been estimated that the damage to forest crops is significant, the dead and partly injured trees costing the lumber industry millions of dollars.

In the sapsucker's favor Bendire notes that this species does consume considerable animal food and W. L. McAtee's studies confirm this. Those studies indicate that, while during most of the year only about 40% of their diet is insects, that increases in fall to over 85% when the birds are stoking up on protein for their flight south. While many of the insects were attracted to the sap wells, others are captured in flight with the sapsuckers adopting the techniques of flycatchers. McAtee also found that a considerable amount of their plant diet is berries. Despite this, however, he indicts the sapsucker as an injurious bird species.

Foresters will have to live with that damage as this bird is among our protected species.

72. Carolina Parakeet

In about 1825 naturalist and artist John James Audubon collected and painted seven Carolina parakeets feeding in one of their favorite plants, a cocklebur. A parakeet, he said, "alights upon it, plucks the bur from the stem with its bill, takes it from the latter with one foot, in which it turns it over until the joint is properly placed to meet the attacks of the bill, when it bursts it open, takes out the fruit, and allows the shell to drop."

Audubon also wrote of these handsome grackle-sized green, yellow and orange birds: "The woods are the habitation best fitted for them, and there the richness of their plumage, their beautiful mode of flight, and even their screams, afford welcome intimation that our darkest forests and most sequestered swamps are not destitute of their charms."

At that time Audubon and others found this a common species throughout the southeastern United States. For example, Alexander Wilson, Audubon's contemporary, found "great numbers" of them feeding at a salt lick near the Kentucky River.

Some Carolina parakeets may even have made it to Erie County. In 1889 a Buffalo attorney, David F. Day, who had good credentials as an amateur botanist and ornithologist, reported that he had once seen thirteen parakeets light on the old city buildings at the corner of Franklin and Eagle Streets and that he knew of many being captured in West Seneca. Audubon too reported that "they could be procured...sometimes as far northeast as Lake Ontario."

But a hundred years after Audubon painted his Carolina parakeets, this species, our only native parrot, was extinct. In fact later in life even Audubon noted their rapid decline.

Early in the twentieth century the final wild parakeet was killed but a few survived in zoos and private collections. George Laycock tells us, "The last known pair were called Incas and Lady Jane. They lived in the Cincinnati Zoo for some 35 years. In the late summer of 1917, Lady Jane passed away, leaving her mate listless and mournful. Alone and the last of his kind, Incas quietly 'died of grief' on February 21, 1918."

We have limited knowledge about why this species disappeared. Some claim that they fed on farmers' crops but few complaints about this kind of behavior survive and farmers often spoke in their favor for controlling those invasive cockleburs.

It has also been said that the introduction of honeybees to North America contributed to the parrot's demise because escaped bees took over nesting cavities they formerly used.

More likely, the birds were simply an attractive and remarkably easy target for hunters and collectors. Their flocking behavior was suicidal. When birds were shot from a group, the others returned to their dead and wounded companions. Wilson described one such episode: "The whole flock swept repeatedly around their prostrate companions and again settled on a low tree, within twenty yards of the spot where I stood. At each successive discharge, though showers of them fell, yet the affection of the survivors seemed rather to increase."

What saddens me is the fact that this extinction was so unnecessary. The caged birds often bred successfully but little care was taken of their offspring and only a few of them survived. And there was clearly no cooperation among owners of the parakeets. Today this would not happen. Not only would the birds' reproduction be carefully supported but, through accurate and widely shared record keeping, individuals would be carefully identified and communicated among owners to avoid the perils of interbreeding. This is another of the positive roles played by modern zoos and circuses.

I occasionally see an escaped parrot while birding and a neighbor's pet parrot occasionally screams from a tall ash tree in his yard when it gets loose. There are also a few colonies of monk parakeets in the New York City area. They are the offspring of parrots originally imported from Argentina as cage birds that somehow found their way to the wild. Unfortunately, in Argentina this species is notorious for its orchard depredations and, since they pose this agricultural threat, they are carefully monitored by our New York State Department of Environmental Conservation.

Those parrots are, of course, all aliens. Our native parakeet is, like the passenger pigeon and the heath hen, gone forever.

73. Stadium Fallout

On the night of October 11-12, 2005, some Ithaca, New York birders had a unique experience.

Mike Harvey and Tim Lenz were associated with Cornell University's Laboratory of Ornithology. Here is Harvey's account: "One of the most spectacular avian spectacles I have witnessed occurred tonight on campus. After a late night at the lab, Tim was dropping me off at my house when we noticed incredible numbers of flight calls overhead. In fact, Tim estimated over 150 calls per minute. We noticed the university football stadium lights were on, and thought that perhaps the combination of this bright light source and low clouds were drawing in large numbers of birds. As we approached the stadium, it was obvious something big was going on. We alerted colleagues and soon a dozen other birders joined us.

"Within and in the trees surrounding the stadium were literally hundreds, perhaps thousands, of migrants. Savannah sparrows blanketed the Astroturf, common yellowthroats flit among the bleachers, and yellow-rumped warblers sallied low overhead. Most of the birds appeared to be feeding, largely on moths, and all were approachable and easy to see in the brilliant stadium lights. Almost as interesting as what we saw were the species not represented on the ground in this flight. Thrushes were very scarce relative to the numbers we were hearing, and vireos and kinglets were completely absent. We canvassed the area between roughly 9:30 p.m. and almost 2 a.m., when the lights were shut off.

Lebbin added: "When I arrived I expected to find many dead birds from collisions but was relieved and amazed that most of the birds seemed to be doing just fine and many were taking advantage of the light to forage. That said, we did rescue several yellowthroats from open lighted doorways when the lights turned off outside and at least one dead ovenbird and one female black-throated blue warbler were picked up. The stadium lights provided sufficient illumination for us to watch the birds and for the warblers to actively forage. The foraging continued and perhaps even escalated when the rain picked up. Although few thrushes were seen on the ground, we did hear a wood thrush low (from a tree) late in the evening and I saw a possible gray-cheeked thrush in a tree by the stadium early in the evening."

A remarkable 17 warbler species were recorded: Northern parula, American redstart, ovenbird, common yellowthroat, and Tennessee, Nashville, chestnut-sided, magnolia, black-throated blue, blackburnian, yellow-rumped, black-throated green, palm, bay-breasted, blackpoll, black-and-white and hooded warblers. At least 500 individual warblers were counted.

Non-birders may not realize how unusual that is. To place that number in perspective, in a lifetime of birding I have seen that many warbler species in a single day less than a dozen times.

The rarest birds recorded were at least four dickcissels and two to three blue grosbeaks. The dickcissel's range is normally limited to hundreds of miles to our west and the blue grosbeak's the same distance to our south. These and many other species were identified by call flying overhead.

The ability to name a bird by its nocturnal call notes is quite new in the ornithological community. But just as many birds are readily identified by song like the robin's "cheery-up, cheery-ee" and the goldfinch's "per-chick-a-ree", species flying overhead in the dark are now identified by serious birders who only hear their brief chips. I have a CD that records many of these calls, none of which I have mastered.

Some of the other birds found were: great blue and green herons, red-tailed hawk, a half dozen shorebird species, kingfisher, phoebe, catbird, pipit, scarlet tanager, rose-breasted grosbeak, indigo bunting and five different sparrows.

Finally, Lebbin summarized: "Is there any other place than Cornell where over a dozen birders — dominated by college students — would gather to watch birds at night in cold rain? The band members and guys playing pickup football on the field surely had no idea what they were missing."

Congratulations to these young ornithologists who grasped this rare opportunity to sample the multitude of birds that pass this way on their semiannual nocturnal migrations.

74. Hawk Owl

In my favorite of the author's *Fables for Our Time*, humorist James Thurber writes of "The Owl Who Was God." Noticing that the owl can see in the dark, the animals of the forest begin to think of him as the greatest and wisest of all animals. They also find that the owl can answer any question. For example, when a secretary bird asks him to cite another expression for "that is to say" or "namely", the owl wisely responds, "to wit." They ask the owl to be their leader.

The owl approaches the other animals in the daylight walking very slowly, which gives him the appearance of great dignity. "He's God," screams a hen and others take up the cry. But the owl, despite warnings, leads his followers onto the highway where most of them are killed by a speeding truck. Thurber's moral: "You can fool too many of the people too much of the time."

I thought of that fable when several years ago a number of us stood watching a Northern hawk owl sitting calmly in the high limbs of a roadside tree. This owl clearly does not fit Thurber's description.

The hawk owl is a daytime owl, its actions much more like that of a hawk than an owl. Thus it is aptly named. Examined through a telescope, this bird appeared very alert, its bright yellow eyes only occasionally looking at us, more often searching the nearby farmlands for its normal prey, field mice.

It even appeared to be talking to itself but I could not hear its vocalizations.

This is a handsome bird. A crow-sized owl, its fluffed out feathers give it a still larger appearance. To me it has an overall gray appearance with its breast barred with chestnut, its face outlined with distinctive black markings. William Brewster has described its flight as "perfectly straight, exceedingly swift, and very graceful."

This species is a very rare visitor to this region. It appears only on the local hypothetical list. In February 1988, Walt Listman reported one in Orleans County very near where this one was found. Unfortunately, he did not provide the verification report necessary to add it to the formal list of regional birds. I recall spending two mornings searching for that bird, cross-country skiing miles across snow-covered fields. In all that time I only had a brief glimpse of what I thought was the owl sailing over a distant hedgerow, far from enough to convince others that I had seen it.

Internet directions led us to that winter 2006 hawk owl along the main road bisecting the village of Lyndonville. When we arrived we found Mike Morgante already observing it. According to nearby homeowners, this bird had already spent several weeks along this road and, like the hawk owl I saw a few winters earlier in the Adirondacks, it stayed for many weeks in that area where it seemed to find easy access to food.

The hawk owl is more at home in the northern forests of countries around the globe. In North America it is more often found at the latitude of Hudson's Bay and Alaska. Why individual birds like this one stray south into the United States is one of those mysteries that baffle ornithologists. Some believe that the birds leave their regular ranges when rodent cycles are at minimum providing them too little food. Others argue that almost the opposite occurs. They suggest that an abundance of mice leads the owls to raise too many offspring and younger or weaker owls are driven by competitors south out of their normal territories.

Because it was unfamiliar with humans, this species is notoriously tame. Whereas other birds would fly off with so many people approaching closely, this owl simply minded its own business giving observers excellent views.

75. Cave Swallows

In mid-November 2002, several of us visited Goat Island just above Niagara Falls to look for an unexpected bird visitor to western New York. Among others already there when we arrived was Bob Andrle. He told me he had a good look at the bird we sought and others agreed with his identification.

But when I looked out over the water, all I could see was a flock of rough-winged swallows. The rough-wings were not common that late in the year, but they seemed to be doing well hawking insects low over the water. Only after we watched for an hour did the rare bird finally appear.

It was a cave swallow.

Even through my binoculars it looked like a cliff swallow, but local cliff swallows had all fled south over a month earlier. Fortunately, observers with better eyesight than mine were able to record the special field characteristics that defined this rare bird.

Rare indeed. The cave swallow is a Central and South American species that only extended its range into the southern United States during the last century. If you wanted to see one, you traveled to Carlsbad Caverns in New Mexico where a few nested.

In about 1970, those local cave swallows began to increase in numbers and expand their range. They were soon found across southern Texas nesting in culverts and under bridges like their cliff swallow cousins. Then late in the century vagrant cave swallows began to appear along the Atlantic coast.

Remarkably, they were next recorded, first in 1989 along the north shore of Lake Erie near Detroit. Those birds appeared to be moving east so local birders kept an eye out for them. One morning in late 1999 Mike Morgante pointed out to a group of us a single swallow winging its way east along the Lake Ontario shore. The timing was right as cave swallows had been reported in nearby Canada just days earlier, but we couldn't make out any field marks and we missed being the first to record one of these birds locally.

Along the south shore of Lake Ontario, one was observed that year near Rochester, 2-3 were seen in 2001, 9-12 in 2003 and 8 in 2004. All of those birds were flying west to east close to the shoreline or out over the water.

That set the stage for the fall of 2005.

Suddenly in early November the region was inundated with cave swallows. Given the weather patterns, knowledgeable birders were out and watching at Hamlin Beach State Park, and the movement was noted and immediately posted on the Internet. I joined a group of birders there watching as dozens flew by. From November 3-6, 761 were recorded and the western New York season total was almost certainly well over 800 birds.

Unlike in earlier years these birds were flying a quarter mile inland from the lakeshore and they were flying east to west, often directly into strong westerly winds.

Other cave swallows appeared all over the northeast. Perhaps the most remarkable of them was the exhausted bird picked up in Algonquin Park, 175 miles north of Buffalo, by Ron Tozer and Dan Strickland. That bird later died as did a few others in Rochester and Ithaca.

This remarkable event, an example in this case of famine to feast, leads naturally to the inquiry: What brought these birds here?

I'm sure that the first thought that occurs to most readers is hurricanes. And indeed southern and oceanic birds are sometimes moved north in the eye of such storms. In 2003, for example, Hurricane Isabel brought oceanic storm-petrels to

Lake Erie. And in October 2005 Hurricane Wilma after bruising the Yucatan Peninsula crossed Florida and sped offshore up the East Coast to Atlantic Canada.

However, most ornithologists doubt that Wilma brought these swallows to the northeast. There is a Caribbean cave swallow subspecies that has begun to appear in south Florida. Since Wilma passed over Florida before heading north, you would expect that subspecies to be represented and that seems not to be the case. It is far more likely the birds observed locally arrived on strong fronts from the southwest on days preceding the observations.

I join Lewis Carrol's Alice in considering this series of events "curiouser and curiouser."

76. Turkey Vulture

I had an unusual experience early one morning several years ago. It happened when I was hiking alone along a section of the Canadian Bruce Trail about 50 miles northwest of Toronto.

The Bruce Trail follows the escarpment over which Niagara Falls flows. What remains of that cliff extends west around Hamilton, then turns north across country up to the Bruce Peninsula. The trail runs up and down the steep slope but where I was walking it passed through a wooded area along the top near the edge of a sharp drop.

Suddenly all around me the forest came alive. A loud rustling noise arose from the undergrowth. It sounded as though large animals or people were moving all around me. I could see only indistinct shapes and the noise kept increasing. Whatever caused the sound seemed to be closing in on me. I could think of no possible source and, quite frankly, I was frightened.

Finally the rustling decreased a bit and I ventured forward. I came to a clear area, which exposed the cliff edge, and I immediately discovered what had scared me. I had come upon a roost of more than a dozen turkey vultures. Instead of spending the night in trees, they had slept on the ground. What had frightened me was the sound of the disturbed birds crashing through the undergrowth to get to the drop off in order to leap out and sail away.

As I watched the last of the big buzzards take off, the tension finally drained from my body.

Setting aside the frightening aspects of my experience, I thought about what I had seen. I decided that I had observed two quite different aspects of this remarkable species.

Sailing overhead the turkey vulture is, I believe, among the most attractive of birds. You can identify them at great distance by their large size — their wingspread is 5 1/2 to 6 feet — and the way they hold their broad wings upswept in a dihedral. They are so aerodynamically well structured that they rarely flap those wings; rather, they are content to soar in circles buoyed only by fickle air currents. That morning I watched several of them, some lower than where I stood, sailing effortlessly on early morning thermals rising into the cool air from the warmer ground.

At first sight turkey vultures appear all black but, when they pass overhead, you notice that only the body and forewings are dark, the rest of the feathers gray with the tips of the primaries silver.

Even when you see these birds perched in the distance they appear massive and when they hold out their wings, as they often do apparently to dry their feathers, this mass gives them a distinguished appearance.

Yet up close there is a striking contrast. Now these are surely among the ugliest of birds. Their heads are bare of feathers and colored the red of raw meat. There are even black areas near their eyes that give the meat a spoiled appearance. And in front of this is a cruel beak. Now that big body appears disproportionately large and hulking. The overall effect is similar to a tiny child wearing a parent's overcoat.

It is appropriate that I write about turkey vultures at this time. They have become the commonest raptor migrating through this region. In 2012 over 8,000 were recorded at the Hamburg hawkwatch site. (To place that number in perspective, the total number of raptors observed there that year was just over 10,800.)

Regional Buffalo Ornithological Society counts also indicate how vulture numbers have increased. Current annual numbers average over ten times those recorded before 1970.

I have talked with a number of birders about why this is happening. One suggested that these birds may be extending their range north as our weather moderates. That may well be true, but I suspect another reason and I will be interested in responses from farmers about my guess. As I understand it, because of the possibility of disease spread, rendering companies no longer collect dead animals from farms. That means that carcasses are often left out longer before burial providing a smorgasbord for vultures.

77. Wind Birds

Peter Matthiessen calls them wind birds.

They are less imaginatively termed shorebirds: plover and sandpiper, snipe and woodcock, yellowlegs and willet, curlew and godwit, whimbrel and phalarope. And by mid-August they are already making their way south through the Niagara Frontier from their breeding grounds in northern Canada. Some, like the tiny sanderling, will fly on to the remotest fringes of South America.

I am reminded of that name, wind birds, and of Matthiessen's beautiful essays as I stand with Mike Galas and Bill Watson watching a small flock of them. For a few moments they move about, each to its own concerns, along the Lake Erie edge. A lesser yellowlegs wades belly deep in the water and occasionally darts a bill at a minnow, semi-palmated and pectoral sandpipers with sanderlings search the rocks and probe the sand for insects, killdeers stand silent, one with its head tucked into its back feathers, and smaller semi-palmated plovers like their obstreperous children dash about among the others.

But suddenly a wind gust picks up most of the birds and at first blown like leaves they quickly become a synchronized team. They wheel with the wind along the shoreline, flash in unison dark backs, light bellies, dark backs, light bellies. Their sharp falcon wings power delicate bodies in perfect formation out over the lake a few feet above the water, first one way then another until, with hardly a minute passed, they return, veer upwind now on drooping wings to touch down gently a few feet from where they rose.

Where we watch these beautiful birds, we stand on what Bill tells me is the Edgecliff member of the Onondaga limestone. This is the shelf rock northern shoreline that juts out into Lake Erie at Rock Point Provincial Park in Canada about 50 miles west of the Peace Bridge. It is clear and sunny with temperature in the mid 70s, another of those days that Niagara Frontier dwellers who have never lived elsewhere too easily forget.

Embedded in the rock are the remaining evidence of rugose and tabulate corals left here when this was an ocean bottom over 350 million years ago. There are also deposits of silica-laden chert, still harder rock that Indians chipped and flaked into arrowheads. On the rocks windrows of the tiny shells of zebra mussels remind us of their aggressive immigration.

Between us and the sand dunes are extensive stands of the handsome purple loosestrife, another dangerous alien, this one choking out native rushes. But near them, seemingly growing out of the solid rock, are the ground-hugging red tentacles of silverweed bearing small green fronds and an occasional tiny yellow blossom.

A few butterflies visit these flowers: a monarch, cabbage butterflies — white with black dots in each wing — and a delicate little blue butterfly, I assume a spring azure.

As I focus my telescope on the shorebirds, I notice that the rough rock face is peppered with thousands of flying insects. As the sandpipers walk among them, the flies retreat, leaving bare a 6-inch radius circle around each bird. Despite this retreat, an occasional thrust picks up a laggard fly.

Bill finally separates a least sandpiper from the more numerous semipalmated sandpipers. I recall color differences between these two species by a mnemonic: the number of letters in SEMI with its GRAY back and DARK legs, the number of letters in LEAST with BROWN back and legs GREEN or, cheating a little, YELLOW (with one L?)

These sparrow-sized sandpipers of the genus *Calidris* are more commonly known as "peeps." We look for their rarer cousins — western, white-rumped, and Baird's sandpipers — without success.

But now the wind birds rise again. Over the days ahead they will drift east along the beaches to Jaeger Rocks at Fort Erie. From there their powerful instinctual drive will join our northwest gusts to urge them on ever south.

78. Cuckoos

Tent caterpillars are the larva of a small moth that is of such minimal importance that, unlike most other species, it gets its name from its own young. It is called the eastern tent caterpillar moth. There is a related species, the forest tent caterpillar which, despite its name, does not erect a tent.

These colonial caterpillars hatch in early March and they immediately spin their silken tent usually in a tree crotch. They are crepuscular, that is most active during early morning or evening twilight when they leave the tent to feed on leaves. They also feed at night in warmer weather. They remain in the tent during the heat of the day or when it rains.

When they emerged from their eggs, those tent caterpillars were small and their tent was an attractive white. Now the caterpillars are large and their tent is soiled with caterpillar feces.

Enter the hero of this essay, the cuckoo, the deadly enemy of the tent caterpillar.

Two species, yellow-billed and black-billed cuckoos, are found here in western New York. They are members of an international family that includes roadrunners, anis and the European cuckoo. That European cuckoo is the bird of the cuckoo clock with its *kuck'-oo* call. It is also the bird from which the word cuckold is derived for it is a brood parasite, like our cowbird laying its eggs in other birds' nests. Our cuckoos are rarely parasitic, although a few nest invasions were identified by early ornithologists. Instead they build their own flimsy nests — not much better than those of mourning doves.

Cuckoos normally remain hidden in foliage. I rarely see them and, when I do, my view is usually a brief glimpse of a blue jay-sized bird flying arrow-straight through the forest, its flight somewhat like that of a mourning dove. They are brown backed and white bellied, the two species with only minor differences in markings.

More often I hear them. The yellow-billed cuckoo's call is described by Peterson as "a rapid throaty *ka-ka-ka-ka-ka-ka-ka-ka-ka-ka-ka-kow-kow-kow-kowp-kowlp-kowlp-kowlp-kowlp* (retarded toward end)". He describes the black-billed cuckoo's call as "a fast rhythmic *cucucu, cucucu, cucucu,* etc." I enjoy listening to these unique sounds just as much as I did listening to their cousins calling in England a few years ago.

Now back to the caterpillars. Tent caterpillars have hairy bodies and for this reason are not attractive as food for many birds. But cuckoos feed on them regularly. As Arthur Cleveland Bent points out, "An abundance of caterpillars in a locality is very likely to bring with it an invasion of cuckoos." Back when ornithologists analyzed such things, one report told of an average of almost 23 caterpillars in each of 121 cuckoo stomachs, a total of 2771 larvae.

Tent caterpillars are not the only species eaten. Bugs, beetles and grasshoppers are consumed as well and cuckoos even devour the poisonous caterpillars of the Io moth. But they are best known for their attacks on tent caterpillars. In 1897, Amos Butler reported that "he has known these cuckoos to destroy every tent caterpillar in a badly infested orchard and tear up all the nests in half a day."

Fall webworms, often mistaken for tent caterpillars, are also taken. In a single stomach 325 of these larvae were found.

Sometimes cuckoos have been observed stripping the hair from caterpillars before eating them but most often they merely eat the entire insect, later disgorging pellets of hair in a manner similar to that of owls.

Most observers rate these birds very positively but they do have a down side. They eat grapes, elderberries and mulberries and one early ornithologist indicted them as nest robbers. In 1896, C. J. Maynard claimed this and added that other species defending their nests would follow the intruding cuckoo, pecking at its tail, so that "by the middle of summer, it is difficult to find a cuckoo which has a full complement of tail feathers." Since then, however, other ornithologists have disputed Maynard's claims.

On balance, I'll take cuckoos.

79. Fall Bird Migration

Among my most popular columns were those that listed approximate dates for spring bird migration. In response to a number of requests I offer now a similar listing for fall. These dates are based largely on the Buffalo Ornithological Society's *Seasonal Checklist of the Birds: The Niagara Frontier Region*, a 2002 compilation by a committee headed by David Suggs.

As should be clear from the following listing, the fall

migration is already well underway by midsummer. I have always been amazed at how soon after nesting shorebirds, cuckoos, flycatchers and even tiny yellow warblers leave. Birds of the year have only been fledged for a few weeks when inbred instincts compel them and their parents to leave on flights of a thousand miles and more to the south.

Leaving Dates for Summer Residents

Aug 1-10: Yellow-billed cuckoo.

Aug 11-20: Black-billed cuckoo, cliff swallow.

Aug 21-31: Alder flycatcher, willow flycatcher, bank swallow.

Sep 1-10: Great egret, least bittern, Eastern kingbird, great crested flycatcher, least flycatcher, yellow warbler.

Sep 11-20: Green heron, American bittern, sora, common moorhen, blue-gray gnatcatcher, warbling vireo.

Sep 21-30: Virginia rail, spotted sandpiper, Caspian tern, ruby-throated hummingbird, barn swallow, veery, red-eyed vireo, chestnut-sided warbler, ovenbird, hooded warbler, indigo bunting.

Oct 1-10: Osprey, chimney swift, Eastern wood pewee, marsh wren, wood thrush, American redstart, common yellowthroat, scarlet tanager, rose-breasted grosbeak.

Oct 11-20: Blue-winged teal, Eastern phoebe, tree swallow, rough-winged swallow, purple martin, house wren, black-throated green warbler, Eastern towhee, savannah sparrow.

Oct 21-31: Wood duck, American bittern, great egret, pied-billed grebe, turkey vulture, common snipe, American woodcock, common tern, belted kingfisher, Northern flicker, brown thrasher, Eastern bluebird, swamp sparrow.

Nov 1-10: Northern harrier, common nighthawk, brown creeper, American robin, gray catbird, field sparrow.

Nov 11-20: Double-crested cormorant, pied-billed grebe, killdeer, hermit thrush, song sparrow.

Nov 21-30: Black-crowned night heron, chipping sparrow.

Dec 11-20: Hooded merganser, great blue heron, American coot.

Migration Dates for Birds Passing Though

Tundra swan: Oct 20-Dec 15, brant: Oct 15-Nov 10, Northern shoveler: Sep 1-Nov 20, American wigeon: Oct 20-Nov 20, blue-winged teal: Jul 20-Oct 15, Northern pintail: Sep 1-Dec 10, green-winged teal: Sep 1-Nov 15, ring-necked duck: Sep 20-Dec 10, lesser scaup: Oct 1-Dec 10, surf scoter: Oct 20-Nov 20, common loon: Oct 15-Dec 15, red-throated loon: Nov 1-20, horned grebe: Oct 15-Dec 15, red-necked grebe: Oct 20-Nov 30, black-bellied plover: Aug 15-Oct 31, American golden-plover: Sep 1-Oct 20, semipalmated plover: July 20-Sep 20, greater yellowlegs: Aug 1-Oct 31, lesser yellowlegs: July 15-Sep 20, sanderling: Jul 15-Oct 15, semipalmated sandpiper: Jul 10-Sep 20, least sandpiper: Jul 10-Sep 10, pectoral sandpiper: Jul 20-Oct 20, dunlin: Oct 1-Nov 15, short-billed dowitcher: Jul 1-Aug 31, Swainson's thrush: Sep 1-Oct 10, American pipit: Sep 20-Nov 10, Nashville warbler: Sep 1-30, Tennessee warbler: Sep 1-20, black-throated blue warbler: Aug 20-Oct 10, bay-breasted warbler: Sep 1-20, black-and-white warbler: Aug 20-Sep 20, white-throated sparrow: Sep 10-Nov 20, white-crowned sparrow: Oct 1-Nov 15, rusty blackbird: Sep 20-Nov 15.

Arrival Dates for Winter Residents:

Oct 1-10: Gadwall, canvasback, redhead, pine siskin.
Oct 11-20: Greater scaup, white-winged scoter, bufflehead, common goldeneye, horned lark.
Oct 21-31: Long-tailed duck, common merganser, red-breasted merganser, ruddy duck, rough-legged hawk, American tree sparrow.
Nov 1-10: Snow bunting, lesser black-backed gull.
Nov 11-20: Snowy owl, Iceland gull, glaucous gull.
Dec 1-10: Little gull.

Permanent Residents

Great blue heron, Canada goose, mallard, bald eagle, sharp-shinned hawk, Cooper's hawk, red-tailed hawk, American kestrel, wild turkey, Bonaparte's gull, ring-billed gull, herring gull, great black-backed gull, rock dove, mourning dove, Eastern screech owl, great horned owl, red-bellied wood-pecker, downy woodpecker, hairy woodpecker, blue jay, American crow, black-capped chickadee, tufted titmouse, white-breasted nuthatch, European starling, cedar waxwing, dark-eyed junco, Northern cardinal, house finch, American goldfinch and house sparrow. Less common: American black duck, ring-necked pheasant, ruffed grouse, pileated wood-pecker, Carolina wren and Northern mockingbird.

Of course none of these dates is set in stone. As the weather has moderated over the past half century, arrival and departure dates are being extended and more and more birds, like robins and bluebirds, overwinter.

80. Goldfinches

If you had an opportunity to be reincarnated as a bird of your choice, goldfinch would not be a bad selection. Winsor Tylor describes them as "high spirited birds, always happy and full of gaiety." Bradford Torrey adds, "To see the devoted pair hovering together, billing and singing — is enough to do even a cynic good." And Roger Peterson sums up, "The responsibilities of life seem to rest lightly on the goldfinch's sunny shoulders."

Indeed, these lovely little yellow and black birds lead what appears to be a good life. In their drab winter garb they are regulars at thistle feeders. Then spring comes and the males change into bright colors. They can now begin to feed on small insects and weed seeds. But while other birds rush to build nests, the goldfinches remain in small flocks through May, June and even July. Not until August do they begin to take things seriously. Only then do they pair up, build nests and raise families.

And so it was, just a week or two before we returned to high school classes, that my friend Tom Killip and I had our experience with a goldfinch family. Tom, now a retired heart specialist and New York City hospital administrator, was then already a fine nature photographer. My service was simply as his assistant and general gofer.

We discovered a goldfinch nest in my backyard and set out to photograph the parents and nestlings. Tom had rigged his camera with an electric connection that allowed him to mount it at a nest, retreat some distance, and then set off the camera flash by touching the wires to complete the circuit. There was a problem in this case, however. The nest was about eighteen feet high in a bush-like willow tree. We could use my family's ladders, but there was no tree trunk to lean a ladder against.

We had a stepladder about ten feet high and a twenty-foot regular ladder. Applying our usual kid logic, we devised a creative solution to our problem. We leaned the long ladder against the stepladder and Tom climbed up to mount the camera. I stood on the bottom rung of the ladder to anchor it.

That seemed to be a good solution. Tom got to the top of the ladder and mounted the camera only about two feet from the nest. But then he discovered that he had forgotten to carry the wire up with him. "Go get it," he ordered me and I stepped off the ladder to pick it up.

At that point the unanchored ladder on which I had been standing swung up like a teeter totter and Tom's top end swung down, dropping him and the camera — and, as it turned out — the goldfinch nest as well.

Fortunately the only injury was to Tom's camera. The bellows was torn and had to be patched with electrician's tape. And Tom wasn't hurt. We were both just chagrined.

We immediately noticed the nest, still attached to the broken limb on which it was mounted, but now empty of birds. We quickly mounted the limb on our fence and set out to collect the young birds. There were four of them, all within a day or two of fledging. We didn't have too much trouble finding them, but keeping them all in the nest was a bit harder.

We finally got them all in and stepped back in hope that the parents would return. Thankfully they did within just a few minutes.

I like to hope that those young goldfinches made it okay. Left out in the open like that surely reduced their chances, but there were young birds in the yard days later after the nest was empty.

81. Alan Klonick

Arguably the rarest bird that ever occurred in western New York was a silver gull, a species whose normal range is the South Pacific near New Zealand and Australia. It appeared shortly after the end of World War II at the mouth of the Genesee River in Rochester.

If that bird were to be found anywhere in North America today, thousands of birders would descend upon that location to add it to their life lists.

Even in the 1940s it caused quite a stir and — in those very different times when photographs didn't play the role they do today — it was decided that the bird should be collected. Translated, that means that it would be shot and the specimen retained in a museum.

And so a group of birders, the shooter carrying a collecting permit, approached the gull, which stood on the Summerville Pier. But when the gun was fired, the bird struggled into the air and, dying, drifted down into the river. Its body then began slowly floating out into Lake Ontario.

While the rest of the group stood stunned by this unexpected occurrence, Allan Klonick stripped off his shoes, jacket and pants, leaped into the water, swam out and retrieved the bird. After he passed the gull's body up to his friends, he had to be helped up out of the ice-cold water as the cement dockside was difficult to climb.

It was later decided that the silver gull had been released from a European zoo during the war.

What brought that episode to mind was the death on February 22, 2003 of my dear friend, that same Allan Klonick. I had talked with him just weeks earlier and his death came as a shock but it brought back other memories as well:

* Of the time when I was a junior high school student and Allan was one of those wonderful birders who patiently helped a youngster whose enthusiasm far outstripped his ornithologi-cal knowledge. I recall riding in the trunk of

Allan's coupe on bird hikes. That wasn't so bad. Others rode in an old Model A. When a rough-legged hawk appeared over a field, they all jumped out, forgetting to bring the car to a full stop. It rolled on and tipped over in the ditch. Luckily cars were so light then that we were able to manhandle it back up onto the road.

* Of the Genesee Ornithological Society of which Allan was a charter member. When they allowed me to join, it was still an informal group meeting in members' homes. Its treasurer was Howard Miller, who sold four-leafed clovers at the meetings for a dime each. Where he came across those lucky charms, none of us had any idea, but that income provided the GOS its tiny fiscal balance.

Allan Klonick was the last of a fine group of Rochester birders and he has now joined his companions, Gordon Meade, Joe Taylor, Hi Clement, John Brown, Ambrose Secker, Elmer Siebert and Bill Edson in some birding paradise.

But even in that company he stood out. When a remarkable local birding spot, Reed Road Swamp, was threatened by development, Allan, whose business was real estate, organized Bird Refuges, Inc., collected money and bought the property. He later acquired additional land including the famous Island Cottage Woods forming the west spit reaching out into Braddock Bay.

Allan was also instrumental in the formation of the Federation of New York State Bird Clubs and he served as the first editor of that organization's journal, *The Kingbird*. That publication is now in its 53rd year.

I will miss this fine friend.

82. Tundra Swans

Most western New Yorkers who make an annual Easter pilgrimage to the Oak Orchard-Iroquois-Tonawanda complex of swamps go there to see Canada geese. And of course they are richly rewarded. Tens of thousands of these geese stand in pasture stubble or ride high on marsh waters, occasionally rising to the skies to join others in skeins or Vs, all the while honking that off-key klaxon.

But some of us, like Warren Button and me, go instead to see white birds: snow geese and tundra (formerly whistling) swans. You have to look hard to pick out these geese and even swans from the thousands of mostly gray and black Canadas, but when you find them you are rewarded. This time you see not one of an uncountable many but one of a very few.

Each spring the total number of all of tundra swans observed in this area may be counted in dozens, sometimes still fewer. In 1992 I was lucky. On April 3, I found 130 tundra swans on Wood Marsh north of Bartel Road in the Tonawanda Wildlife Management Area.

Tundra swans may also be observed along the Canadian side of the Niagara River. Varying numbers stay through the winter in those open waters. Often hundreds are recorded there on the January waterfowl counts of the Buffalo Ornithological Society.

These are majestic birds. They stretch well over four feet long and enjoy a wingspread of seven feet, about the same as that of an eagle. When they sit on the water, their necks rise arrow-straight, giving them a posture that is both regal and graceful. Watching them drifting in stately groups, you realize how right for the finest ballerinas is Tchaikovsky's *Swan Lake*.

Several years ago I was standing in the yard of my Amherst home when I heard goose-like calling but softer and lower in pitch. I turned just in time to see three tundra swans in perfect echelon shoot overhead only a few feet above the trees. They were so close that I could hear the *howf howf howf* of their wing beats.

That was the first time I realized how very fast they fly. Their wing beat is slower than the smaller geese and ducks, giving them the appearance of proportionally slower flight, but in truth their powerful wings are driving them forward at a high rate. One migrating group averaged 51 mph on an eleven-hour flight!

They need that powerful flight. The swans that pass through this region have come from the Chesapeake Bay area. They will continue west from here to North Dakota before they turn north or northwest to fly on to the farthest boundaries of continental North America.

I close these comments about tundra swans by recounting the saddest event in local ornithological history. On March 15, 1908, more than one hundred of these beautiful birds, as James Savage reported, "journeying toward their summer home near the Arctic Circle, came to an untimely end. A severe rain storm, accompanied by thunder and lightning, prevailed during the greater part of that day. About 11 o'clock in the morning, between showers, William LeBlond of Niagara Falls, Ontario, was engaged in removing from the ice bridge a temporary structure that had been used during the winter as a souvenir and refreshment stand, when he was startled by a loud cry. Turning around, his attention was first attracted to a swan struggling in the water at the upper edge of the ice bridge, but on looking toward the falls he saw a great company of swans in distress, coming toward the bridge. These splendid birds, helpless after their terrible plunge over the cataract, were dashed against the ice bridge by the swift current, amid cakes of loose ice, which were constantly coming down from the upper river. Some had been killed outright by the falls. Others, unable to fly because of injury to their wings, attempted to stem the rushing waters, but here their wonderful swimming powers were to no avail. They were soon imprisoned in the ice where their pitiful cries were heartrending. It was not long before men and boys, armed with guns and sticks, became the chief factors in the closing scene."

83. Windows

One of my common contacts is a request for help. A bird — most often but not always a beautiful male cardinal — is attacking a window day after day and won't stop. Invariably the caller is not concerned about the window or the noise of the bird's thumping and scratching; rather, they worry about the bird injuring itself. Rarely does a serious physical injury result but it is a possibility. Psychological injury is another matter: the bird is clearly frustrated.

This is territorial behavior. Male birds establish personal homelands, in the case of songbirds one to ten acres in size. Then they spend much of their time announcing their hegemony, inviting in willing female partners through song and coincidentally defending their yard against other males.

Ornithologists who study territorial behavior find that they can plot the borders of these small kingdoms with great accuracy. Males in adjacent bailiwicks know their mutual borders as though a fence separated them.

The window the bird is attacking serves as a mirror and the bird, not schooled in physics, doesn't understand that its anatiomorphic image the other side of that glass isn't real. (That technical word anatiomorphic means the same size and shape but reversed like two gloves. Mirrors do that. The only time you see an exact copy of yourself is when you look into two mirrors that meet at right angles.)

Please understand: I don't offer all that information to my callers. It simply doesn't solve their problem. In fact I have very little advice to provide.

One suggestion is offered by feeder watchers: "Clean your feeders but keep your windows dirty." You might even spray the area the bird attacks with window cleaner and leave it whitened. (As you might expect, this response is only acceptable to men.) Other possibilities offer similar problems. Windows are for you to look through and covering them in any way should not be a choice.

In any case, I tell my callers, you're not alone. Here are some stories posted on the Internet:

* Westerner Francis Toldi told of a California Towhee "repeatedly trying to feed its reflection in the rear view mirror of my car. The bird would fly up with bug or whatever and try to stuff it into the mouth of its reflection." His solution: he put a hat over the mirror.

* Floridian Cheri Pierce found a Yellow-throated Warbler attacking its reflection in the side view mirror of the car parked next to hers. "The bird let me approach to within about 4 feet before flying over the top of the car to the side view mirror on the other side where it resumed its attack." Several hats evidently required there.

* And Minnesotan Roger Everhart described a cowbird that spent little time fluttering against his window, instead putting its effort into trying to stare down its reflection. I give that cowbird credit: this was at least a less physically exhausting response.

This kind of behavior is, of course, quite different from birds flying into windows simply because they could not interpret this invisible barrier. This is a still more serious problem as the bird is often killed, like the two lovely fox sparrows that hit Mrs. Fastinnati's Williamsville window this spring.

I can appreciate this problem as I once walked into a glass door. The experience was like being flattened by Mohammed Ali.

Most callers tell me that they have little success putting up those hawk silhouette cut-outs. One suggestion offered by Dr. Christine Sheppard, Bird Collisions Campaign Manager for the American Bird Conservancy is to paint a pattern or design on the outside of your windows with tempura paint. Although the paint lasts quite well, it also washes off easily with soap and water.

Reader Response. In my column on birds attacking or flying into windows I invited readers' suggestions and I was overwhelmed by the volume of response — and I must add, most delighted. Dozens wrote, e-mailed or called since I posted that invitation. It seems to have opened the floodgates as many of the communications took us in different directions from the original request. As in the past, I have responded privately to each inquiry, but in this essay I will share as many of those interesting messages with you as space permits.

* Unfortunately, most of the responses followed the pattern of Suzanne Barber's call for help with her window-attacking cardinal. "I have tried everything," she says. "I have hung everything you can imagine out there — [imitation] cats, snakes, owls — and nothing helps. I haven't tied my live cat out there yet, but this cardinal has about driven me crazy. It is a bold bird.

  And she adds in frustration: "I am thinking of trying to hit it with a broom. I hate to do this as I am a bird lover. I have two canaries that brighten each day for us. If you get any advice, would you please forward it to me as I am getting desperate."

* Ms. Barber's experience is unlike that of Brian Griep, one of several out-of-state respondents and one of those who offered what works for them: "I live in North Carolina where the cardinal is the state bird, but this one was very annoying being at my office window every day. I put up newspapers and tried several other things that are too stupid to mention, but the plastic owls did the trick. You may need a couple of them."

* Several other solutions were offered. Jim and Karen Landau string vertical monofilament lines with gull feathers attached in front of the window being attacked, the feathers evidently distracting the attention of these aggressive birds. (Fluttering feathers may also suggest a recent hawk attack.)

* Marilyn Peccoraro O'Connell, owner of the Wild Birds Unlimited store in Blasdell, provided a number of suggestions. (I consider Marilyn's always forthcoming advice the best available for this kind of inquiry as she enjoys close

personal contacts with many birders whose experiences she carefully absorbs.) Motion is important, she tells me. Brightly colored flags or ribbon streamers that flutter in the wind have been successful. She also agrees with the Landaus' suggestion about stringed gull feathers and adds that dying them bright colors might work even better. These kinds of things - spirals called wind divas among them — are marketed, but not by her: she considers their prices excessive.

* For the other problem — birds trying to fly through windows — Marilyn suggests purchasing the kind of mist net sold by golf pros as a guard against golf balls hitting the windows of houses located near fairways. They also turn away birds and, equally important, their thin filaments are virtually invisible to us.

* My favorite of all the responses was from Mrs. S. Richter: "We haven't any solution to offer but want to share our story with you. We have had an experience with a frustrated bird here in Lockport. What appeared to be a sapsucker began attacking our front window for three or four days. After fluttering against the window for a few minutes, he would sit in a nearby shrub and, turning his back to the window, would flash his rump to his 'rival.' The activity amused us for several days before stopping without intervention."

It seems even the birds indulge in mooning.

84. House Wren

One of the cheeriest songs heard around country homes is that of the house wren. Neltje Blanchan describes it well: "Like some little mountain spring that goes rippling along over the pebbles, tumbling over itself in merry cascades, so this little wren's song bubbles, ripples, cascades in a miniature torrent of ecstasy."

The presence of a pair of these energetic little birds in a yard can amuse and delight the meanest spirit. They are the developers of the bird world, each individual, whether male or female, frantically building homes in every niche it can find. A male may even continue to construct nests when his mate is incubating.

Wrens build in birdhouses but they also construct nests in almost any available crevice — in a tin can, a teapot or flowerpot, an old boot or shoe, a pump nozzle, the end of a hollow railing or the pocket of a scarecrow. They sometimes drive off, take over and reconstruct the nests of other birds — even the hanging nests of orioles and the bank burrows of kingfishers. One observer reported on what must have been the most unusual pair, however. These wrens nested on the rear axle of a car that was used daily. When the car was driven, the wrens followed along. Remarkably, the eggs in this strange nest were successfully hatched and the resulting brood all fledged.

Another strange pair of wrens was observed raising young in two nests at the same time — one in a gourd, the other in a birdhouse. They acted like a divorced couple, the male and female incubating and then caring for separate families.

The nesting materials are equally interesting. Twigs, feathers, leaves, twine, pieces of cloth, bark and weed stalks are often used but odd materials may also be found. An inventory of a single nest listed, among other things, "52 hairpins, 68 nails (large), 120 small nails, 4 tacks, 13 staples, 10 pins, 4 pieces of pencil lead, 11 safety pins, 6 paper fasteners, 52 wires, 1 buckle,

2 hooks and 3 garter fasteners." This pair of wrens could easily have stocked a flea market table.

When they build in birdhouses, they often face initial difficulty getting a longer stick through the small entrance hole, but these intelligent little wrens soon learn to turn the twigs lengthwise and, once they have mastered this method, they use the technique without hesitation.

The mating instinct of these feisty birds is obviously strong and occasionally it is extended to support for other species. For example, one house wren was seen bringing food to a pair of rose-breasted grosbeaks at their nest. The grosbeaks readily accepted the food, sometimes eating it themselves instead of feeding it to their young.

There is also a down side to wren behavior — their frenetic activity too often turns to aggression. A journal article entitled "Down with the House Wren Boxes" found house wrens guilty of destroying the eggs or killing the young of other birds — and bluebirds in particular. Indeed this is a serious problem, especially for those who care for trails of bluebirdhouses.

A few weeks ago I joined Steve Labuszwski in Amherst's Nature View Park where we visited the dozen bluebird nest boxes he had built and set out. Unfortunately, none had been used by bluebirds; most were filled instead with the identifiable sticks of the far more feisty and opportunistic house wrens. (One produced something quite different. When Steve opened the box, a little white-footed mouse jumped out onto my chest and scampered down my leg into the underbrush. Unprepared for this surprise, I jumped even farther than it did.)

But many serious ornithologists come to the house wrens' defense. In particular their food is almost exclusively grasshoppers, beetles, caterpillars and spiders with over 95 percent of these invertebrates considered pest species. One economic ornithologist went so far as to argue that wrens are more beneficial than "most of the species whose eggs it occasionally destroys."

I suspect that some readers will have trouble with that argument, but we have come to accept predators like hawks and owls. We'll just have to put up with an occasional act of infanticide from these otherwise welcome neighbors.

85. Common Bird Questions

In its May-June 2003 issue the editors of *Bird Watcher's Digest* celebrated their 25th year of publication with an article listing the 25 most frequently asked questions addressed to them by "backyard birders." Because I have also been asked so many of these same questions, I offer a half-dozen of theirs here with my responses — drawing only in part upon their wisdom.

* *What is the best time of year to put out a bird feeder?* Anytime. Most bird feeding is done in winter but, especially during and after the breeding season, birds will visit feeders and often bring their young. However, do not expect birds to visit a new feeder immediately: it may be weeks before your first customer arrives.

* *I don't see as many birds as I used to. What's happening?* There are many reasons for this. Bird populations fluctuate and local populations change as land use changes. If your neighborhood is filling in and lawns are replacing meadows and woodlands, you should expect these changes. (For example, our pheasants left when a road was built behind our home.) But individual observations of such changes are often untrustworthy: seasonal censuses by the Buffalo Ornithological Society taken for over 60 years suggest that the regional bird population is more stable than may seem apparent. A number of species like the brown thrasher are indeed threatened but others, like the wood thrush about which I am often asked, appear to be holding their own or even increasing across the area.

* *How can I keep birds from flying into my windows?* I add their

answer to my own given in earlier essays: "Silhouettes of flying hawks...do work but they perform best when applied on the outside of the glass. Hanging ornaments such as wind-chimes, wind socks, and potted plants in front of windows also helps. Misting the outside of the window with a very weak detergent or soda solution will eliminate the reflection but will also impair visibility for you. Awnings, eave extensions and window screens will eliminate all reflection.... Plastic cling wrap applied to the inside or outside of the window can also be effective."

* *How can I get birds to visit my birdbath?* Moving water is a good attractant. Suspend a water container punctured with small top and bottom holes over it to provide a continuous drip. Note: winter birdbaths regularly refreshed with warm water are especially well received.

* *I found a bird with a band on its leg. What should I do?* Contact the Bird Banding Laboratory at the Patuxent Wildlife Center in Maryland. Their phone number is 800-327-2263 and their web address is www.pwrc.usgs.gov/. Eventually they'll send you information about where and when the bird was banded.

* *I found an injured bird. What should I do with it?* Although they are not always strictly enforced, the regulations regarding the handling of any wild animals have become increasingly strict. If you handle a bird, you are probably breaking the law and in some cases endangering yourself as well. Dead or dying birds may be afflicted with a disease like West Nile virus. Your best bet is to leave any animal alone and let nature take its course. You may wish to report dead birds, especially crows, to the Department of Environmental Conservation and injured animals of any kind to a licensed rehabilitator. You can obtain a referral from your veterinarian.

Readers who want answers to a list of similar inquiries should contact *Bird Watcher's Digest* at PO Box 110, Marietta, OH 45750 to order their *Backyard Bird Watcher's Answer Guide*.

86. Hummingbird Myths

Several publications have recently included lists of hummingbird myths. The latest appeared on Bill Hilton's website, www.hiltonpond.org, which I recommend to you. Hilton is arguably the most knowledgeable hummingbird specialist in the eastern United States. I will draw upon his in developing my own half dozen myths.

* *Myth 1. Colored water is necessary for hummingbird feeders.* Here I quote from Hilton's excellent response: "Virtually all commercially-made hummingbird feeders have red plastic parts that negate any need for food coloring. Although the jury isn't in about possible dangers of red dye to humming-birds, such chemicals are additives that might cause harm; since the dye is not needed, why take the risk? Keep your sugar water fresh and curious hummingbirds will eventually find and frequent your feeder - no matter what color it might be."

* *Myth 2. You should not feed hummingbirds after Labor Day because you will delay their migration, possibly threatening their lives.* Nonsense. The compulsive force of birds' migration instinct, acquired over thousands of years of evolution, will not be modified by a few cups of sugar water. Hilton maintains feeders year round at his North Carolina preserve and has found that they have never affected hummingbird migration.

  Also, if you leave your feeder out, it may serve as a stopover diet supplement for birds coming through from farther north or it may even save lingering birds that, possibly because of injury, cannot migrate. For example, we have had Baltimore orioles winter in this area, obtaining part of their food from hummingbird feeders providing these off-season supplies. (If an oriole does stay in your yard, you can further assist it by setting out halved oranges or apples.)

  Moreover, by continuing to supply your feeder late in the

year, you may attract a vagrant hummingbird such as the rufous hummingbird, a rare visitor from the far west that has been recorded here several times in recent years. These birds, whose normal range is along the Pacific coast, seem increasingly inclined to wander east in fall and often appear at feeders after our native ruby-throated hummingbirds have left. In November 1998, several of us visited a home in Binghamton where we saw a still rarer westerner, an Anna's hummingbird, visiting a feeder.

* *Myth 3. If I go on vacation and stop feeding my hummingbirds they will die.* No, they will simply find other food sources. If they don't return when you come back, it is probably because they have found a neighbor's feeder to which they have accommodated.

* *Myth 4. Hummingbirds are monogamous.* Far from it. Observers find that hummers are sexually 'loyal' to their mates for about the second it takes them to copulate. Neither males nor females are discriminating in their mating and many nests contain eggs fertilized by different fathers.

* *Myth 5. Small baby hummingbirds are feeding on my flowers.* Hummingbirds do not leave their nest until they are as large as the mother that has cared for them. There are two possibilities for those midgets. If it is coming to your feeder, it is most likely a bumblebee or giant hornet. If it is coming to your flowers it is almost certainly a hummingbird clearwing moth. This remarkable hummingbird look-alike also mimics hummers by rapidly beating its wings, quite unlike most other moths.

   Hilton points out that reports of hummingbirds from Europe are almost certainly moths like these as hummers are native only to the Western Hemisphere.

* *Myth 6. Hummingbirds hitch rides on the backs of larger birds like hawks or geese when migrating.* This is my favorite hummingbird myth because, although no such hitchhiking has ever been observed, some ornithologists formerly argued for it. Their reasoning: hummingbirds migrate almost 500 miles

across the Gulf of Mexico, too far for these tiny birds to last on their limited supply of energy; thus, they must hitch rides. Now, however, it has been shown that, like other long-distance migrants, before setting out on this challenging marathon, hummingbirds gain 25-40% extra body fat, just enough to supply them.

But even this is sometimes not enough. A hummingbird cannot make forward progress in a 20 mile per hour headwind and weather changes lead to many deaths. Less than half of newborn hummers survive their first year.

87. Woodpecker Physiology

Most of us have had the unfortunate experience — usually in the dark — of walking into a wall. It is not a pleasant misadventure. Thankfully, few — at least of those who live to tell of it — have run full tilt into a tree.

Yet that is what a woodpecker does hundreds of times each day. It pulls its head back as far as it can and then thrusts it forward in a straight trajectory, its eyes closing an instant before it strikes solid wood. The bill hits that wood at about fifteen miles per hour. That may seem slow but an automobile hitting a wall at that speed would suffer a great deal of damage while its front seat passengers would be bounced violently by air bags.

Why then don't woodpeckers at least suffer terrible head-aches? The answer is complex. First and most important, they enjoy the advantage of smaller size. Their lesser mass-to-surface ratio makes the deceleration force at impact corres-pondingly less. This is the same property that allows an ant to fall from a tabletop to the floor with no ill effect. The ant's drop is proportional in distance to that of a human falling from the top of City Hall, but size is on the smaller animal's side.

Like those of all birds, woodpeckers' brains are even smaller than their body size relative to humans, thus adding to this advantage. This difference alone makes them fifty to one hundred times less vulnerable to brain trauma.

Size is not enough, however, and woodpeckers also enjoy physiological adaptations that allow them to use their heads and bills as pickaxes. Their brains are not in line with their bills; thus the strongest collision forces are transmitted to bones below the brain. Tough brain casings and associated muscles act as shock absorbers. Also there is less fluid in and around their brains than in ours, reducing the damaging shock waves that we suffer in accidents. Finally, some of the shock is diverted by their bills being held slightly open at impact.

A less obvious feature of woodpeckers is their tongue. Like that of frogs and anteaters, it is very long but it differs signify-cantly from theirs in structure. The cartilage supporting a woodpecker's tongue is coiled down into the throat and from there up over the top of the skull. In some species it is finally attached to the bill, in others it is wound around the eye socket. Straightening this lengthy coil extends their tongue well beyond the end of their beak.

Most woodpeckers' tongues are sharply pointed and barbed, helping them to reach deep into crevices to draw out boring insects. Their salivary glands secrete a glue-like fluid on the ends of their tongues that also helps to hold prey. These glands are especially well developed in flickers, which probe anthills to feed on those colonial insects.

Unlike their relatives, sapsuckers have tongues with brush-like tufts appropriate to their sap-drinking habits.

Woodpeckers also enjoy special adaptations to their lives spent clinging to tree trunks. Stiff tail feathers give them that tripod-like prop and well-developed claws a firm grasp on even the smooth surfaces of beech and birch trees. As should be expected, in most species all four toes are well developed and they are directed at right angles, thus providing excellent stability. This is especially important because woodpeckers do not walk but leap from one position to the next, sometimes even doing this on the bottom side of branches. (The more sedentary three-toed woodpeckers lack that rear toe.)

Finally, the especially tough skin of woodpeckers protects them against the stinging insects they meet in foraging.

Woodpeckers are surely among the most remarkably adapted of all wildlife.

88. America's Other Audubon

Probably no one noticed the young woman who stood for so long before the exhibition of Audubon's *Birds of America* paintings at the 1876 Philadelphia World's Fair. Her face was scarred by illness and her parents' rejection of her former suitor added gloom to her countenance. But the bird art that captured her attention was to change not only her life but that of every member of her family as well.

Genevieve Jones returned to her home in Circleville, a central Ohio town, her mind set upon producing her own volume of art. She would complement Audubon's bird portraits by illustrating their nests and eggs.

She had shown artistic talent in elementary school, a talent encouraged by her mother, an amateur artist herself, but Genevieve had no formal art training and no experience whatever with lithography. Although her father, a physician, had nourished her interest in natural history, taking Genny with him on long buggy-rides to visit his country patients, she had no formal science training. But her family rallied around her and supported the enthusiasm and excitement that replaced her earlier depression.

The scene that followed must have been like one of those early Judy Garland-Mickey Rooney movies in which they say: "Let's put on a play." Genevieve's father would provide financial backing. A childhood friend would paint too. Genny's brother Howard, a Hobart College graduate, would write species accounts. Their mother and neighborhood women would color the plates. Everyone had a role.

A company in Cincinnati sold them lithographic supplies and even instructed the women in the techniques of lithography — by mail! Dr. Jones developed a prospectus for the work to be entitled *Illustrations of the Nests and Eggs of the Birds of Ohio* and sold subscriptions. Their project was underway.

Remarkably, the first set of plates — the nests of Baltimore oriole, wood thrush and black-billed cuckoo — were soon completed and copies sent out to leading ornithologists for review. The responses were overwhelmingly positive: Elliott Coues said that there was "nothing since Audubon...to compare with the present work" and William Brewster added, "The Baltimore oriole seems...almost if not quite faultless;...the wood thrush is...a perfect masterpiece."

But now, almost immediately after receiving these encouraging accolades, 32-year old Genevieve Jones contracted typhoid and died. On her deathbed, however, she extracted promises from her family to continue her work.

As a memorial to her daughter, Virginia Jones reorganized the project and took over major responsibility for the original art. The 68 plates depicting 129 species were finally completed in 1883 and, together with Howard's narratives, they were bound in two volumes.

The timing could not have been worse as the country was deep in a depression. Fewer than ten sets were sold by the time Genevieve's father died in 1901. By then his entire investment, the equivalent of over a million dollars today, had been depleted. Seemingly a sad ending to an extraordinary story.

But all was not lost. Joy Kiser, head librarian of the Cleveland Museum of Natural History, was writing a book about this project and also sought a publisher to bring this art to the public attention it so richly deserves.

I visited the Cleveland Museum in 1998 where Ms. Kiser gave me an opportunity to examine Virginia Jones' original copy. I second the remarks of those early ornithologists. The lithographs are exquisitely detailed with every leaf vein, every twig, every egg marking perfectly etched. This is not a collection of illustrations; it is fine art in the tradition of Audubon.

And now I have in hand the 2012 book, *America's Other Audubon* by Joy Kiser, published by Princeton Architectural Press. I believe that a copy should be shelved in every birder's library next to Audubon's own paintings.

As the Smithsonian Institution's Natural-History Rare Books Curator Leslie Overstreet says in his Foreword: "For over one hundred years, ornithologists have consulted the book's meticulously detailed and scientifically accurate illustrations, but few beyond this specialized group even know that the book exists. Now you will have the pleasure of seeing all of the illustrations and reading the story behind them."

Despite her untimely death, Genevieve Jones goal has now been achieved. Joy Kiser, now the librarian for the National Endowment for the Arts in Washington, D.C., has served not only the Jones but us as well by publishing this handsome book.

89. Botulism

A symbol of wilderness is the common loon. I hope that some of you had a chance to interact with these wonderful birds on their nesting grounds this past summer. Did you have the opportunity to observe the adults' handsome black and white pattern with their distinct necklace, their big bill and their bright red eye as they fearlessly approach your boat or campsite? Did you also see young birds clinging to their backs or paddling around their parents? And even more satisfying, did you hear the loons' distinctive yodeling and wailing and laughing through the evening and early morning hours or just before and after a storm?

I hope you did indeed interact with those birds because your chances of being able to do so in the future are decreasing significantly. Loons are threatened by a disease that is killing thousands during their migration through this region between their summer breeding grounds to our north and their wintering grounds in the southern states and the Gulf of Mexico.

Rick Taylor has summarized the problem in an essay that appeared on several Michigan websites. I draw on his analysis here.

The recently introduced zebra and quagga mussels filter lake water very rapidly. Today we can see much deeper into our Great Lakes than we did in the past. Unfortunately, what appears to be a positive feature has a downside as well. The problem is that the clearer water allows the sun to penetrate to the bottom of shallow water lake regions allowing algae mats to photosynthesize and grow there. Those mats are now many feet thick. While the top layer of algae is getting sunlight, the lower layers are not and they die and decay. Currents and wave action especially during storms skim off the live surface of these beds, driving it near shore and leaving tons of algae decomposing on the lake bottom. It is in that soup where the Botulism E bacteria grows and produces its deadly toxin. According to Dr. Kurt Newman of the Great Lakes Science Center in Cleveland, Ohio: "Botulism E toxin is the most toxic substance known to man. One gram of purified toxin could kill hundreds of thousands of people."

The round goby, an introduced fish that grows to about the size of your thumb, swims through this decomposing algae to feed on worms and bugs that have ingested the toxin from the rotting algae. Then waterfowl like the loon and double-crested cormorant dive down to eat the goby and other deep swimming baitfish. Working up the food chain, the Botulism E neurotoxin affects the central nervous system of any bird or animal that ingests it.

Botulus is Latin for sausage, the etymology deriving from the fact that preserved meats gone bad have historically been a source of human food poisoning. The affliction occurs when a toxic bacterium, *Clostridium botulinum*, is ingested.

Death for an infected duck or gull follows a slow but inevitable progression that is pathetic to observe. Muscles become progressively paralyzed. Early in the course of the sickness, paddling through the water tilts the bird's body back and forth as its reluctant legs are coerced into service. Then when the legs fail completely, it is forced to employ a kind of breaststroke with its wings. But meanwhile neck muscles fail. Avian botulism is often called "limber neck," because the neck of a bird picked up at this stage is limp and its head hangs down. If the bird cannot reach shore, it drowns. If it does manage to pull itself onto land it soon suffocates as its lungs become paralyzed.

The only positive aspect of this decline is that parallel nerve destruction probably prevents the dying bird from feeling pain.

One estimate has 100,000 birds killed by this virulent toxin in Lakes Erie and Michigan through which the loons migrate in 2009 when the disease was especially severe. Although most years fewer die, the disease continues to take its toll.

This is just one of the serious problems associated with Lake Erie. (Recently T. J. Pignataro summarized many of them in a fine series of articles in the *Buffalo News*.) As with so many of our current problems, we are the cause. We are, in effect, fouling our own nest. We need our governments to address some of these issues, but we too need to contribute to solutions as well as to stop creating still more.

If you live near Lake Erie or in fact any nearby body of water, here are two things you can do:

* Participate in the Annual Beach Sweep near you. These are the largest volunteer environmental events in the world. For more information visit the website Greatlakesbeachsweep.org.
* Use care in choosing the fertilizer you use on your gardens and, yes, on farm crops as well. Fertilizer is labeled with three numbers, like 4-8-6. Those numbers represent the percentage

of nitrogen (N), phosphorus (P) and potassium (K), with the remainder – in this case 82% — other ingredients and filler. Nitrogen and phosphorus contribute to the growth of algae and you should choose fertilizer with low or zero potassium (the middle number) and with slow-release nitrogen.

90. Colorado Trip

In 2009 I went on a ten-day trip with my son through the Rocky Mountains west and south of Denver, Colorado. Part of the trip was a thousand mile meandering tour of the state from Denver to Durango by car and the rest a pleasant stay at my son's camp near La Veta.

The Rockies certainly take some getting used to. The country is very different from here in western New York. Much of our trip followed roads at 8000 to 12000 feet. This gave me a real appreciation for the problems of people beset with emphysema. Ten steps and I found myself breathing hard.

The name Rocky perfectly describes the ground. The thin soil layer atop those rocks is meager sand, quite unlike our thick clay. Adirondack climbers can appreciate what this is like: the whole western half of Colorado is like the barren areas atop Adirondack peaks. Because of this, Rocky Mountain trees are small and widely separated. Most of them are conifers but with some aspens and scrub oak mixed in, the oaks seldom growing more than six feet high. Beneath those trees the ground is generally covered with a flimsy growth of hardy grasses and weeds.

One outcome of this is that the country is remarkably open. There are very few of the lush tangles though which we have to pick our way and walking into what passes for a Colorado forest is like walking into a Buffalo city park except for the steepness of the terrain.

The scenery was, as you might expect, spectacular, but so too was the wildlife. Dave Friedrich had suggested that I check out a website called BirdingPal that lists birders willing to help visitors to a region unfamiliar to them. This led to several especially informative contacts. In one case I was told that a Lewis's woodpecker, a species I had never seen, was to be found in the neighborhood near the corner of Brookdale and North Pleasant Avenues in Buena Vista. We drove to that intersection, got out of the car and immediately saw the bird.

Although I had been to Colorado several times before, I found five other species on our driving trip that were new to me: black-chinned hummingbird, acorn woodpecker, Hammond's flycatcher, western bluebird and canyon towhee. The hummingbird was most startling. It was on a feeder across from a broad-tailed hummingbird, both birds displaying brightly colored throats.

My son's camp is built into a mountainside at 8450 feet. It is surrounded by scrub oak. These are stunted trees, in fact really shrubs that grow to about seven feet. Some pines and spruce rise above this undergrowth. Higher up are slopes of open rock with conifers hanging on precariously.

From a second level porch you look south across a long valley to more mountain peaks and east at a line of crags along which Rocky Mountain bighorn sheep pick their way. On one cliff face is a golden eagle aerie.

Although we hiked, always on the lookout for rattlesnakes, and rode ATVs around the area, we spent much of the four days I visited on that porch. On one morning my son-in-law pointed out two bear cubs cavorting in a meadow a quarter mile downhill. But the best attraction for me was the beautiful 35-foot blue spruce that grew only about ten yards from where we sat facing its upper branches. That is where I saw a remarkable number of handsome birds we rarely if ever see here in the East.

* *Mountain bluebird.* Our eastern bluebird is among my favorites, the male with a rich blue unequaled in the bird

world and a breast of almost equally rich chestnut-orange. This western cousin is all blue, its blue much softer but still very attractive. A pair nested under the porch and they were regular visitors to the spruce.

* *Steller's jay.* Our blue jay is rarely seen in this part of Colorado. Locals were very excited when several years ago I found one even further west near Park City, Utah. The Steller's jay is a striking bird. It looks as though our eastern jay had stuck its head and shoulders in black ink. When I finally got beyond looking at that startling head and crest, I could see that it didn't have the wing bars of our jay and that the blue of the rest of its body was brighter than ours. This bird often perched in the top branches of the spruce from which it liked to stare us down.
* *Western scrub jay.* Easily identified as a jay, this bird looks nothing like the blue jay. It has less blue than ours, with gray on its back and belly, dark gray cheeks and a white throat. Its habits were quite unlike the Steller's jay. It visited the lower branches of the spruce or worked its way through the stunted ashes.

You might think by now that all the western birds are blue and most of them are jays. But other quite differently colored birds also appeared in this spruce.

* *Spotted towhee.* Black with chestnut sides like our eastern towhee but with, as you might expect, white spots on its back.
* *Bullock's oriole.* This is the widespread western replacement for our Baltimore oriole. It has orange extending from the stomach up the side of its head. It appeared only once at mid-height in the spruce.
* *Black-headed grosbeak.* Another orange and black bird, this one with the thick bill that gives it its name. Like the towhee and scrub jay, it spent its time in the lower branches and out in the oaks.
* *Hammond's flycatcher.* Westerners too have trouble

distinguishing their empidonax flycatchers. You have to wait for them to sing. Fortunately, I heard this bird's sharp two note chips.

* *Broad-tailed Hummingbird.* Last and indeed least, this is the noisiest hummer, quite similar to our ruby-throated. It alternated with the Steller's jay in the treetop.

That was just one tree. Nearby were ravens, a green-tailed towhee, pine siskins, violet-green swallows and a red-shafted flicker.

91. Windmills and Birds

An important debate is being waged between the proponents of wind turbines and naturalists concerned about birds that may by killed by those windmills.

Both sides agree that, like solar power, wind power is an important alternative to fossil fuel-burning generators that pollute the atmosphere and lead to health problems. This issue is especially timely because, as this is written, 94 new coal-fired power plants are planned in 36 states. Erie and Chautauqua Counties have already been cited for sub-standard air quality and these new plants, many of them upwind from us in the Midwest, would add still more mercury and greenhouse gasses to our atmosphere.

Beyond their agreement about the need for the benign energy production of wind turbines, however, disagreements arise and we could be headed for gridlock. Perhaps the best example of this was to be seen in the headline over an otherwise reasonable newspaper statement by Elmer Marien, then president of the Buffalo Audubon Society. It read: "Keep Wind Turbines out of Migration Routes". Since birds migrate across broad fronts that cover all of North America, that order could effectively end wind power.

Indeed wind turbines can kill birds. In fact as many as 50,000 birds are killed each year by wind turbine collisions across this continent?

Today's windmills are giants. You can see some of them in action in the Wyoming County Town of Wethersfield. Each 213-foot turbine tower there supports three 77-foot blades. Thus they reach a height of about 290 feet, still, however, well below the usual flight path of both day and night-flying bird migrants. In significant wind their blades turn at 28.5 revolutions per minute but, while they appear to be moving slowly, that is an illusion. Their tips swing at over 150 miles per hour and no bird could survive being hit by a blade at that speed.

The often-cited worst case for windmills is Altamont Pass in California where many hawks and eagles have been killed. But even at Altamont, an early windmill location with technology and turbine proximity judged inappropriate today, the Center for Biological Diversity's lawsuit against its operators states: "We are not suggesting closing the Altamont wind farms, rather that turbine owners take reasonable measures to reduce bird kills and adequately compensate for impacts to imperiled bird populations."

As I have presented that information, wind turbines seem to represent a serious problem. Indeed, many people argue that such a total of annual kills calls for a moratorium on wind power. One individual, upset by the location of a wind farm on Ontario's Amherst Island near a woodland where owls winter, even called for a boycott of Canadian products and travel to that country.

I reject those calls for action and consider the latter an inane indictment of our Canadian friends. It represents an extreme and irrational response based on little or no understanding of the identified problem. Unfortunately, however, it also represents a kind of thinking widespread among well-meaning people.

As it happens, a 2013 paper published in *Avian Conservation and Ecology* by a group of Canadians headed by Anna Calvert of Environment Canada recently summarized a series of controlled research studies of human-related causes of bird deaths in that country. Their paper gives us the best currently available data comparing the specific causes of bird death and I have drawn on their report for the following comparisons.

Fifty thousand birds killed seems like a great many until you consider the total number of bird deaths each year. It turns out that only one out of 14,000 is due to those turbines. That should make it clear that the general effect of wind turbines on our bird populations is infinitesimal.

Well, just what is killing those birds? For every one windmill death the Calvert paper indicated that the following approximate numbers are killed by other means: feral cats, 6000; domestic cats, 4000; striking private homes, 1200; vehicle collisions, 750; the game bird harvest by hunters, 200; pesticides, 150; transmission tower kills, 101; striking commercial buildings, 90; transmission line collisions, 65.

It is worth considering a few of those numbers more closely.

Almost 3/4 of all of these human-related deaths are caused by cats: 43% by feral cats, 29% by domestic cats. Another way to think about those numbers is to compare them with the effect of hunting. For every game bird shot, 19 birds are killed by domestic cats, 28 by feral cats. Can you understand then why I strongly support the "Cats Indoors" program of the American Bird Conservancy and equally strongly oppose the Trap-Neuter-Return program that supports thousands of cats that are killing birds and small mammals?

And think too about transmission towers, those towers that support your cell phone as well as radio and television stations. They kill over 100 times as many birds as do wind turbines yet turbines are far more strictly regulated.

Okay, tower kills represent a very small fraction of the hazards we erect for birds. But research is suggesting ways to reduce those deaths as well.

Tower height and the use of guy wires to support the structure have an effect on bird deaths. A Michigan study found that guy wires increased the number of fatalities by a factor of 16, and that tower height quadrupled that factor. By constructing only un-guyed towers of medium height, many bird lives would be saved.

Most bird migration takes place at night, the birds foraging during the day to stoke up the energy needed to continue. And at night they are easily confused by lights. The results of one study suggests that avian fatalities can be reduced by over 50% by replacing steady-burning lights with flashing lights. Here is where you may be able to help. If you observe such a structure lighted at night with steady lights, communicate the need for the simple but effective change to flashing lights to local authorities.

Here is another way to look at the information now collected. A summary indicates that the average number of birds killed annually across North America is between one and two per turbine. Arguably the best of the intensive studies was carried out by Canadian Ross James. His year-long field work at a Toronto wind turbine sited in the middle of a fall migration route turned up three birds killed. He also watched birds change course to avoid the turbine blades, an observation shared by many other observers. His final conclusion: "The greatest threat to all wildlife is still loss and degradation of habitat."

Against this data we have scare statements like one from a dedicated hawk-watcher in the Chautauqua town of Ripley: "If a bird doesn't get killed in Ripley, he may get killed in Rochester, if not there then at Derby Hill, Prince Edward Island, Toronto...." Statements like this together with intensive lobbying by such deeply concerned birders is deterring the development of wind farms.

But consider what development at Ripley would mean. Over 20,000 hawks, vultures and eagles pass that location each spring to say nothing of passerine migrants. If 35 wind turbines were erected there (more than the number contemplated), the national average would suggest annual deaths of about 60 birds of all species, an infinitesimal fraction of the total number traversing that region.

There is clearly a trade-off here but I believe that a cost-benefit analysis comes down on the side of the wind turbines. I join my birding colleagues in their concern for the death or injury of any bird, but I suggest that wind turbines represent the least of their worries. For example, a single feral cat kills more birds in a week than the average wind turbine kills in over three years.

92. Crows

In that long litany of group names — a pod of whales, a gaggle of geese, a murmuration of starlings, a pride of lions — I find it significant that the list designates a murder of crows. I am not a crow enthusiast and I find the implication of that collective name satisfying. I am glad that the author did not choose, for example, the quite reasonable and entertaining but more neutral alternative, a caucus of crows.

Frankly, I don't know how my vote against them would fare in a popularity contest for there are many people who like crows. There is, for example, an excellent website devoted to them. Cornell corvid researcher Kevin McGowan answers many questions about them at www.birds.cornell.edu/crows.

There is even an American Society of Crows and Ravens, a rather strangely named group but perhaps understandable when its (presumably human) members call themselves corvies. At any rate crows do have their supporters.

Admittedly, they are among our smartest and most sophisticated birds. Individual crows have definite person-alities — when it was legal to keep them, they often made delightful pets — and their interactions with each other are playful and humorous. An interesting experiment demon-strated that they can count — admittedly, however, only up to two. When two observers entered a blind and one left, the crows shied away, but when three entered and two left, they approached without hesitation.

Why then don't I like crows? I am not enthusiastic about nest robbers in general, but crows I assign to a special purgatory for having wiped out our local population of nighthawks.

Nighthawks are those long-winged birds that formerly flew gracefully overhead catching insects attracted to the lights of night baseball games. (The hawk in their name is misleading for nighthawks are not raptors but are instead close cousins of whip-poor-wills.) Watching more closely, we could occasionally see nighthawks "booming." Booming is an acrobatic display flight in which they soar higher and higher then dive steeply, finally pulling up to make a roar with their wings. In any case nighthawks are now only seen here during migration and this year I missed them entirely.

Both circumstantial and observational evidence suggests that the villain of the nighthawk demise is the crow. Nighthawks nest in the open on the gravel roofs of city buildings and when crows extended their range into urban areas about 35 years ago, they immediately sought out those nests to consume nighthawk eggs and young. I suspect that they and their jay cohorts represent a problem for other city dwelling birds as well, but the evidence is less clear about them.

Only older observers realize that crows never ventured into urban areas until the 1970s. Why did they do so? Quite simply, because they are very intelligent birds. They may only be able to count up to two, but they quickly realized that they are now safer in cities than in the countryside. Most urban and suburban areas have passed laws against discharging firearms and the crow shoots I watched years ago along flight lines to their fall and winter roosts have been disbanded.

Another factor — as suggested in the movie "The Graduate" — plastics, in this case those familiar trash bags that are even manufactured in the crow's favorite color. Crows in my neighborhood know the garbage collection schedule better than do local homeowners. A couple of pecks gains entrance to the dining room where a smorgasbord is spread before them.

No matter what I think of them, I am certain that crows will win out. They are the ultimate survivors.

Added note: As trash bags are replaced by large containers, there is less incentive for crows to visit urban and suburban areas. Perhaps over time this will allow the return of those nighthawks. Only time will tell.

93. Bird Flocks

Every fall skeins of Canada geese fill the sky, their mournful honking reminding us, as if the falling temperature did not, of the end of another growing season. Meanwhile other bird species gather into vast flocks that rise and wheel in the wind almost like smoke.

There are many questions that intrigue me about such aggregations. For example, I once watched a peregrine falcon approach a huge flock of starlings in flight. The response of the smaller birds was immediate. They tightened from a loose collection into a mass so dense that it was nearly black. I could also see the resulting conglomeration rotate as a single entity. Individual birds seemed to exchange positions within the flock so that each was on the side toward the predator only briefly. The hawk was apparently confused by this remarkable activity because, after flying parallel to the flock for several minutes, it veered off and dropped into a tree.

How in the world could the starlings accomplish these spectacular feats? The birds appeared to move as one with no apparent signal. Any marching band conductor would be extremely jealous of their precision. Surely there must be some signaling going on within the flock, but how is it transmitted with such split-second timing? And how do the birds learn these maneuvers? Do they practice at night when we aren't watching?

Just as intriguing is the V-formation flight of those geese. Are there physical savings to individual geese to be gained from such flight patterns? If there are, does the leader share in those gains or is that goose simply imposed upon? On a less serious note: is the leader goaded into accepting this role as a kind of show-off macho behavior?

I was hospitalized briefly during World War II with several Navy pilots and I asked them if they felt that their planes gained from flying in close formation. Their response was that energy gains were illusory and that the tight company was solely for military purposes. And they even provided evidence: they told me that on long flights there were no differences in fuel consumed between leaders and wingmen (it was strictly men in those days).

I remained convinced by their argument until recently when twice I had bicyclists closely follow my motor scooter. I asked each of the bikers if they felt they gained significantly from this and they both claimed a real advantage. They told me that they didn't have to pedal as hard.

So intrigued have I been about these matters that I have read several books on flying. My favorite is Henk Tennekes' *The Simple Science of Flight: From Insects to Jumbo Jets*. I like everything about his book except that word "simple," as the ideas seem most complex to me.

Then I found an article that was published in 1988 in the American Ornithologists' Union journal, *The Auk*, by John Badgerow of Syracuse University. It is titled, "An Analysis of Function in the Formation Flight of Canada Geese". In the article Badgerow reports on carefully controlled studies that compared formation and solo flight on two factors: energy consumption and the associated visual communication. Although many of his tests proved inconclusive, the results he does claim (partly from prior studies) are most intriguing.

"The geese realized an average savings of about 10% over solo flight," he tells us and he continues, "The advantage could translate as greater flight range [or] greater reserves at the end of a flight."

Part of the evidence he brings to bear on this claim is the discipline in distance and angle maintained by following birds that keeps them in reasonable position to maximize their gains.

So evidently the geese are indeed bouncing along on those air pillows compressed by their leader's wings.

94. Disappearing Birds

In September 2014 a reader wrote to ask, "Why is there a big drop in bird activity in the village of Sloan?" That's a question that might well be asked about any local community at that time of year. There are a number of answers to this question and I offer a few here.

First, some species like bobolink are molting into their basic plumage and for that reason have retreated to hiding places in regional marshes.

I offer an aside here about plumage names for adult birds. Some species molt just once each year and their single plumage is called basic plumage. Examples of such birds are chickadees, swallows and thrushes. Other species molt twice a year and their often-drab winter plumage is also called basic. When we see these birds in their spring colors, they are in what is called alternate plumage. This may seem backwards to some readers but these species are in their winter basic plumage much longer each year than they are in their bright springtime alternate plumage. Examples of species that fit this second category are tanagers and warblers. Among feeder birds the goldfinch is a perfect example. I won't even try to describe the further plumage complications of gulls.

Back to birds disappearing.

Second, some have already left on their southward migration. Those yellow warblers that were so prominent through spring and summer headed south beginning in mid-August.

Third, many species are organizing into family groups and larger flocks. Thus you find all or none situations. One woodlot may have no birds whatsoever and the next one may be full of birds. Also, because birds like cedar waxwings wander in search of the best berry crops, you may be inundated with them today and find none in your neighborhood tomorrow when your grapes have all been eaten.

Larger flocks indeed. At the suggestion of Alec Humann a group of us went one evening to Buckhorn Park on Grand Island to watch a huge flock of purple martins gather before dropping into a small cattail marsh in the middle of the Niagara River. This was one of the largest groups of native birds I have ever seen and I found it impossible to estimate their number. I am told, however, that one estimate made by photographing them, counting a small section and extrapolating from that to the entire area of the flock produced well over 10,000 birds.

One thing I noticed about the martins. There seemed to be no pattern to their flight. They were moving every which way and it is a wonder they didn't bump into each other. Only when they finally dropped into the marsh did they seem to act in concert.

What also amazed me about the numbers of these birds is the fact that I don't think of martins as very common. Increasing numbers of people erect those multiple houses for these birds but I would never have estimated our regional birds to add up to this mob. It looked to me as though we had all the martins in North America overhead.

But I have seen still larger flocks. Among non-native birds starlings are surely the champions in flock formation. Not only are their numbers amazing but their flock behavior is absolutely remarkable. Flying a foot or two apart at most, they act in concert. The entire flock appears like a single entity, turning and twisting through the sky.

For a film of a spectacular flight of starlings in Gretna, Scotland, see www.youtube.com/watch?v=8vhE8ScWe7w.

A lesser grouping of birds before they leave for the south are the lines of swallows you find on any drive along the shores of Lakes Ontario and Erie. It is not uncommon to find five swallow species represented among a group of 50-100 birds.

And a final reason for the disappearance of birds at this time of year. Many species are fattening up for migration and for that reason they abandon feeders for the greater protein diet provided by insect prey.

95. Coot

"Stupid as a coot!" You may have heard an expression like that. If you have, I hope it wasn't directed at you.

Now, research is suggesting, that epithet is misdirected even for coots because they have suddenly joined crows on the roster of our smartest animals. Scientists now tell us that they are among those rare non-humans that can count.

Crows are already on that list of counters because of an old often-repeated story. Angry at a bothersome crow roosting in his silo, a landowner sought to shoot it. He set up a blind and hid in it but the wily bird saw him enter the blind and stayed away. Thinking that he would fool the crow, the landowner got a friend to enter the blind with him and return alone. Still the crow wouldn't come back. Increasingly irritated, the farmer repeated the experiment with two friends, then three. Not until then was the crow fooled. It seems that the bird could not count beyond three: a fourth man remaining while three departed finally was too much for the crow. It returned to the silo and its demise, an unhappy ending for a counting bird.

Since then, experiments with other crows, jackdaws (crow relatives) and parrots suggest that at least a few individual birds can show number understanding still higher.

But back to coots. They are slate-grey marsh birds with a white bill, at once chicken-like and duck-like. The most commonly observed members of the family of rails and moorhens, they are often seen at any time of year swimming in open water with flocks of ducks. Another name for them is spatterer for their awkward take-off: Bent describes a coot "rising noisily from the water; running along its surface, it beats the water with wings and feet, splashing alternately with its heavy paddles and making the spray fly, until it gains sufficient momentum to fly."

In an early April issue of *Nature*, an article by biologist Bruce Lyon appeared with the off-putting title: "Egg recognition and counting reduce costs of avian conspecific brood parasitism." I'll try to translate that headline.

Like some other waterfowl, coots are guilty of egg-dumping, that is laying eggs in the nests of other birds of the same species. (In another striking example of this, nesting wood ducks are occasionally overwhelmed with dozens of extra eggs foisted on them by other female woodies.)

Coots respond to egg dumping in quite remarkable ways that are apparently unique to this species.

They normally lay 8-12 eggs and here is where their counting comes to bear. When they are parasitized by other coots, the females are about equally divided between what Lyon calls acceptors and rejecters. The acceptors incorporate the foreign (parasitized) eggs and reduce the number they lay themselves to retain the 8-12 clutch size. The rejecters push aside or bury the foreign eggs and lay their own 8-12 eggs. In each case their brood remains the same as that of non-parasitized coots.

Lyon claims that this demonstrates two things: (1) that some coots are able to identify the foreign eggs even though they are very similar to their own, and (2) that they can count. Those claims make sense to me, but you'll have to decide whether or not you agree with them.

In any case, Lyon tells us, the rejecter's strategy has evolutionary importance, because about half of coot chicks in his study died of starvation. This "indicates that each successful parasitic chick survives at the expense of a host chick — a one-for-one substitution."

If we accept either of those interpretations, we'd better change that designation to "smart as a coot."

96. Our Other Swans

Each spring tundra swans appear on the Niagara Frontier as they pass through on their way to and from their breeding grounds in the far north. In fall they again visit, this time on their way to their wintering grounds along the Atlantic Ocean coast.

The other two species, the mute swan and the trumpeter swan, do not migrate and they pose serious problems.

Unlike those other introduced bird species, the starling and the house sparrow, the mute swan is a handsome bird, perhaps best known to us from Hans Christian Anderson's story of *The Ugly Duckling*, that matures to become, in Anderson's description, "the most beautiful of all the birds."

This species comes to us with another legacy. In England's past, mute swans were domesticated for food. Farmers identified their birds by nicking their bills or feet and registering those marked birds with the Crown's representative, the Royal Swanherd. Birds not so marked were considered Crown property and so the mute swan has become known as the Royal bird.

Mute swans were first brought to North America in the late 19th century. Until about 1970 they remained uncommon, most found in park ponds where they had been introduced. From that time on, however, their population has increased exponentially, doubling every seven or eight years.

Today in New York State there are over 2000. Well over half of them are found on Long Island and in the lower Hudson valley but their numbers are increasing rapidly in western New York as well. For example, 15 were recorded recently in Wilson

Harbor where for many years there were only two and you can then find 65 in Irondequoit Bay near Rochester. One possible reason for this increase may be the recent replacement of lead fishing sinkers and shot with less toxic substances. The swans had been among the waterfowl poisoned by discarded lead that they swallowed when feeding.

To many people that all sounds fine. Here is another beautiful bird to be seen more often.

Unfortunately, the mute swan is a problem species. These big birds rapidly deteriorate the quality of any marsh they inhabit. They feed year round almost exclusively on submerged aquatic vegetation, each day consuming over a third of their body weight. Their voracious appetites quickly deplete this important marshland component that supports fish and other wildlife. They overgraze an area, destroying its value, and then simply move on, leaving the aquatic equivalent of a desert. In this they differ from tundra swans that feed mostly on mollusks and land-based crops.

Mute swans are also intolerant of other species, driving away or even killing rails, ducks and geese. They are even aggressive toward people. And where these swans congregate their feces significantly increase the coliform count.

In response to these problems, the New York's Department of Environmental Conservation (DEC) recently proposed a management plan for mute swans. Here is the key wording of that plan: "DEC has been operating for close to 20 years under a management policy that permits removal of mute swans from lands administered by [the state], prohibits release of captive mute swans into the wild and authorizes issuance of permits for swan control by others on a site-specific basis. This new plan supports further action by DEC to eliminate free-ranging mute swans from New York by 2025, while allowing responsible ownership of these birds in captivity."

The response to this plan has been, as I expected, very strong. Here are just a few reactions: "You better not mess with them." "First the deer, now the swans, next it will be the poor." "Man is the invasive species." "Doesn't anyone respect God's creatures?"

I side with the DEC. I see their proposal as thoughtful, appropriate and necessary. Yes, the mute swan is beautiful but it deserves the same consideration as those less attractive invasives: the Norway rat, the European starling and the Emerald Ash Borer.

The third swan now beginning to be recorded here is the largest of the three, the trumpeter swan. I consider it the most beautiful bird in North America. Once completely gone from the United States and rare even in Canada, it has now been reintroduced to our northwestern states where it is doing quite well. I was awed a few years ago when I observed three of these swans flying along the Yellowstone River in Montana.

Although most ornithologists agree that this species never bred east of Michigan, a "restoration" program was begun a few years ago in Ontario and another was attempted near the Iroquois refuge. The latter included an attempt to lead the swans to migrate by showing the way with light aircraft. The experiment failed with some birds severely injured in the process and the remaining swans were finally relocated to Maryland.

Although the Ontario birds are non-migratory and, like mute swans, usually tamely respond to handouts, they have begun to wander in fall and winter. A few have made it to New York State and seven pairs were confirmed nesting in *The Second Atlas of Breeding Birds in New York State* within the period 2000-2005.

Many people will be glad to see these majestic birds and birdwatchers are delighted to add this species to their local lists but, as is the case with the smaller mute swan, they are voracious eaters and their presence will further endanger our eastern marshlands that are far less extensive than those of the west.

I hope that the future history of mute and trumpeter swans will not replicate that of the Canada goose. Migrating Canada geese are still uncommon and welcome, but those migrants are now far outnumbered by resident geese that are undesirable pests of golf courses and parklands.

97. Yellow Warbler

The yellow warbler, our most abundant warbler on the Niagara Frontier during spring and summer, is also one of the prettiest of these avian jewels.

But because it is so common, many bird watchers record their first yellow warbler of the season and then devote little attention to those that follow. They are too busy looking past the bright yellows in migrant flocks to seek out rarer species like Kentucky, cerulean and Cape May warblers or parulas and waterthrushes. For many years I was like that, but now as age has mitigated my desire to accumulate long lists, I have come to appreciate the extraordinary beauty of common birds like this.

I saw my first yellow warbler this year on May 6. It was singing its sweet *chip chip chippa chippa chip* from an ash thicket in Nature View Park in North Amherst. With no leaves to hide it, the brightly colored bird was easy to pick out rapidly flitting about looking for insects. I watched it for several minutes. In its bright new spring plumage the dainty red feathers that form breast streaks were evident and identified it as a male. Females lack these streaks and are a duller yellow.

Although their overall yellow coloration is quite distinctive, yellow warblers are sometimes confused with four other largely yellow birds. Of these, the prothonotary warbler has a gray back, the blue-winged warbler a black eye line, the Wilson's warbler a black yarmulke and the goldfinch black wings.

The yellow warbler's singing varies widely and I often have difficulty distinguishing it from the songs of two other summer residents: the chestnut-sided warbler and the American redstart. This is troublesome in Southern Tier areas where the three are equally common.

Because this year winter lingered, that yellow warbler was almost a week later than usual. During the previous eight years my first was recorded between April 29 and May 2. But by May 10 the same area was alive with them. I counted thirty in just two hours of birding. All were males busy establishing and defending boundaries of their half-acre territories. Females — and more males as well — will continue to trickle in for several weeks. Many will continue north, but the species will remain common here throughout the summer.

The yellow warbler is among our most beneficial birds. It feeds almost exclusively on insects, among them some of our worst pests: tent caterpillars, gypsy moths, bark and boring beetles, cankerworms, locusts, grasshoppers and weevils.

By early June resident yellow warblers will be homemakers, usually weaving their nests in shrub or sapling forks three to seven feet above the ground. Their materials are mostly grasses and plant fibers. As at my own home, the female does 90% of the work.

She then lays four or five eggs and tends them carefully until they hatch in about eleven days. The base color of the ovate eggs is variously pale blue, green or gray, splotched with darker browns or olives, these markings often forming a wreath around the large end.

Heavily parasitized by cowbirds, some yellow warblers fight back by building additional nest layers and covering over earlier eggs — their own as well as the cowbird's. A record nest was found with six stories burying 11 cowbird eggs.

Both parents feed the young, the female twice as often as her mate. Within a week of hatching the young birds weight is multiplied sevenfold and they are ready to fly in three days.

Among the first migrants to leave in the fall, yellow warblers are uncommon by August 25. After that it's a long family holiday in Central America.

98. Thrasher

One of our finest songbirds may soon disappear from the Niagara Frontier. The brown thrasher, once common here, appears headed for extirpation from this region within a very few years.

Our knowledge of this unfortunate situation derives from three kinds of records kept by the Buffalo Ornithological Society: May and October migration counts and June breeding bird censuses. All three data collections show sharp population declines since the 1960s. Even worse, their regression lines predict zero population for these birds locally within a few years. (Regression lines are graphs that average out the effects of data variation.) Confirming this trend is statewide breeding bird census data from the Fish & Wildlife Service that shows a 79% drop in New York brown thrasher numbers between 1966 and 2014.

Anyone who knows this handsome bird must view this situation with serious concern. Most often we experience extinction far off in time or distance. For example, the passenger pigeon was last recorded in this area in 1899, the final dodo on an island in the Indian Ocean in 1662. But the thrasher is not like them; to many of us it was once a familiar friend.

The brown thrasher is brown and white, its body robin-sized, its tail much longer than a robin's. It has a large, slightly decurved bill. I think of it as a bird of hedgerows. Arthur Cleveland Bent of Massachusetts agrees: "Here the thrasher is essentially a bird of the rural, woodland, and farming districts, living in bushy pastures, sproutlands, brier patches, tangles along fences, dry thickets, brushy hillsides, and the edges of woodlands, almost always far from human habitations. On large estates and in parks or reservations, where there are scattered woodlands and plenty of shrubbery, the brown thrasher may find a congenial home, and here it may build its nest close to a house; but such cases are exceptional."

Thrashers belong to the family of mimic thrushes together with catbirds and mockingbirds. Their song repertoire — Bent calls it "one of our best and most spectacular" — is less extensive than the mockingbird's and few thrashers imitate other birds. Winsor Tyler describes the song as "a long series of short, sparkling phrases given rapidly, sometimes repeated two or three times in quick succession, but as the song goes on it displays a great variety of phrases." He adds, "To sing, the thrasher mounts to a conspicuous perch where, with the tail pointing to the ground, a characteristic pose of the wrens while singing, he devotes himself to his song, pouring out his loud, spirited concert, like a vocalist singing a solo."

The thrasher is largely beneficial, its food two-thirds insects, the rest mostly mast — beechnuts and acorns — and other wild fruits.

Why is this delightful bird declining so rapidly while birds with similar habitat — cardinal and catbird — are doing so well? I find few clues. The thrasher is rarely parasitized by cowbirds, but its low nest is vulnerable to cats, raccoons, skunks, squirrels and snakes like the blacksnake shown in Audubon's thrasher portrait. Grackles, crows and blue jays also rob their nests and they are parasitized by lice, mites, ticks and flies. But so too are those other species.

With farmland decreasing and fallow fields returning to woodlands it may be that thrasher habitat requirements are no longer being met. If this is indeed their problem, I wish we knew those requirements as we could then try to fulfill them.

It has been over a year since I last saw a brown thrasher lustily singing from a fence near a rural airport runway. I hope that will not be my final experience with this lifelong favorite.

99. Flycatchers

When spring migration winds down in mid-May is a good time to focus on an interesting bird group, the flycatchers, because many are summer residents in this region.

More technically these are birds of the family *Tyrannidae*, the tyrant flycatchers. Tyrant may seem an odd title for a group most of which are shy retiring birds. After all, the Oxford dictionary defines a tyrant as "a cruel and oppressive ruler." But a single species, the kingbird, earns them all that title. In fact it repeats versions in its own scientific name, *Tyrannus tyrannus*.

Even that is a stretch, however. This handsome bird of our orchards and field edges does indeed rule its nesting area. Birds or animals that come near the tree in which the female incubates eggs are attacked by these pesky birds. Size doesn't matter: you'll see them chase away crows, red-tailed hawks or even great blue herons; you too if you walk nearby. But it is still hard to assign this behavior to "cruel and oppressive."

The kingbird is easy to identify. Slightly smaller than a robin, it has a dark gray head, back and tail, white throat, breast and the tips of its tail feathers. Look for this common bird on fence posts at roadsides.

About the same size is the great crested flycatcher, a bird heard more often than seen as it inhabits treetops from which you can hear its *wheep* note or a rougher burry call similar to that of the red-bellied woodpecker. If you do see this attractive bird, you will note its olive back, gray throat, yellow belly and rufous tail. I find this species most often in wooded swamps.

Our other seven resident flycatcher species are all drab gray birds the size of house sparrows but that perch with a more upright posture. It takes good field birders to tell them apart by their insignificant plumage differences: more or less distinctive wing bars, tinges of yellow, a gray wash in the breast. I don't even try.

Fortunately, these little gray birds are reasonably easy to

distinguish by their simple songs. Where you see them can help as well. For example, the most common species, the phoebe, is a bird of streamside that very often nests near bridges. Listen there as it pronounces its name in a buzzy two-note high-low *fzzz-bzzz*. Then watch for it and you will soon see it perch on a twig overhanging the water from which it dashes out occasionally to capture insects.

This species enjoys an interesting role in ornithological history. In 1803 Audubon attached silver threads to the legs of phoebe nestlings and showed that the birds returned the following year to the same locale. This was the first episode of bird banding which continues today to provide information about bird populations and migration.

A phoebe-like bird of open forests is the wood pewee, which also gets its name from its notes, this time a high clear whistled but downslurred *PEEawee* or a shorter upslurred *pawee*.

And then there are the species birders call the "empids," flycatchers of the genus Empidonax. Two are so similar that they were, when I was young, considered one species. Even in the hand bird banders cannot tell them apart. They still call them Traill's flycatchers but, as with phoebes and pewees, these two, willow and alder flycatchers, are easily distin-guished by their songs.

I consider the willow flycatcher the more common. Its song is a buzzy two-note *fitz-brew*. The alder flycatcher's is in three slurred notes, *fzzz-bzzz-fzz*, with the middle note higher.

Another empids I find far less common in summer. Most of the least flycatchers pass through in migration when their distinctive *che-beck* calls identify them.

And we are on the northern edge of the Acadian flycatcher's range. This species is found only locally here, for example, along the Onondaga Trail of Iroquois National Wildlife Reserve. Its very distinctive song is an explosive *pit-see* that some describe as that of a child's squeeze toy.

I wish we had olive-sided flycatchers here, because theirs is my favorite bird song, best described as a clear whistled *Hick, three beers.* Unfortunately even on Canadian canoe trips I have found them rare, but one did put in that order in Forest Lawn Cemetery a few weeks ago.

100. Korean Trip

Like many birders University at Buffalo librarian Chris Hollister keeps lists of the species he sees. As of September 2012 his world life list stood at 565 species. Having seen that many birds, it is not often that he adds new ones. But in early October he had an opportunity to do just that.

Hollister's daughter, Jessica, was studying anthropology and history at the university and that semester she accepted an invitation to study in South Korea. Her dad jumped at the chance to visit Jessica for a week while she was there. And, of course, he went with a hidden agenda: he would take the opportunity to add Asian birds to his life list.

As is true of many librarians, Hollister is well-organized so he planned for his trip. He obtained a copy of Mark Brazil's *Birds of East Asia* to use as a field guide. He contacted international birders, people who keep similar world lists. Unfortunately none were of much help. In fact, they warned Chris that he would have serious trouble since he didn't know the Korean language. Beyond Korea University in Soeul where Jessica was studying he would find few Asians with whom he would be able to communicate. And no one could identify a single Korean birder who could help him. Somewhat daunted, Chris realized that he would be birdwatching on his own.

Despite these problems, however, Hollister did remarkably well. The remainder of this column is based on his notes.

Arriving at the Incheon airport exhausted from 24 hours without sleep, Chris saw his first Far Eastern species: a bit of a let-down, it was a rock pigeon, the same bird we see in our city parks picking up bread crumbs. But on the drive to Soeul along

Yellow Sea shallows he picked up his first lifers: great white egret and gray heron.

On a brief tour along the Han River in the Soeul city center with Jessica and Professor Choon Shil Lee from Sookmyung Women's University, Chris added several more species including a Mongolian gull, very similar to our herring gull.

Refreshed by a much-needed night's sleep, he set out the next morning hiking through the city up into one of Soeul's richly forested mountain parks. "As if I didn't already stand out enough, using my binoculars on bustling city streets certainly brought stares." Among the common urban birds he found Eurasian tree sparrows, replacement for our ubiquitous house sparrows.

The mountaintop proved to be remarkably remote and peaceful in the middle of this vast congested city of over ten million. In these wild surroundings he found more than a dozen new species including ones with strange names like mugimaki flycatcher and vinous-throated parrotbill.

The next day Hollister visited Bukhansan National Park where he found still more new species including an elegant bunting, a bird with plumage similar to our dickcissel. This was more than a birding expedition, however. He found this "one of the most beautiful hikes of my life." Along the way he came upon the magnificant Cheonchuksa Temple.

The next day Chris reentered the academic world. He gave a talk to the Sookmyung Women's University's library school students, all of whom he found conversant in English. He notes: "Now I know what the term 'treated royally' really means."

Back to birding the following morning, this time in another of Soeul's mountain parks. More lifers including a striking red-flanked bluetail, somewhat like our bluebird. He and Jessica visited the King's Palace that afternoon.

On Hollister's final day, Chris and Jessica traveled to the Demilitarized Zone between North and South Korea. There they joined a strictly controlled tour: they had to sign a waiver indicating that, if they were killed, the United Nations would not be responsible. This waiver was serious: our Camp Boniface there is named for an army captain axe-murdered by North Korean soldiers in 1976 and during the tour similar soldiers constantly "pointed their guns at us." Jessica responded by pinning a peace ribbon to one of the 30-foot security fences.

An exciting tour with birding sidelights: the number of life birds added on Hollister's Asian trip, 48; his world list is now, in August 2016, 894; and his North Korean list, seen across the border, is six.